Gladiator
Film and History

Gladiator
Film and History

Edited by
Martin M. Winkler

Blackwell
Publishing

© 2004 by Blackwell Publishing Ltd

350 Main Street, Malden, MA 02148-5020, USA
108 Cowley Road, Oxford OX4 1JF, UK
550 Swanston Street, Carlton, Victoria 3053, Australia

First published 2004 by Blackwell Publishing Ltd

Library of Congress Cataloging-in-Publication Data

Gladiator: film and history / edited by Martin M. Winkler.
      p.   cm.
Includes bibliographical references and index.
    ISBN 1-4051-1043-0 (alk. paper) – ISBN 1-4051-1042-2 (alk. paper)
    1. Gladiator (Motion picture : 2000)   I. Winkler, Martin M.

    PN1997.G532G49 2004
    791.43'72 – dc22

                                                        2003017578

A catalogue record for this title is available from the British Library.

Set in 10 on 12.5 pt Photina
by SNP Best-set Typesetter Ltd., Hong Kong
Printed and bound in the United Kingdom
by MPG Books Ltd, Bodmin, Cornwall

For further information on
Blackwell Publishing, visit our website:
http://www.blackwellpublishing.com

Contents

Illustrations

Notes on Contributors

KATHLEEN M. COLEMAN is Professor of Latin at Harvard University. She has edited and translated Book IV of Statius' *Silvae* and published a number of articles on Latin literature and Roman spectacle. She was a consultant to DreamWorks SKG on the script of *Gladiator*.

MONICA S. CYRINO is Associate Professor of Classics at the University of New Mexico. She is the author of *In Pandora's Jar: Lovesickness in Early Greek Poetry* and has published articles on Greek lyric, Euripides, and Greco-Roman mythology. She frequently gives lectures on and teaches courses in classics, film, and popular culture.

ARTHUR M. ECKSTEIN is Professor of History at the University of Maryland. He is the author of two books on the great age of Roman imperial expansion (*Senate and General: Individual Decision Making and Roman Foreign Relations, 264–194 B.C., Moral Vision in the Histories of Polybius*) and of numerous scholarly articles on related topics. He is also co-editor, with Peter Lehman, of *The Searchers: Essays and Reflections on John Ford's Classic Western*.

ARTHUR J. POMEROY is Associate Professor of Classics at Victoria University of Wellington, New Zealand. He has published on Latin poetry, ancient historiography (*The Appropriate Comment: Death Notices in the Greco-Roman Historians*), Hellenistic philosophy (*Arius Didymus: Epitome of Stoic Ethics*), and Roman social history.

David S. Potter is Professor of Greek and Latin at the University of Michigan. His publications include *Prophets and Emperors: Human and Divine Authority from Augustus to Theodosius*, *Literary Texts and the Roman Historian*, and articles on textual criticism and on Greek and Roman history and epigraphy. He is also co-editor, with D. J. Mattingly, of *Life, Death, and Entertainment in the Roman Empire* and has appeared in various programs for the History Channel on Roman entertainments.

Peter W. Rose is Professor of Classics at Miami University of Ohio. He has published articles on classical literature and on Cuban cinema and has written analyses of films for various leftist political newsletters. His book *Sons of the Gods, Children of Earth: Ideology and Literary Form in Ancient Greece* applies Marxist critical perspectives to the Greek literary canon.

Jon Solomon is Professor of Classics at the University of Arizona. He is the author of *The Ancient World in the Cinema* and the editor of two collections of essays, *Accessing Antiquity: The Computerization of Classical Studies* and *Apollo: Origins and Influences*. He has also published a translation, with commentary, of Ptolemy's *Harmonics*.

Allen M. Ward is Professor Emeritus of History at the University of Connecticut – Storrs. He is the author of *Marcus Crassus and the Late Roman Republic* and of several articles on that period of Roman history. He is also co-author, with Fritz M. Heichelheim and Cedric A. Yeo, of *A History of the Roman People*, recently published in its fourth edition.

Martin M. Winkler is Professor of Classics at George Mason University in Fairfax, Virginia. His books are *The Persona in Three Satires of Juvenal*, *Der lateinische Eulenspiegel des Ioannes Nemius*, and the anthology *Juvenal in English*. He is also the editor of *Classical Myth and Culture in the Cinema*, a revised edition of *Classics and Cinema*, which had been the first collection of scholarly essays on the subject of antiquity and film. He has published articles on Roman literature, on the classical tradition, and on classical and medieval culture and mythology in the cinema. He frequently lectures and teaches courses on classical literature and film.

Editor's Preface

"On this day we reach back to hallowed antiquity"
                 – Cassius, announcing the Battle of Carthage

Immediately upon its release, Ridley Scott's *Gladiator* proved immensely successful with audiences, if less so with critics. Its gigantic box-office success has made epic cinema a promising venue for commercial film-making, with several historical films in various stages of preparation or production. Regardless of the different opinions that have been voiced about *Gladiator*, everybody seems to have been surprised by its worldwide appeal. The first ancient epic produced for the silver screen since the mid-1960s, *Gladiator* had to battle prejudices against a film genre long discredited for the elephantine size of its last exemplars and for their often lumbering, if inspirationally minded, plots. Equally, hardly anybody believed that a film set in ancient Rome could hold its own against the special-effects thrills of horror or science-fiction films currently in favor, although some of the latter, such as George Lucas's *Star Wars – Episode I: The Phantom Menace* and *Episode II: Attack of the Clones* (1999 and 2002) and Steven Spielberg's *A.I.: Artificial Intelligence* (2001), exhibit quasi-Roman overtones. And for action pure and simple, the military of World War II, for instance, could presumably deliver more satisfying battle sequences and inspiring heroism than Roman legionaries or gladiators. So why the attraction to *Gladiator*, even among those who are aware that the film contains numerous historical inaccuracies and distortions of fact? Does *Gladiator* really reach back to hallowed antiquity?

The contributions to this volume address these and related questions and examine *Gladiator* in connection with Roman history and in its modern contexts. Essays on history deal with Emperor Commodus, the Roman Empire, the Colosseum, and the Roman games. The others raise issues of historical authenticity in film, the origins and cinematic traditions of *Gladiator*, and its place in contemporary society and politics. The contributors, all classical scholars, may express different points of view, but all are agreed that the film demands serious attention and intellectual engagement. *Gladiator* provides us with a unique opportunity to reexamine, at a particular moment in our own time, certain issues important to history and to modern society and popular culture. So the moment is right for the kind of inquiry we present here.

Readers we hope to reach include those interested in film and history, in the importance of cinema as a kind of cultural or social seismograph, and students and teachers of Roman history and culture. But we also address those in related areas of the humanities, such as Film Studies, Comparative Literature, and Cultural Studies. Our contributions are therefore written in non-specialized English and without the jargon that most readers have rightly come to dread in academic writing. We explain all technical terms, and all quotations from Greek and Latin texts appear in translation. We annotate and give references where appropriate, so that curious readers can further pursue individual topics. The most important passages on the life and reign of Commodus that have come down to us in our ancient sources supplement the essays. A chronology of Rome at the time of Commodus follows these ancient sources, as do suggestions for further reading. If we succeed in persuading our readers to think anew about Roman history and culture or about historical cinema, to watch *Gladiator* with a deeper understanding of its historical and social contexts, or to watch some of the other films we discuss with the points we raise in mind, our book will have accomplished its purpose.

As editor of this volume, I am indebted first and foremost to my contributors for their willing and enthusiastic participation. They formed a veritable *familia gladiatoria academica*. I am also grateful to Harvard University Press, Liverpool University Press, and Penguin Books for permissions to reprint copyright material. I owe thanks to William Knight Zewadski, Esq., for allowing me to use a number of photographs from his personal collection of film stills and to Alexander Oliver of the Hermitage Foundation Museum in Norfolk, Virginia, for permission to include Edwin Howland Blashfield's painting of Commodus. Al Bertrand, commissioning editor at Blackwell, deserves my gratitude for his ready support of this project from its inception. I thank the Blackwell staff who worked with me in the selection and acquisition of some of the illustrations and in seeing the book through the production process quickly and efficiently.

CHAPTER ONE

Gladiator from Screenplay to Screen

Jon Solomon

Everyone interested in tracing the development of *Gladiator* has access to various sources: two preliminary versions of David Franzoni's screenplay; several Internet interviews with Franzoni, director Ridley Scott, and co-producer Douglas Wick; the film itself; extra footage on its DVD issue; numerous comments on the World Wide Web; and, finally, the ancient historical sources for the life of the villainous Commodus – Cassius Dio, Herodian, and the *Augustan History*.[1] The following essay offers a study of the development of *Gladiator* based on these sources, from its original artistic concept to its release version.

To most of us, this may seem like a common or easy enough task: reading interviews with filmmakers, examining their notes or drafts, and finding additional material on a DVD or on the Web. But nothing could be further from the truth when these methods of research are applied to an ancient story. For example, Homer is not available for interviews, and we have none of Virgil's notes or drafts. On his deathbed, Virgil reportedly requested his friends to burn the one copy of his not quite finished *Aeneid*, Rome's national epic. We are fortunate to have his poem, but we cannot examine his notes or drafts.

---

1   The two drafts of the screenplay are published electronically at *http://www.hundland. com/scripts/Gladiator_FirstDraft.txt* (revised and dated April 4, 1998) and *http://www. hundland.com/scripts/Gladiator_SecondDraft.txt* (revised by John Logan and dated October 22, 1998). My quotations are from these sources.

In fact, we do not have these kinds of resources for studying the development of any ancient literature, be it epic, tragedy, comedy, lyric poetry, satire, or novel. We do know in some cases what previous authors or versions of a story, often a myth, influenced an author, but this is a particular work's literary tradition, not its inception. And by comparison with ours, ancient writing materials were crude, and methods of writing depended, much more than ours, on an author's memory. But even if they had had all the writing tools available to modern authors, ancient writers could never have imagined that someday in the distant future someone would want to study their first drafts, let alone post them on the Web or even purchase them on eBay.

This situation is not unique to ancient authors and is true, to varying degree, for all literature down to at least the nineteenth century. With *Gladiator* we can, perhaps for the first time ever, build a comprehensive understanding of how an author and his subsequent collaborators developed a story set in antiquity.

The original author of the screenplay of *Gladiator* is David Franzoni, whose most significant previous work was Steven Spielberg's *Amistad*, a 1997 historical film which helped establish the reputation of Dream-Works SKG, the new production company of Spielberg and others. On the strength of *Amistad*, which deals with the plight of Africans illegally sold as slaves in 1839, Franzoni was given a three-picture deal with DreamWorks as writer and co-producer. Franzoni's next submission was *Gladiator*, another fact-based historical film about slaves, tyranny, and freedom. Franzoni had been inspired by Daniel P. Mannix's novel *Those About to Die* (1958; published again in 2001 as *The Way of the Gladiator*), which Franzoni had read while living along the banks of the Tigris River almost thirty years earlier when he was on a motorcycle trip around the world. Franzoni mentioned the idea for his film to Steven Spielberg, who asked "three basic questions":

> My gladiator movie, it was about ancient Roman gladiators – not American, Japanese, whatever else? Yes, I said. Taking place in the ancient Coliseum [*sic*]? Yes. Fighting with swords and animals to the death and such? Yes. Great, let's make the movie.[2]

Franzoni is not a classical scholar. He is a storyteller capable of finding inspiration in historical sources and adapting them for the screen. In his

2   The quotation is from an interview conducted by John Soriano for the Writers Guild of America. My source here and below is its electronic publication at *http://www.wga. org/craft/interviews/franzoni2001.html.*

first version of the script, dated April 4, 1998, Franzoni named his protagonist Narcissus, using the *praenomen* (first name) of the wrestler who strangled Emperor Commodus to death on the last day of A.D. 192. Franzoni read what he called "the *Augustan Histories*," a collection of Roman imperial biographies, as his inspiration for choosing Commodus as his historical focus. But the biography of Commodus by Aelius Lampridius in the *Augustan History* does not offer any name for the athlete responsible for killing Commodus. Narcissus is, however, named by Herodian and Cassius Dio, so we are immediately put on alert that Franzoni may have used a variety of ancient sources in preparing his screenplay.[3]

In this first draft, Franzoni's General Narcissus wins the war in Germania. Immediately after the death of Emperor Marcus Aurelius, which is neither shown nor described, Narcissus is shipped as a condemned prisoner to the Colosseum, where he becomes a huge popular success. A superstar gladiator sponsored by the Golden Pompeii Olive Oil Company, Narcissus ultimately strangles Commodus in the Colosseum sands and then sails off into the sunset with his wife and two daughters. Anachronistic and trite, this was the original storyline that was nurtured and developed into the film which won multiple Academy Awards including Best Picture, cost over $100 million, and grossed over $200 million.

The original screenplay opens with Commodus, his sister Lucilla, and their family physician, the historically appropriate Galen, in two enclosed wagons. Commodus is eager to catch up with his father on the German frontier. There we meet Juba, leader of the Numidian archers, and Narcissus Meridas, the general of the Spanish Gemina Felix VII Army. Merida is the modern name of Colonia Augusta Emerita in Spain, a colony founded by Emperor Augustus in 25 B.C. as a reward to the *emeriti* (veterans) of two Roman legions. Later, it became the capital of the province of Lusitania and the most important city in Roman Spain. The placement of Numidian and Spanish troops and auxiliaries in Germania did not evolve into the Spanish and North African settings we see in the final version until the second draft of the script, but it did create both the character of the African Juba, played ultimately by Djimon Hounsou (from *Amistad*), and Narcissus' *cognomen* (second name) Meridas, later to become Meridius.

Visitors to Merida can today see the remains of a Roman theater, amphitheater, and circus and monumental statues of Romulus, Remus, and the she-wolf, the latter a reference to the foundation legend of Rome: Romulus and Remus were abandoned as infants and rescued by a

3   Herodian 1.17.11; Dio 73.22.5.

she-wolf who became their wet nurse. In the scene mentioned above, we now also meet the Roman general's mascot. Most viewers of the film think that Maximus has a pet dog, who runs alongside him into battle, but it is really a wolf. In the original screenplay it is called the "Wolf of Rome."

In the first draft, Marcus Aurelius addresses his troops in a cinematically impossible speech about two pages long. Here are its opening paragraphs:

> Today may be the last day in the life of Rome . . . For nine hundred years Rome has lived! For nine hundred years architects, mathematicians, poets, and philosophers have fled within her arms sheltered from superstition, prejudice, hate, and every form of cruelty. We Romans have become a light in the barbarian night!
>
> For nine hundred years this one heart of humankind has been defended by the likes of Pompeii [*sic*], Mark Anthony [*sic*], Julius Caesar, The Divine Augustus, Claudius, Trajan, Hadrian, and my own father Antoninus Pius. Now, it has come down to us! It has come down to this one day . . .

This history lesson would hardly inspire any soldiers about to be sent into battle. The author is instead sending us, the viewers, the message that Rome, like the USA, is the "land of the free." As Franzoni has said:

> the movie is about our culture, our society: promoter Proximo (Oliver Reed) is sort of a Mike Ovitz, and Commodus (Joaquin Phoenix) is sort of a Ted Turner. And Maximus (Russell Crowe) is the hero we all wish ourselves to be: the guy who can rise above the mess that is modern society.

Twenty-two pages later, Narcissus is visited in Germany by his wife, two daughters, and their pedagogue Lindo, who is teaching them a more populist attitude. Here is the dialogue:

> Manto [daughter]: Father, is it true the Germans are just fighting to protect their land?
> *Narcissus and Selene [his wife] swap a fast look.*
> Selene: Well, you wanted the girls to have the best teachers.
> Narcissus: Greeks?
> Selene: Athenians . . .
> *That sounds even worse.*
> Manto: Teacher says that the divine Julius used the Germans as a pretext to dissolve the Republic.

Narcissus: Did he now . . . ?

Manto: And that the Germans are only struggling to keep their honor and the ways of their people. And that throughout history Rome has always been the aggressor.

Narcissus: Well, remind teacher: once upon a time it was the Hebrews over the Philistines; the Babylonians over the Hebrews; Egypt over Babylon; the Greeks over the Trojans; Persians over the Greeks; Etruscans over the Latins; Sabines over the Latins and Etruscans. Now it's Rome over everyone and I don't know when the world has known such peace.

Manto: I can't wait to tell my teachers [*sic*] all that.

Can see Narcissus feels better about this already.

Narcissus: What about their philosophy lessons?

Selene: They're studying with Cynics.

Narcissus: Of course . . .

The liberal Greek teachings grate on the father, a career military officer. His response to learning that the children are studying the Cynic philosophers is a sarcastic comment. But Lindo's views nicely parallel the politics of visiting Senators Gaius Cantus, Falco Verus, and, later, Gracchus – the last a name associated since 1960 with republican ideals thanks to the character portrayed by Charles Laughton in Stanley Kubrick's *Spartacus*.

In between such observations on Roman–American freedoms and Greek Marxism there occurs the battle against the Germans. Franzoni has done some homework here, as his descriptions show:

A red 'flag' on a long pole goes up answering the trumpet, and the line of the fresh cohort parts in segments revealing ONAGERS – portable catapults – and SCORPIONS – powerful precision-fire crossbows that launch javelins.

THE ARTILLERY FIRES . . .

cannonball-size shot driven at a hundred miles an hour rip over the heads of Narcissus' troopers and slam against the fort walls.

ONAGER CREWS

reload with incredible speed from wagons filled with hand-picked rocks – some bear SCRAWLED EPITHETS essentially the Latin equivalent of "EAT THIS HANS!" [*sic*] Onagers launch barrage after barrage, their backs leaping off the ground like recoiling 45 millimeter field guns.

Franzoni here specifies and defines the use of Roman artillery pieces. The German fortification he mentions did not make it into the film, nor did his description of the Romans scrawling mottoes onto hand-picked catapult rocks. (No doubt he meant them to write the equivalent of "Eat this, Huns!") Elsewhere he wanted to have the Romans use two-sided, quick-release spears.

Apparently one of Franzoni's messages was that armies with superior technology defeat locals who have only an admirable defiance and love of liberty. Clearly he wanted ancient Roman military power to be vividly realized on film. The battle sequence at the opening of the film, part of which is computer-generated, relies visually on the "barrage after barrage" imagery described in the first draft. Franzoni also called for an authentic Roman *testudo* ("turtle") formation, in which the soldiers protect themselves on all sides with carefully arranged shields, as depicted on Trajan's Column and re-created in Joseph L. Mankiewicz's 1963 version of *Cleopatra*. The *testudo* is used twice in *Gladiator*, once during the German battle and later in the Colosseum. There is no evidence that the Roman army used catapults to hurl exploding clay pots at their enemy, but visually this segment in the forest is spectacular, even if more trees than Germans are hit. And while authenticity and plausibility – cavalry in a forest battle? – are questionable, such free invention makes for thrilling footage.

In the first draft of the script the wolf saved Narcissus' life in the middle of the battle sequence, and this still occurs in the film. In the second draft, "a cage full of ferocious wolves" appears in the Colosseum, prompting Commodus to rave madly about "the great She-Wolf of Rome," who "will again suckle us, again ravage our enemies – AND BRING US A WORLD REBORN!" But in the film, these wolves have disappeared, as has Maximus' wolf after the opening battle. What happened to him? As soon as the wolf appears and helps save Maximus' life, Hans Zimmer's music modulates from the rousing "battle waltz" in 3/4 time to an adagio victory hymn. The Wolf of Rome has saved the hero, and this is the turning point of the battle. There are many wounded and exhausted Romans, and the gritty, smoky texture of the images on the screen in the last stages of the sequence reflects a bitter-sweet relief over battle's end. At this point General Maximus can proclaim triumphantly, and in Latin, "Roma victor!" ("Rome is victorious!") The battle for Germania is over, and the emperor can return to Rome. The wolf, who made all this possible, now vanishes. In this way it takes on an almost supernatural quality, one entirely appropriate for such a reincarnation of one of the founders of Rome and her empire.

In the first draft of the screenplay we do not see Commodus murder Marcus Aurelius, although we suspect that he does, as does Narcissus. Galen was probably involved as well. There is a verbose scene in which Commodus, Narcissus, Senator Gaius, and Galen discuss the emperor's health:

> Narcissus: Do you expect Marcus to be well enough by morning for an audience?
> Commodus: That's difficult to say, general.
> Narcissus: Perhaps, Master Galen, you may say.
> Galen: It's difficult to name a time . . .
> Commodus: May I remind everyone that Master Galen is the finest medical philosopher in the Empire and his detailed assessment of the Emperor is delicate and confidential and is the business of the immediate family alone.
> Narcissus: I would venture, with all respect: the Emperor's health is the business of every soul in the empire.
> Gaius: Yes! The days of Imperial Prerogative and disdain for the Senate are over – thanks to your father! Now report to the Senate, Master Galen: what is Marcus' state?
> Commodus: Report, Master Galen, by all means. The Senate demands it · · ·
> Galen: We are talking simply about a disturbance of the hues [*read*: "humors"]. Nothing more. In precisely one hour I will analyze the Emperor's bile and then my assistants and I will stand by in an unfailing vigil until his fever breaks. Now with your permission [–] Caesar, Senators? I must return to my patient.
> *Commodus gestures him out as if he were just amused.*
> Commodus: One doctor now knows his place in the empire. Congratulations, general, your victory seems to inspire courage everywhere.

The ambiguity intended in these exchanges is eliminated in the film when Commodus smothers Marcus Aurelius in his tent. Often, literary details of a script are eliminated once a more vivid, if less subtle, visual replacement is discovered. That the final choice was to show this murder is not surprising in the case of a director known for preferring the visual to the verbal. A simple but discomforting scene, it verifies for the viewer beyond any question Commodus' guilt and establishes a motive for Maximus to avenge Marcus Aurelius and fight for his dream of a *res publica restituta*, a restored Roman republic.

Commodus stands in the way of Marcus Aurelius' ideal vision of Rome. Dio describes Commodus as extremely naïve and full of ignorance.[4] To combat such innate inability, the historical Marcus attempted to provide Commodus with astute advisors. Franzoni effectively drama- tizes the disappointment that Marcus must have had in his son. He describes Commodus' faults as ignorance and arrogance and has Marcus plan to transfer power from the Antonine dynasty to the senate and people of Rome:

> It's not because he's young, it's because he's ignorant and arrogant. His sister is a better man. That's why I have undertaken to begin sweeping changes in the relationship between the emperor and the Senate . . . If the Emperor and the Senate can share power then the people will be ready to take their share.

In the film, some engaging dialogue inspired by the real Marcus Aurelius' *Meditations* has been added. Marcus wrote: "If mortal life can offer you anything better than justice and truth, self-control and courage . . ."[5] In *Gladiator*, Commodus says to his father:

> You wrote to me once, listing the four chief virtues. Wisdom, justice, for- titude, and temperance. As I read the list, I knew I had none of them. But I have other virtues, Father. Ambition. That can be a virtue when it drives us to excel. Resourcefulness. Courage. Perhaps not on the battlefield, but there are many forms of courage. Devotion. To my family, to you. But none of my virtues were on your list. Even then, it was as if you didn't want me for your son.[6]

This is an effective piece of writing. Franzoni or one of his later collabo- rators lists specific virtues from the *Meditations* and has Commodus sup- plement them with plausible virtues of his own. The scene makes it clear that it was Marcus Aurelius' failure as a father to recognize the most important of Commodus' virtues, devotion to his family and his father. This failure, which both now regret, ultimately results in parricide and leads Rome into tyranny and oppression.

---

4   Dio 73.1.
5   *Meditations* 3.6.1; quoted from Marcus Aurelius, *Meditations*, tr. Maxwell Staniforth (Harmondsworth: Penguin, 1964; several rpts.), 57.
6   Quoted from *Gladiator: The Making of the Ridley Scott Epic*, ed. Diana Landau (New York: Newmarket, 2000), 135. This book contains photos, interviews, and more and should be consulted alongside my essay.

Herodian tells us that at first Commodus was highly popular in Rome, and so he is for the most part in the film.[7] Commodus' triumphal entry on his return from Germania, introduced by the now famous "fly-over" of Rome, was enhanced by computer-generated visual effects. Actually, our ancient sources give us mixed and confusing statements about the Roman people's attitude towards Commodus, and the film reflects this during his triumph by contrasting the (computerized) formal arrangement of soldiers with a montage of (real) angry Romans. This contrast is the result of Franzoni's original conception of the Roman populace as a lower-class and even bizarre rabble in the manner of Federico Fellini's *Satyricon* (1969), a film based on a Roman novel from the time of the early empire. Franzoni had the Colosseum surrounded by relic hawkers selling memorabilia of deceased gladiators, merchants selling lion paws and leopard ears as aphrodisiacs, bare-chested and gaudily painted prostitutes, and an albino dwarf with "Jimmy Winters white hair and almost crimson eyes." In fact, at one point Franzoni describes a detail which, in one of only three footnotes in the screenplay, is attributed to Fellini's film:

> Some slaves of the upper-class 'fans' smack long WOODEN HANDS together overhead as their MASTERS recline in luxurious padded seats. Others – equally wealthy – leap up cheering and one even grabs the 'souvenir hands' away from his slave and whacks them together himself.

The note states: "Borrowed from Fellini but may be an historical artifact." Some of this urban color is preserved in the final version, where we see a juggler, prostitutes, an elephant, caged wildcats, and finally a frenzied sportsbook.

Balancing this socio-economic circus is a wonderfully human touch in the clay figures of his gods that Maximus keeps with him. These are either divine *Penates*, protective divinities of the Roman family, or other-worldly *Lares*, figurines of minor Roman guardian spirits, and that is how Franzoni originally conceived them in his first draft. But in the film they have been turned into figurines of his wife and son. Franzoni's conception would have lent the film another legendary-heroic touch in that the original figures would have been analogous to the statuettes of the gods that Aeneas, the ancestor of the Romans, first brought to Italy centuries before the time of Romulus and Remus. Virgil mentions this detail in the opening sentence of his *Aeneid*. Franzoni's figurines were a kind of

---

7   Herodian 1.7.

Virgilian *Lares* in their authentic emphasis on worship of one's ancestors. Regrettably, the change made them far less Roman and much more
Californian in the worship of one's wife and child.

Throughout the arena sequences, the first draft authentically portrays Commodus as remaining in his imperial box, as Herodian says.[8] But
Franzoni excludes the Buffalo Bill-like marksmanship and skill at slaugh-
tering large numbers of animals for which the historical Commodus was
admired by the mob. Commodus is alleged once to have allotted himself
just 100 spears to kill 100 lions and did not miss with a single throw!
But to modern audiences, killing people is one thing, acceptable and even
expected in action films; but killing scores of lions, tigers, and bears, not
to mention the ostrich that the albino dwarf rides – that is barbaric.
Modern taste would never tolerate it in a film. Instead, Commodus uses
his Praetorian Guard in an impressive show of protection to descend
into the arena when he confronts Maximus, the gladiator he has not yet
recognized. The scene once again reminds us that the visual impact of
the cinema almost always outweighs both historical authenticity and the
scriptwriter's specifications.

The latter third of the first draft clearly demonstrates how Hollywood
works from visual conceptions much more than from historical texts.
Here are some examples: Narcissus throws rocks up at Commodus in
the imperial box, an act which the mob loves. This is when the owners
of the Golden Pompeii Olive Oil Company begin using Narcissus'
endorsement on their advertising with the slogan that "Narcissus
would kill for a taste of Golden Pompeii Olive Oil." Promoter Proximo
munches on live butterfly chips; the Roman senate disintegrates into
squabbling; Narcissus is told that his family is dead, but later Lucilla
surprises him by informing him they are alive – a dramatic trick used
in countless seventeenth- and eighteenth-century French plays set in the
ancient world; and a reporter for the *Daily Action*, as Franzoni calls it –
the *Acta Diurna* were the Roman equivalent of our daily newspapers –
interviews Narcissus after a match and writes an anti-imperial,
pro-republican article:

> . . . encased in the armor of a demigod, Narcissus The Good continues his
> impossible climb in the arena where he was unjustly cast by the emperor
> of Rome. This writer asks: between a Senate that debates truth until they
> choke, an Emperor who has the birth sign of a woman, is it possible there
> is more virtue within the arena than without?

8   Herodian 1.15.7.

There are also numerous crass comments and bits of bathroom humor in this draft, and Narcissus poses before the crowds as if he were Arnold Schwarzenegger – who had once, billed as "Arnold Strong," been the hero in a Z-grade epic, Arthur Allan Seidelman's *Hercules in New York* (1970). Narcissus frequently entertains the mob with his catch line "Surrender or I'll kill you!" which was replaced in the film by the more somber and heroic "Strength and Honor." For the climax, Commodus immolates Lucilla and a number of senators in a brass bull – much as the notoriously cruel Greek tyrant Phalaris had actually done centuries before on Sicily – and then replaces these senators with chimpanzees dressed in purple-trimmed togas. Narcissus finally strangles Commodus and sails off into the sunset with his family.

Franzoni claims that he envisioned the film as a tragedy, but this is obviously not the case, unless by "tragedy" he meant a story with a dramatic catastrophe. He said elsewhere: "My vision from the beginning was [:] this is not *Ben-Hur*. It's *All Quiet on the Western Front*. This is a grownup movie about war, death, and life in Rome – the life of a gladiator."[9] But the preliminary screenplay demonstrates that Franzoni planned the final third of the film to be a grotesque, if still heroic, joy-ride somewhat along the lines of Simon West's *Con-Air* (1997), Michael Bay's *Armageddon* (1998), or the contemporary *Mummy* films. He even regrets the elimination of the olive oil endorsement: "I would have liked to have had more fun with this."

The film version, of course, is much more serious, so let us now turn to the second draft of the screenplay, finished six months later, to see if the heroically tragic ending was conceived there. The revisions in the second draft are attributed to a second writer, John Logan, whose credits include Benjamin Ross's HBO film *RKO 281* and Oliver Stone's *Any Given Sunday*, both from 1999 and containing notable allusions to classical antiquity. In this second draft the protagonist's name is now "Maximus Meridas," perhaps named after the Sextus Quintilius Maximus who is mentioned in the *Augustan History*.[10] He was one of the consuls in A.D. 172 and a successful military leader. He fell victim to Commodus around A.D. 183.

The first act still takes place in Germania, Maximus' wife and son are killed on their Spanish farm, Maximus then trains for the arena in North Africa, and the story shifts to the Colosseum. The people of Rome love his independent spirit, and Lucilla and several senators seek him out to

9   Quoted from *Gladiator*, 31.
10   *HA Comm.* 11.14.

free Rome of the tyrannical Commodus. Commodus threatens the life of Lucilla's son Lucius Verus, forcing her to inform him of the plot against him. In a montage Commodus rounds up the senatorial conspirators as well as a slew of such disrespectful or liberal types as actors, Christians, and scholars. (Arrests of intellectuals occurred several times in Roman history.)

All of this, except for the round-up of those mentioned, is used in the filmed version. (The outtakes in its DVD edition include Maximus' and our brief glimpse of some Christian prisoners in the Colosseum.) But the ending of this second version of the screenplay is very different from the film, yet superior to that in the first draft. Maximus escapes through the labyrinthine Roman sewer system, the Cloaca Maxima, stabs to death the general who betrayed and replaced him, leads the Felix regiment on horseback into the city of Rome, and wins the battle against Commodus' Praetorian Guard. Commodus has already stabbed Lucilla to death and is now going after young Lucius Verus. Maximus arrives with the Roman cavalry in the nick of time, pursues Commodus through the network of dark corridors and air shafts beneath the Colosseum, and kills him. Cutting one of the counterweight ropes, Maximus then lets an elevator platform carry him and the slain tyrant up to the arena floor to the delight of 50,000 screaming Romans. As he had promised Marcus Aurelius and Lucilla, Maximus instructs the senate to establish a new government. He takes the orphaned Lucius back to his farm in Spain with him for a new beginning.

Franzoni's concept for the film – "war, death, and life in Rome" – allows him much flexibility. It leaves him free to make the decision most theatrical writers have had to face, not only ancient ones – whether to provide a tragic or a happy ending. For example, Euripides decided to give happy endings to several of his tragedies, among them *Alcestis* and the lost *Antigone*, and Pierre Corneille battled the Aristotelian purists of his time to make his Roman history dramas end happily. As we have seen, the two versions of Franzoni's screenplay ended quite happily, too. The film, however, is different. It ends with the death of Commodus and the restoration of Roman freedom, but Maximus has to sacrifice his life for Rome, and we mourn his death.

Clearly this semi-tragic and heroic ending was decided upon late in the development of the story, as we know from its absence in the two versions of the screenplay. But the change well accords with Ridley Scott's working method. He usually continues the story-development process in the editing room and throughout post-production. Co-producer Douglas Wick verified this in an interview:

Last minute tweaking of the script and a new ending helped the production to stay on track. "Literally until the last two or three weeks of shooting, we were making adjustments," says Wick.[11]

Franzoni, too, reports that the final editing process changed the story yet again:

Creatively, I was concerned when the family was dropped out of the script. As originally written, that's a big part of what motivates the hero. And then when I saw the first cut, suddenly, the "family" was back in – Ridley had shot some pickups in Italy while scouting *Hannibal*, and there it was, the emotional element I wanted.

Hannibal refers to the modern cannibal Hannibal Lector, the subject of Scott's next film, not to the ancient Carthaginian general, Rome's greatest enemy. "Pickups" are brief segments shot before or after principal photography that are inserted during the editing process. So it seems rather likely that it was Scott who turned the film from Franzoni's sociopolitical, delightfully bizarre action film into a more somber study of war, death, and life in Rome. Scott's films tend towards semi-tragic endings, in which he almost always kills off at least one important character. This is the case in some of his best-known films: *Alien* (1979), *Blade Runner* (1982), *Black Rain* (1989), and most notably *Thelma and Louise* (1991), in which both heroines die. Almost all the protagonists of *Black Hawk Down* (2001) die in action. Although it sometimes seems that Hollywood films as a rule end happily, there had been highly influential recent precedents for killing off the protagonists in semi-tragic endings, most notably James Cameron's *Titanic* (1997), Steven Spielberg's *Saving Private Ryan* (1998), and George Lucas's *Star Wars – Episode I: The Phantom Menace* (1999). All three were the top grossing films of their respective year; the first two also garnered Best Picture Oscars.

Scott reshaped the story line of *Gladiator* and significantly improved its tone. The film now opens with Maximus' vision of death as an endless field of wheat, a plant long associated with Proserpina, queen of the land of the dead. (Proserpina's mother is Ceres, the goddess of agriculture.) Maximus' hortatory speech to his soldiers before battle is now not about Roman politics, as Franzoni originally wrote it, but about death and eternity:

---

11   Liane Bonin, "No Roman Holiday," *Entertainment Weekly* (May 5, 2000); quoted from its electronic publication.

Fratres, three weeks from now I will be harvesting my crops. Imagine where you will be, and it will be so. Hold the lines, stay with me. If you find yourself alone, riding in green fields with the sun on your face, do not be troubled, for you are in Elysium, and you're already dead! Brothers, what we do in life echoes in eternity.

Every time Maximus prepares for combat, be it military or gladiatorial, he rubs dirt into his hands, a primordial reminder that he is a farmer and a warrior, a kind of Cincinnatus in touch with Mother Earth. This, too, was a late addition to the film, although in the second draft of the screenplay Juba had said:

> Among my people we honor the soil of our home. Our ancestors are in that soil. All their dreams live there. I will never see my home again. The soil is dead and no one honors them, so the dreams die.

With these words we may compare the film's final scene in this draft, which expresses the circle of life, death, and rebirth. We are on Maximus' Spanish estate at dawn:

> *Maximus stands with Lucius at his old vineyard. It is still scorched and dead, weeds overgrowing the vineyards, the house ruined. Maximus puts a hand on the boy's shoulder, this boy so like his own son.*

> Maximus: It doesn't look it now . . . but soon we'll have it growing again . . . Next year there will be vines, and then there will be grapes . . . It will be alive.

> *We leave them, dreaming of the future.*

> FADE OUT.

> THE END

This ending shows us that Juba's simple agrarian values have been transferred to Maximus. In the film, they make him fearless of death. Once he learns that his wife and son have been killed, Maximus' eagerness to join them in Elysium is tempered only by his commitment to his creed ("what we do in life echoes in eternity") and his promise to Marcus Aurelius to restore the republic. Death takes Maximus to the gates of Elysium and the joyously expectant shades of his wife and son. Not at all awash in Christian eschatology, as most films set in the Roman Empire used to be,

Gladiator leaves us with a pagan tranquility in regard to death and the afterlife. Neither the first nor the second draft of the screenplay, neither story boards nor principal photography had contained such a perspective on life and death. From Franzoni's original conception in Mesopotamia thirty years earlier to Scott's visit to Italy in preparation for his next film, *Gladiator* was always a work in progress – a modern work about antiquity that rewards our study of its narrative development. From its beginnings as a satire of modern life set in antiquity, it became the first heroic tragedy on the cinema screen set in the Greco-Roman world at the turning point of two millennia.

CHAPTER TWO

Gladiator and the Traditions of Historical Cinema

Martin M. Winkler

As did audiences worldwide, classical scholars and teachers tended to regard the release of *Gladiator* with favor, not least in the hope that its popularity would lend support to their teaching of Roman history and culture. Classicists have held such hopes since the earliest days of cinema, but they have rarely if ever been fulfilled.[1] The same classicists, however, have criticized *Gladiator* for its distortions of historical fact, which occurred despite the involvement of an expert from an Ivy League university as consultant to the production. But such criticism is short-sighted. Although it is necessary for historians to identify and point out historical inaccuracies, charges of inauthenticity do not contribute to our understanding of the artistic and intellectual issues underlying historical cinema. Indeed, lack of authenticity is unavoidable in historical films. Why should this be the case?

1. Film and Historical Authenticity

Films which re-create antiquity, which rebuild its ruins – even if their restoration is frequently rather fanciful – and give them new life by

---

1   I have addressed this subject in more detail in my "Introduction" to *Classical Myth and Culture in the Cinema*, ed. Martin M. Winkler (New York: Oxford University Press, 2001), 3–22, at 3–9. I refer interested readers to this discussion, some points of which I am taking up again here.

making them inhabited by historical and fictional people, can go a long way toward showing us what life back then could have been like and what some of it actually *was* like, provided that we are able to abstract from the worst stereotypes or anachronisms that may be present on the screen. Films are by necessity a mixture of fact and fiction.

The same is true for any kind of re-creation of any era of the past in any medium, be it literature, painting, or opera. The appeal of such works rests at least as much on their fictional as on their factual side. Most of the time, the fiction is even more important than the facts because the story being told is what primarily interests us. If this fiction is based on or embellished by historical or archeological facts, so much the better, but the appeal of such authenticity is limited. For example, who among the audiences of Cecil B. DeMille's *The Sign of the Cross* (1932) or Mervyn LeRoy's *Quo Vadis* (1951) paid attention to, or remembered afterwards, that most of the decor of these films was highly authentic and had been re-created lovingly and at great expense? Were not the climactic arena sequences much more fascinating through their visceral appeal? Most audiences would have the same reaction to or memories of these films if their sets and decor had been utterly inauthentic. Clearly, the story takes precedence, as it always must do, and any story is just that: a story, not history. Most people read a novel primarily for the plot, and they watch a film mainly for its storyline.

The makers of historical films are actually in good, even distinguished, company, that of ancient historians. Greek and Roman historians also re-created the past. They shaped it artistically through their inventions, most famously speeches delivered by historical characters. What Thucydides, commonly regarded as the greatest of all classical historians, has reported about his own approach to historiography is revealing in its modern applicability. While he emphasizes the importance of historical truth, he also admits that certain parts of his account are invented, if still adhering to the spirit of the times or circumstances being described. Thucydides' account of his historical method is worth quoting at some length:

> In investigating past history, and in forming the conclusions which I have formed, it must be admitted that one cannot rely on every detail which has come down to us by way of tradition . . . We may claim instead to have used only the plainest evidence and to have reached conclusions which are reasonably accurate, considering that we are dealing with ancient history . . . In this history I have made use of set speeches . . . I have found it

difficult to remember the precise words used in the speeches which I listened to myself and my various informants have experienced the same difficulty; so my method has been, while keeping as closely as possible to the general sense of the words that were actually used, to make the speakers say what, in my opinion, was called for by each situation . . . It will be enough for me . . . if these words of mine are judged useful by those who want to understand clearly the events which happened in the past and which (human nature being what it is) will, at some time or other and in much the same ways, be repeated in the future.[2]

Without such a procedure, classical historiography would have read much more dryly to its ancient readers and to us today and would probably have been considered much less useful.

So the ancient historians give us facts inseparable from their inventions.[3] In a well-known passage of his *Poetics*, Aristotle contrasts and compares historiography and fiction – "poetry," in his terminology – and evaluates their authors:

The poet and the historian differ [in that] one relates what has happened, the other what may happen. Poetry, therefore, is a more philosophical and a higher thing than history: for poetry tends to express the universal, history the particular.[4]

2   Thucydides 1.20–2, quoted in the translation by Rex Warner, *Thucydides: The Peloponnesian War* (Harmondsworth: Penguin, 1954; several rpts.), 46–8.

3   On the wider ramifications of this topic see, e.g., Charles William Fornara, *The Nature of History in Ancient Greece and Rome* (Berkeley, Los Angeles, and London: University of California Press, 1983; rpt. 1988), 120–34 (section on "Pleasure"), 134–7 ("Historical Amplification"), and 142–68 (chapter on "The Speech in Greek and Roman Historiography"); John Marincola, "Genre, Convention, and Innovation in Greco-Roman Historiography," in *The Limits of Historiography: Genre and Narrative in Ancient Historical Texts*, ed. Christina Shuttleworth Kraus (Leiden, Boston, and Cologne: Brill, 1999), 281–324; Frank W. Walbank, "Profit or Amusement: Some Thoughts on the Motives of Hellenistic Historians," in *Purposes of History: Studies in Greek Historiography from the 4th to the 2nd Centuries B.C.*, ed. Herman Verdin, Guido Schepens, and Eugénie de Keyser (Leuven: Leuven University Press, 1990), 253–66, rpt. in Walbank, *Polybius, Rome, and the Hellenistic World: Essays and Reflections* (Cambridge: Cambridge University Press, 2002), 231–41. All provide additional references. On Thucydides cf. the now classic study by F. M. Cornford, *Thucydides Mythistoricus* (1907; rpt. Philadelphia: University of Philadelphia Press, 1971). For a wider examination see now Joseph Mali, *Mythistory: The Making of a Modern Historiography* (Chicago and London: University of Chicago Press, 2003), with further references.

4   Aristotle, *Poetics* 9.2–3 (= 1451b1–7); quoted from S. H. Butcher, *Aristotle's Theory of Poetry and Fine Arts*, 4th, corrected edn (1911; rpt. New York: Dover, 1951 and later), 35.

Before Thucydides, Herodotus, the Father of History, had been famous – or, to more analytical minds, infamous – as a master storyteller.[5] Herodotus ultimately also became the father of the historical novel and a precursor of all other creative reconstructions of the past. The greatness of a Herodotus, Thucydides, Sallust, Caesar, or Tacitus derives from *what* they report in combination with *how* they report it – how they approach their topics, how they structure their works. Similar points can be made about modern historians from the eighteenth century on.[6] Recent scholarship, reflecting on the nature of history and of the historian's craft, has come to comparable conclusions:

> Historians are not . . . only concerned to explain the past; they also seek to reconstruct or re-create it – to show how life was experienced as well as how it may be understood – and this requires an imaginative engagement with the mentality and atmosphere of the past . . . historians are time and again confronted by gaps in the evidence which they can make good only by developing a sensitivity as to what might have happened, derived from an imagined picture that has taken shape in the course of becoming immersed in the surviving documentation . . . imagination is vital to the historian.[7]

One of the most influential modern works on the nature of history and historiography, E. H. Carr's *What Is History?* (1961), had already addressed this subject in detail in its opening chapter ("The Historian and His Facts"). Carr further observed:

> To learn about the present in the light of the past means also to learn about the past in the light of the present. The function of history is to promote

5   The term "father of history" (*pater historiae*) as applied to Herodotus comes from Cicero, *On the Laws* 1.1.5. On fictional and related aspects of Herodotean historiography see, e.g., the following contributions in *Brill's Companion to Herodotus*, ed. Egbert J. Bakker, Irene J. F. de Jong, and Hans van Wees (Leiden, Boston, and Cologne: Brill, 2002): Deborah Boedeker, "Epic Heritage and Mythical Patterns in Herodotus" (97–116), Suzanne Saïd, "Herodotus and Tragedy" (117–47), Vivienne Gray, "Short Stories in Herodotus' *Histories*" (291–317), and Paul Cartledge and Emily Greenwood, "Herodotus as a Critic: Truth, Fiction, Polarity" (351–71), all with further references.

6   The subject is too large to be dealt with here, but interested readers may wish to consult Hayden White, *Metahistory: The Historical Imagination in Nineteenth-Century Europe* (Baltimore and London: Johns Hopkins University Press, 1973; rpt. 1990), as a starting point.

7   John Tosh, *The Pursuit of History: Aims, Methods and New Directions in the Study of Modern History*, rev. 3rd edn (London: Longman, 2002), 175–6 (in a chapter entitled "The Limits of Historical Knowledge").

a profounder understanding of both past and present through the inter-relation between them.[8]

What T. S. Eliot had observed about poets in his 1919 essay "Tradition and the Individual Talent" applies here, too:

> the historical sense involves a perception, not only of the pastness of the past, but of its presence . . . the past should be altered by the presence as much as the present is directed by the past . . .[9]

In a further step down a path that would have appeared impossible or even absurd to previous generations of historians, alternatives to actual history have now become a legitimate object of scholarly inquiry. This "What if . . . ?" approach to the past even has a scholarly name in Latin: *historia eventualis* (roughly, "alternative history").[10] So strict emphasis on factual accuracy, perhaps in the manner of Dickens's schoolmaster Gradgrind in *Hard Times* ("All I want is facts"), has come to be regarded with suspicion. Adherence to facts is only one of several aspects of serious work on history, if a major one, and imaginative combinations of fact and fiction have acquired a kind of intellectual legitimacy. Historiographical narratives thus begin to come closer to fictional narratives. But this is nothing new, for the historical novel took over some of the traditional functions of historiography long ago:

> The segregation of historical from fictional narrative was a by-product of late-Renaissance concern about the validity and accuracy of historical sources . . . And as history retreated to the arid confines of empirical rigour, novelists took over the richer if more fanciful aspects of the past that historians relinquished . . . The most pellucid pearls of historical narrative are often found in fiction, long a major component of historical understanding . . . All accounts of the past tell stories about it, and hence are partly invented . . . The truth in history is not the only truth about the

---

8　The quotation is taken from the 40th-anniversary edition: E. H. Carr, *What Is History?* (Basingstoke: Palgrave, 2001), 62.

9　T. S. Eliot, "Tradition and the Individual Talent," in *Selected Essays*, 2nd edn (London: Faber and Faber, 1951; several rpts.), 13–22; quotations at 14–15.

10　The best and most up-to-date starting point for anyone interested in this is Alexander Demandt, *Ungeschehene Geschichte: Ein Traktat über die Frage: Was wäre geschehen, wenn . . . ?*, 3rd edn (Göttingen: Vandenhoeck and Ruprecht, 2001), with additional references. *What If? The World's Foremost Military Historians Imagine What Might Have Been* and *What If? 2: Eminent Historians Imagine What Might Have Been*, both ed. Robert Cowley (New York: Putnam, 1999 and 2001), provide a wide variety of case studies.

past; every story is true in countless ways, ways that are more specific in history and more general in fiction.[11]

Aristotle could have found himself in agreement with this. The last sentence quoted here is particularly Aristotelian. All this also applies to visual history. Film scholar Pierre Sorlin has put the point well:

> Historians who tr[y] to list the historical inaccuracies in [a film] would be ignoring the fact that their job should not involve bestowing marks for accuracy, but describing how men living at a certain time understood their own history. An historical film can be puzzling for a scholar: everything that he considers history is ignored; everything he sees on the screen is, in his opinion, pure imagination. But at the same time it is important to examine the difference between history as it is written by the specialist and history as it is received by the non-specialist.

Just as Thucydides had identified usefulness as the chief goal of historiography, so Sorlin points to "the use of historical understanding in the life of a society" in regard to film.[12] The demand for strict historical authenticity fails to take into account the very nature of film as a narrative medium – that is to say, as a medium which is primarily dramatic (telling stories) and creative (in order to tell its stories the most effectively) and which is not indebted to or dependent on principles of authenticity.

Gladiator is a case in point. On the one hand, the production team had an expert consultant with impeccable academic credentials. On the other, the film is full of historical inaccuracies and anachronisms. As much as one may have preferred it to have adhered more closely to Roman history, a plot showing "what really happened" at the end of the rule of Marcus Aurelius and during the rule of Commodus is an impossibility. Historical cinema has lived with this dilemma since its inception.

Points and conclusions such as these may be illustrated by another example in which a scholar was technical advisor to a Roman film. P. M. Pasinetti, then associate professor of Italian at a major American

---

11   David Lowenthal, *The Past Is a Foreign Country* (Cambridge: Cambridge University Press, 1985; rpt. 1993), 225, 224, and 229. The entire section, entitled "History, Fiction, and Faction" (224–31), is important for the present topic.

12   Both quotations are from Pierre Sorlin, *The Film in History: Restaging the Past* (Totowa: Barnes and Noble, 1980), ix, in connection with D. W. Griffith's historical epic *The Birth of a Nation* (1915). Cf. Sorlin, 19–22 (section entitled "What is an 'Historical' Film?").

university, served as consultant to Joseph L. Mankiewicz's *Julius Caesar* (1953), an adaptation of Shakespeare's play. In a report on his experience in Hollywood, Pasinetti addressed aspects of historical filmmaking that are still being debated:

> Why are experts hired? One version is that the producers want to feel "protected": that the historical allusion, the armament detail, the duelist's motion, or whatever, will bear the stamp of specialized approval. This attitude is largely fictitious, unrelated to actuality; for the producer knows very well that his historical reconstruction is not going to be exact and "scholarly" and, which is more important, that there is no reason why it should be so. A film is being made, not a contribution to a [scholarly] journal; the requirements are those of the film as an artistic whole . . . The moment we stop and think, if nothing else, that those ancient Romans speak English blank verse, we have a wide basis upon which to build as "unhistorical" an edifice as we may wish.[13]

In the case of *Julius Caesar*, the filmmakers' guiding idea was "that of giving a modern man's vision of ancient Rome and of the feeling of a city alive and functioning" and as "a 'lived-in' place." For this reason the film's producer preferred "a person of Italian origin and education" to an ancient historian or archeologist as his advisor.[14] Pasinetti's research made him realize the "crucial difference between scholarship and film making: while the former can afford to be vague in its results, the latter cannot." Scholars may not like to be told that what they do may be vague in certain important respects, but the fact is there. As is always true for historical fiction or film, "the artistic truth of characters within the drama is what counts, not their relation to history."[15]

A good ten years later, director Anthony Mann addressed the subject in connection with his film *The Fall of the Roman Empire* (1964), the source of the plot of *Gladiator*. To Mann, the most crucial aspect of filmmaking is the successful combination of fact and fiction, something that is equally true for all kinds of artistic re-creations of the past in any medium. About his Roman epic Mann observed:

> all we were trying to do was dramatize how an empire fell . . . if everything [in such a film] is historical, then you don't have [dramatic] liberty . . . inaccuracies from an historical point of view . . . are not important. The

---

13   P. M. Pasinetti, "*Julius Caesar*: The Role of the Technical Adviser," *Film Quarterly*, 8 (1953), 131–8; quotation at 132–3.
14   Pasinetti, "*Julius Caesar*," 134.
15   Pasinetti, "*Julius Caesar*," 135 and 136.

actual facts, only very few people know. The most important thing is that you get the feeling of history.[16]

Mann's word choices are telling. Dramatization of the past is its re-creation in a compelling story, to which historical authenticity is subordinate. Mann's last sentence here quoted contains a key phrase: "the feeling of history." This is the only standard by which to measure a historical film's level of achievement.

Ridley Scott, whose first feature film was *The Duellists* (1977), a historical drama set in the Napoleonic era, and who later directed *1492: Conquest of Paradise* (1992), was and is aware of all this. "With history, your challenge, really, is to see how accurate you can be," he has said, and: "you have to do massive research." Nevertheless, Scott firmly sided with the primacy of storytelling over history: "I felt the priority was to stay true to the spirit of the period, but not necessarily to adhere to facts. We were, after all, creating fiction, not practicing archaeology." As a result, he, too, wanted a "Rome that looked lived in," as one of his staff members has said.[17] Scott himself elaborated on this in "The Making of *Gladiator*," a promotional documentary included in the film's DVD edition: "One of the biggest challenges when you're doing a period film is not to let it feel like it's a period film, but in fact to allow the audience entrance to that world and feel absorbed by that world."

Ancient historians and modern creative artists equally strive to bring history to life. This is the common ground they share. Today, there is no further-reaching or more effective medium to achieve such a goal than the cinema. This makes it important for classical scholars and teachers to deal with film as part of their educational responsibilities, because they, too, want to make the past come to life, if in different ways and with different emphases. As classicist Lily Ross Taylor is reported to have said: "my aim as a teacher is to make my students feel that they are walking the streets of Rome, and seeing and thinking what Romans saw and thought."[18]

16 Anthony Mann, "Empire Demolition," in *Hollywood Directors 1941–1976*, ed. Richard Koszarski (New York: Oxford University Press, 1977), 332–8; quotation at 336. Mann's essay originally appeared in *Films and Filming* (March, 1964).

17 Quotations from *Gladiator: The Making of the Ridley Scott Epic*, ed. Diana Landau (New York: Newmarket, 2000), 28 (twice), 64, and 120.

18 Quoted from Richard Saller, "American Classical Historiography," in *Imagined Histories: American Historians Interpret the Past*, ed. Anthony Molho and Gordon S. Wood (Princeton: Princeton University Press, 1998), 222–37; quotation at 225. Saller, 234 note 15, gives its source.

While it is a commonplace today to assert that "the past is a foreign country," popular art and culture often succeed in keeping the past alive by making it modern. Historical film does so in many ways, most fundamentally by the unavoidable fact that characters from the past, both fictional and historical, are being portrayed by modern actors who speak in a modern language. In addition, the plots of such films tend to follow certain patterns that are able to make almost any period of history or any locale familiar to viewers, even to those with little or no first-hand experience of different times or places. From this perspective, one might say, historical film is the greatest leveler of past and present.

Besides his interest in the historical and other creative challenges posed by as large-scale a project as *Gladiator*, Scott was also pleased to be able to "revisit the genre" of historical epic films, as he put it.[19] But there are many more correspondences between *Gladiator* and film history than between this and other films set in ancient Rome. They are the more conspicuous because *Gladiator* takes obvious recourse to archetypal hero tales.

2. Plot Patterns: "A Hero Will Rise"

> So David prevailed over the Philistine with a sling and with a stone, and smote the Philistine, and slew him. – 1 *Samuel* 17.50

Maximus, the hero who rises in *Gladiator*, single-handedly takes on an evil emperor who is the absolute ruler of a world power. The hero, who represents Right, prevails against overwhelming Might. Occasionally, he pays with his life, as he does here, but to the audience he is still victorious in having vanquished the bad and served justice. The world is a better place because of his heroism, at least temporarily. The lone hero's fight against great odds is as old as the story of David and Goliath or Homer's *Odyssey*. In the cinema, these archetypal or stereotypical tales duly recur, especially in historical epics. The stories of Ben-Hur and Spartacus – one a fictional, one a historical character – are obvious parallels to Maximus' story. But the pattern has much wider ramifications. By the time *Gladiator* was released, variations of the theme in which an underdog who seems at first to have little if any chance of success takes on a large power, military or corporate, and wins had come back to prominence in historical and contemporary American cinema. Such stories could be set

19   Quoted from *Gladiator*, 50.

in mythical or biblical antiquity – John Musker and Ron Clements's *Hercules* (1997), Brenda Chapman and Steve Hickner's *The Prince of Egypt* (1998), both animated features – in European and early American history – Mel Gibson's *Braveheart* (1995), Steven Spielberg's *Amistad* (1997), Roland Emmerich's *The Patriot* (2000) – and in contemporary society – Michael Mann's *The Insider* (1999), Steven Soderbergh's *Erin Brockovich* (2000). Russell Crowe played the hero of *The Insider* just before playing Maximus. The phenomenon has continued unabated before and after *Gladiator* with individuals or small groups, as in the *Terminator*, *Lord of the Rings*, and *Matrix* films. These and other comparable heroes all come from the same romantic American mold, according to which rebels, loners, or outcasts follow a vision, dream, or calling to build or achieve something great. They usually go against the status quo that is represented either by some faceless juggernaut of a bureaucracy, conglomerate, or even the Mafia or by a particularly villainous individual in power. Variations on these archetypal constellations are legion.

Such protagonists are more effective figures of audience identification if they exhibit and then overcome an initial reluctance to heroism. This is a common theme in the quintessentially American heroic genre, the Western: "A man got to do what a man got to do." So does any man on a mission. Cinematic knights errant, samurai, soldiers, private eyes, rogue cops, and countless others are their brothers – and now sometimes sisters – in spirit. The titular hero of Sergei M. Eisenstein's *Alexander Nevsky* (1938) is an example from the Eastern-European tradition. All this works for Roman heroes as well. An American example that bridges several archetypal traditions illustrates this point by its generic affinities to *Gladiator*. In Elia Kazan's *Viva Zapata!* (1952), the eponymous Mexican hero is a historically remote and somewhat exotic figure for contemporary viewers, but he and his story have clear modern overtones. Zapata's words early in the film could as well have been spoken by Maximus as a message to Marcus Aurelius, the good emperor who wants Maximus to be his successor:

> Tell him to get another leader. Tell him to get another man. I have private affairs. I don't want to be the conscience of the world. I don't want to be the conscience of anybody.

Maximus and Zapata are farmers – one married, the other still courting but later marrying – who have heroism and greatness thrust upon them. Pancho Villa, former farmer and revolutionary and current president of Mexico, wants Zapata to be his successor. He explains his reason in terms that remind us of *Gladiator*: "I'm going home. I have a nice ranch now, and I'm going to be president of that ranch." Such dreams of the simple agricultural life cannot, of course, become reality for Villa, Zapata, or Maximus. Villainous General Huerta, lusting for power, is behind an assassination plot against Zapata, of whom he has said earlier: "He believes in what he's fighting for." Huerta characterizes Zapata in terms now again familiar from *Gladiator*: "Zapata is a tiger. You have to kill a tiger." After Zapata has been treacherously killed, another officer says: "The tiger is dead."

Among recent films, *The Patriot* is closest in spirit to *Gladiator*. (It was released the month after Scott's film.) Widower Benjamin Martin is a peaceful farmer and devoted father with a heroic past. The forces of history – in this case, the American Revolution – thrust him back into the thick of battle. Not unlike Mad Max, a film hero to be discussed shortly, Martin has a tendency to yield to furious and uncontrollable violence. (Since the same actor, Mel Gibson, plays both, we may be tempted to call the patriot Mad Martin.) Max, Martin, and Maximus all become tigers. Even the meek may do so, as a reverend in *The Patriot* shows. Armed and ready to march off to fight for liberty, he explains to his surprised parishioners: "A shepherd must tend his flocks. And at times fight off the wolves." His pastoral terminology finds an appropriate agricultural analogy later when, victory won, we hear the patriot saying in voice-over: "My hope, and prayer, is that the sacrifices of so many will spawn and fulfill the promise of our new nation." Martin has been fighting for the creation of this nation; Maximus has fought to restore an old nation's greatness. He dies, but the patriot lives to realize the agricultural idyll that Maximus desires. The two and their films are comparable even in certain details. Maximus wins the crowd; Martin "has the loyalty of the people" and of "his men," as someone says. Both kill their evil foe in hand-to-hand combat by delivering a fatal blow through the enemy's throat. And just as Maximus races home to save his wife and child from slaughter but finds them killed, so does a member of Martin's militia.

Alexander Nevsky and Emiliano Zapata start out as farmers. Many of the hard-working protagonists of the American Western work the land, too. In this regard, socialist Russia and capitalist America share a predilection for lower-class heroes in harmony with the soil. Martin and Maximus are two of several recent examples. Their films' perspective on the social status of their heroes is virtually identical with that found in another blockbuster epic, one released three years before *Gladiator*. James Cameron's *Titanic* has been described as a "populist" film which propagates the view that "greed is bad, elitism wrong, freedom a virtue, self-sacrifice noble, and, above all, that true love transcends death."[20] Maximus might well agree. The heroes of *Titanic* and *Gladiator* both sacrifice themselves nobly. As has been said about Scott's entire body of work: "His films project a set of values that at once reflect left-wing liberalism and an essentially neoclassical conservatism that insists on tempering passion with reason, choosing wise and intelligent courses of action, and acting with honor, virtue, and concern for the good of society at large as well as for the individual . . . Scott often celebrates the working classes over the privileged classes" with their "self-important individuals in positions of authority [who tend] to subvert the sincere and altruistic work of their underlings."[21] The plot of *Gladiator* in general and Maximus' motto "Strength and Honor!" in particular exemplify this. Equally, liberty at the risk of death is a common theme for Scott, too, most notably in *Blade Runner* (1982), *Thelma and Louise* (1991), and *Gladiator*.

The plot of *Gladiator*, however, is indebted primarily to *The Fall of the Roman Empire*, whose story it lifts wholesale, if with some variations. (The archetype of the reluctant hero is prominent in Mann's film, too.) Other films that strongly influenced *Gladiator* are William Wyler's *Ben-Hur* (1959), with the double reversal of the protagonist's fortune from exalted position in society to slavery to victory over his powerful opponent; Stanley Kubrick's *Spartacus* (1960), with the similar ordeals as gladiator-slaves which both films' protagonists endure and with their association with a black fellow-gladiator; Delmer Daves's *Demetrius and the Gladiators* (1954), directly with its tiger fights and indirectly as a model for *Spartacus*; and Bob Guccione's and Tinto Brass's *Caligula* (1980) in regard to the villain's sexual depravity. The plot of *Gladiator* contains little that is new.

Nor do some aspects of the film's look. The armor and weapons of several gladiators owe more to the world of medieval and fantasy films than to Roman epics. In regard to one of the most spectacular special effects in the opening battle sequence of *Gladiator*, Scott's trip down the memory lane of film history goes back even farther, if perhaps unconsciously. The real Roman army never had the kind of fiery balls that we see flying through the air and exploding on impact. Their cinematic

20   David M. Lubin, *Titanic* (London: BFI [British Film Institute], 1999), 14.
21   Richard A. Schwartz, *The Films of Ridley Scott* (Westport and London: Praeger, 2001), viii. Schwartz also notes the importance of teamwork in Scott's films, best seen in *Gladiator* and *Black Hawk Down* (2001).

predecessor is the huge flame thrower that appears in the Babylonian sequence of D. W. Griffith's *Intolerance* (1916), a venerable ancestor to most of Hollywood's historical epics. The pillars on display in the Colosseum are *metae*, turning points for chariots in the Circus Maximus, and are out of place here; their appearance is due to historical paintings and earlier films, especially LeRoy's *Quo Vadis*. DeMille had female arena fighters in *The Sign of the Cross*, as did, more prominently (in every sense of the word), Steve Carver's *The Arena* (1973; retitled *Naked Warriors*), produced by exploitation master Roger Corman. The success of *Gladiator* made a video remake of Carver's film possible; it was directed by Timur Bekmambetov and has *Gladiatrix* as an alternate title. The music score of *Gladiator*, composed by Hans Zimmer, carries overtones of Carl Orff's *Carmina Burana* and is heavily influenced by orientalizing film scores ranging from Pier Paolo Pasolini's *Medea* (1969) to Franc Roddam's television *Cleopatra* (1999). This list can easily be expanded. In its use of silly Latin, however, *Gladiator* is on its own.

But more revealing of the cinematic ancestry of *Gladiator* are its close resemblances to films which have, on the surface, nothing to do with Rome and are not set in the past but in the future. Even in such alien worlds viewers familiar with heroic stories, especially those set in antiquity, may readily feel at home. Since 1977, George Lucas's *Star Wars* films have restated archetypal heroic themes with particular success.[22] Closer parallels may be found in another futuristic trilogy, the Australian Mad Max films directed by George Miller: *Mad Max* (1979), *Mad Max 2* (US title: *The Road Warrior*, 1981), and *Mad Max Beyond Thunderdome* (1985). Mel Gibson had even been the first choice to play Maximus, whose name seems to have been abbreviated to "Max" as a matter of course during the production of *Gladiator*.[23] A dual summary of Miller's and Scott's films shows their plot affinities:

> The hero (Max/Maximus) is happily married and the loving father of a little boy. He has a responsible position upholding the society to which he belongs (as policeman/as general) and defends it against outward threats (savage outlaws/savage Germans). While he is carrying out his duties, his family is massacred, and our hero becomes a social outsider himself (outlaw/slave-gladiator), away from civilized society (the desert of the

22   On these films and their recourse to archetypal Roman images and themes cf. my "*Star Wars* and the Roman Empire," in *Classical Myth and Culture in the Cinema*, 272–90.
23   Cf. *Gladiator*, 47. An abbreviation like this is not surprising, as examples such as "Herc" for Hercules, "Phil" for Philoctetes, and "Meg" for Megara show. Those mentioned here all occur in Musker and Clements's *Hercules*.

Australian outback/the desert of Africa). He is intent only on revenge. He becomes an invincible warrior, returns, and achieves his goal. The two stories now diverge somewhat. Max survives, to continue being a savior of people in need, while Maximus is treacherously wounded and heroically dies in the arena. Their heroic reputations survive.

The main difference between the two stories lies in the fact that *Gladiator* tells a pseudo-historical tale while the Mad Max films are almost pure myth. When he was collaborating on the screenplay for his second film, director Miller watched a number of Westerns and samurai films to learn about story construction from these archetypal genres. What he has said about the worldwide appeal of his hero applies to Maximus in equal measure:

> It was then that it occurred to us that here was the explanation, that until now had eluded us, of why 'Mad Max' [the first film] had worked so well in such diverse cultures – from Berlin to Tokyo, Paris to Mexico City. For this reason . . . we decided to be much more aggressive in exploring the history and function of storytelling . . . We realized that we were twentieth-century storytellers, and while the technology at our disposal was more sophisticated than in any other age, the aim was still the same: to weave stories which would satisfy those longings within other people and at the same time confirm certain values that we all hold dear.[24]

Miller may not have been aware that he used an archaic Greek metaphor when he described himself as a weaver of stories. The ancient storyteller was a *rhapsôidos*, a "weaver of songs," i.e., of stories recited orally. But the term is appropriate for visual stories as well. Moreover, the Mad Max films carry explicit ancient overtones, although not Greek but Roman ones. In the third film, Max enters a circular arena, the Thunderdome, which is part of a post-apocalyptic city named Bartertown. This action sequence has several quasi-Roman components. The female ruler of Bartertown reminds dedicated viewers of several Italian muscleman epics featuring Amazons and their queens. Here, she has a grand entrance into the arena before the games begin, and she presides over the bloody combats just as Nero, Caligula, and Pontius Pilate did in *Quo Vadis*, *Demetrius and the Gladiators*, and *Ben-Hur*. (Other examples could be added.) Her posture on her throne-like seat is the one that is almost *de rigueur* for a Roman emperor or governor: arms stretched out on arm

---

24 The quotation is taken from a text by Miller included on the DVD edition of *The Road Warrior*.

rests in a posture of power and arrogance. Frank Thring, the actor who, as Pontius Pilate, had started the chariot race in Wyler's *Ben-Hur*, here announces the games in the Thunderdome. The soldiers keeping guard are identified as "Imperial Guards" on the DVD issue, if not in the film itself. Max's opponent, called The Master, wears pseudo-Roman armor. The spectators still use the Thumbs Up or Down signs and yell and scream in excitement as do those in Roman films. Like Demetrius and others before him, Max nobly spares the life of his defeated enemy. He thereby breaks the rules of the games and is exiled to a penal colony which looks suspiciously like the quarry in which Spartacus toils at the beginning of *his* film.

Both *The Fall of the Roman Empire* and *Gladiator* introduce us to the wise philosopher and statesman Marcus Aurelius, the last of the "good emperors" who ruled Rome in the second century A.D. His two cinematic reincarnations are, of course, fictionalized. But the historical Marcus Aurelius seems to have known something about the relation of history to the story patterns of hero tales. He was referring to historical fact, not to works of the imagination, when he observed in his *Meditations*: "Look back over the past, with its changing empires that rose and fell, and you can foresee the future too. Its pattern will be the same."[25] With these words he virtually predicted the future of popular narrative.

25   Marcus Aurelius, *Meditations* 7.49; quoted from *Marcus Aurelius: Meditations*, tr. Maxwell Staniforth (Harmondsworth: Penguin, 1964; several rpts.), 113.

CHAPTER THREE

Gladiator in Historical Perspective

Allen M. Ward

Ridley Scott's *Gladiator* has already taken its place in a long line of books, plays, films, and works of art that keep alive interest in the ancient world among the general public, something at which artists and writers have been far more successful over the centuries than professional historians. Unfortunately, the creative minds who do the most to shape popular views of the past often have little regard for the level of accuracy that preoccupies professional practitioners of Clio's craft. Artists and writers mine the past for raw materials that support their own creative agenda. Few writers other than the most scrupulous of historical novelists will ever let the facts that concern professional historians get between them and paying customers.

Gladiator provides a perfect illustration. Professor Kathleen Coleman of Harvard University found her work as a historical consultant to have had such little effect that she asked not to be mentioned in the credits. Ultimately, she was thanked, but without any mention of her function. Right from the opening scene, the film's historical inaccuracies are, well, legion. First, there was no last great battle with the Germanic tribes on the eve of Marcus Aurelius' death. There was a great day-long battle late in the campaigning season of A.D. 179, but Marcus died on March 17 of 180, just as he was about to launch another great military campaign in his scheme to annex the lands of the Marcomanni, Quadi, and Jazyges across the

Danube.[1] One could say that the scriptwriters needed to foreshorten the chronology here to save time in a long movie, but they certainly played fast and loose with some other aspects of the battle. I have found no attested parallel to the war dog of the Roman commander Maximus Decimus Meridius, the movie's hero. If there were one, it would not have been a German shepherd, a breed that did not exist in antiquity. The use of fire-hurling catapults (*catapultae, ballistae*) and mechanical dart launchers (*scorpiones*) against the oncoming barbarians was certainly dramatic but probably unhistorical and pointless for use in a forest. By and large, such weapons were too cumbersome for use even on an open battlefield and were confined to more static siege warfare.[2] On a more mundane note, Roman horsemen are shown using stirrups, which were not introduced into Europe until the sixth or seventh centuries A.D.

The whole movie radically compresses the chronology of Emperor Commodus' reign. He became sole emperor upon his father Marcus Aurelius' death and was assassinated almost thirteen years later on December 31, 192. Although the time encompassed by *Gladiator* is not precisely indicated, it appears that no more than two years could have passed before Commodus was killed. Within that time-frame, the script does use some historical facts: Commodus was fascinated with shows of beast hunting, chariot racing, and gladiatorial combat; he did train himself in those skills; and eventually, to the ultimate scandal of all classes, he fought in the public arena as the kind of light-armed gladiator known as a *secutor* ("pursuer").[3] His public feats after A.D. 182 were to reinforce his identification with Hercules, which he officially proclaimed with coins and statues.[4] Indeed, he even had his own head sub-

---

1   In this and the following notes, references to the *Roman History* of Cassius Dio, as surviving in the excerpts by Xiphilinus, will include the book number assigned by U. P. Boissevain and a slash followed by the book number given by Earnest Cary in the Loeb Classical Library edition. The *Augustan History* (*Historia Augusta*) will be abbreviated as *HA*, followed by an abbreviation of the name of the biography's subject. On the historical situation mentioned here see Dio 71/72.33.4, *HA Marc.* 27.9–12 and 28.8–10, and Herodian 1.3.1–4.8. – An earlier version of this article was published as "The Movie 'Gladiator' in Historical Perspective," *New England Classical Journal*, 28 (2001), 112–23. I thank my student Lara Langer for helping me start this project and my friend Wilda Van Dusen for helping me finish it.

2   Cf. Livy 21.11.7, 26.6.4, and 46.2 and Caesar, *Gallic Wars* 7.25.2. See in general Eric William Marsden, *Greek and Roman Artillery: Historical Development* (Oxford: Clarendon Press, 1969).

3   Herodian 1.13.8–15.9, Dio 72/73.16.3–22.3, and *HA Comm.* 2.9, 8.5, 10.10–12, 12.10–12, and 15.3–8.

4   References in *Herodian in Two Volumes*, tr. C. R. Whittaker (Cambridge: Harvard University Press; London: Heinemann, 1969), vol. 1, 94 note 2.

stituted for that of Helios, the god of the sun, atop the colossal statue that had originally depicted Emperor Nero in front of the Colosseum. Commodus added the lion skin and club of Hercules and attached an inscription proclaiming his 620 victories in gladiatorial combat.[5]

In real life, Commodus' eldest living sister, Lucilla, plotted with a number of senators to kill him within the first two years of his reign.[6] Born Annia Aurelia Galeria Lucilla on March 7, 150, she had just turned 30 at the time of Marcus' death. As in the movie, she had been married to Lucius Verus, Marcus' former co-emperor. After that, however, specific historical details and the movie part company. Only fourteen when she married Verus in A.D. 164, Lucilla had borne him three children before she was widowed in 169, three months before her nineteenth birthday.[7] Obviously, the character identified in the movie as their eight-year-old son Lucius Verus is unhistorical. In fact, their only son and one of their two daughters had died as infants. Their other daughter (of unknown name) survived to be engaged to Claudius Pompeianus Quintianus, either a nephew or son by a previous marriage of Lucilla's second husband, Tiberius Claudius Pompeianus.[8] Both this daughter and Quintianus participated in a plot against Commodus in A.D. 182 but appear nowhere in the movie. Lucilla did have a young son by Pompeianus at the time in which the movie takes place. About six years old in 182, he was Aurelius Commodus Pompeianus, who lived to become a consul in 209 under Septimius Severus, only to be murdered under Caracalla.[9] He had survived earlier because his father had never opposed Commodus.

Lucilla had nothing in common with her son's father. Both she and her mother, Empress Faustina, bitterly resented the marriage that Marcus had hastily arranged between her and Claudius Pompeianus.[10] It had taken place only nine or ten months after Verus' death and before the proper mourning period had ended. Lucilla was unhappy with the extreme difference in their ages. She was only nineteen and a half, and he may have been over fifty. Both she and her mother found him socially beneath their dignity since he was the son of a provin-

---

5   Herodian 1.15.9, HA Comm. 15.8, Dio 72/73.22.3. The *Augustan History* gives the correct figure of 620; cf. Whittaker, *Herodian*, vol. 1, 107 note 2.

6   Herodian 1.3–8, Dio 72/73.4.4–6, HA Comm. 4.1–5.8.

7   Anthony R. Birley, *Marcus Aurelius: A Biography*, 2nd edn, rev. (1993; rpt. London and New York: Routledge, 2000), 131 and 196. Birley, 44–5, gives a chronological overview of events during the lifetime of Marcus Aurelius.

8   Birley, *Marcus Aurelius*, 196. Cf. Whittaker, *Herodian*, vol. 1, 48 note 1.

9   HA Carac. 3.8. Cf. Birley, *Marcus Aurelius*, 196 and 247 (F4).

10   HA Marc. 20.7, Dio 72/73.4.5.

cial Equestrian from Antioch in Syria.[11] This marriage was the source of the cold relations between Lucilla and Marcus that the movie never adequately explains.

Having been an Augusta as the wife of Verus, Lucilla probably wanted to be one again. Marcus, however, had chosen Pompeianus because he was a loyal and valuable military officer who could protect the imperial family but whose social station made impossible any ambitions of his own for the throne.[12] He was one of those whom Marcus left to form Commodus' council of advisors, and he remained completely loyal to his young emperor.[13] Even though his son or nephew Quintianus, his wife, and his stepdaughter were at the center of the plot in A.D. 182, he was completely uninvolved. This was fortunate for him, for, unlike in the movie, the unsuccessful conspirators were executed, even Lucilla after she was briefly exiled on the isle of Capri.[14] Having escaped the bloodbath, Pompeianus prudently retired from public life to his villa at Terracina and twice refused offers of the purple after Commodus' assassination.[15]

Except for his love of the games, there is not much that is historical about the Commodus we see in *Gladiator*. He appears to be in his mid-to-late twenties, is of average build, has dark hair, and fights with his right hand. In reality, he was only eighteen and a half when Marcus died, had a very strong physique, sported golden blond hair, and fought with his left hand.[16] Moreover, he was not single, as the movie represents him, but had been married to Bruttia Crispina in A.D. 178 at the age of sixteen. It was not until after the conspiracy of A.D. 182 that he divorced her for adultery and had her executed.[17]

The picture of Commodus as a man starved for paternal affection, lusting after his sister, and even murdering his father to avoid the ultimate rejection of being passed over as his successor has some support in the often tendentious and sensationalistic ancient sources. The *Life of Commodus* in the notorious pastiche of fact and fiction known as the *Augustan History* takes almost pornographic delight in depicting the drunkenness and sexual excesses that every ancient rhetorical hack stereotypically ascribed to a tyrannical ruler. Ironically, Lucilla is the only

11   *HA Marc.* 20.6.
12   Birley, *Marcus Aurelius*, 161–2.
13   Herodian 1.8.4.
14   Dio 72/73.4.3–6, Herodian 1.8.3–8, *HA Comm.* 4.1–5.7.
15   Dio 72/73.4.1–2, 72/73.20.1, and 73/74.3.1–2; *HA Pert.* 4.10 and *Did. Jul.* 8.3.
16   Herodian 1.7.56 and 17.12, Dio 72/73.19.2 and 22.3.
17   *HA Marc.* 27.8 and *Comm.* 5.9, Herodian 1.8.4, Dio 71/72.33.1 and 72/73.4.6.

sister with whom he is not accused of incestuous relations. However, the filmmakers are to be commended for not focusing on the biographer's unreliable charges and for not turning *Gladiator* into another cheap sexploitation epic of Roman imperial orgies.

Historical evidence does not support Anthony Birley's speculation that "Commodus may have been a lonely figure."[18] Although he correctly points out that Commodus lost a twin brother at the age of four, a younger brother at eight, and his mother at fourteen, Birley wrongly claims that four of Commodus' five living sisters were considerably older. Fadilla was only two to two and a half years older and Cornificia no more than a year and a half.[19] They may well have entered marriage at about the time his mother died, but he himself was married only two years later. It is true that Marcus was often away on campaigns between Commodus' eighth and thirteenth years from A.D. 169 to 175.[20] Nevertheless, Marcus lavished great care on providing Commodus with the best tutors and doctors and brought him to the front by June of A.D. 172 at the latest.[21]

One might argue that his serious nature, evident since boyhood, and the self-control of a Stoic philosopher, demonstrated at the death of Commodus' twin brother, would not have made Marcus Aurelius a warm or demonstrative parent.[22] Nevertheless, the picture that emerges from his correspondence with his beloved teacher Cornelius Fronto and from his *Meditations* is that of a kind, sympathetic, and affectionate man. Indeed, it is hard to imagine that he had at least fourteen children with his wife of thirty years simply out of a grim sense of Stoic duty.[23]

The idea presented in the movie that Marcus had decided to pass over Commodus and restore the old free republic is an instance of pandering to an American audience. Nobody, not even the senators who plotted against Commodus, wanted to restore the Roman republic. The office of emperor was a necessity universally recognized. The main source of friction between the emperors and a number of senators was the question of how that office should be filled. Leading senators wanted to be able to

18   Anthony R. Birley, *Septimius Severus: The African Emperor*, 2nd edn, rev. (London and New York: Routledge, 1999), 57.

19   Birley, *Marcus Aurelius*, 247–8 (F8–9).

20   Birley, *Septimius Severus*, 58.

21   Herodian 1.2.1, 4.3, and 5.3; *HA Comm.* 11.14. See also Whittaker, *Herodian*, vol. 1, 24 note 1; Birley, *Marcus Aurelius*, 174 and 284 note 31.

22   *HA Marc.* 2.6 and 21.3–5.

23   For the number and names of their children see Birley, *Marcus Aurelius*, 239 and 247–8 (F1–14).

choose a mature man of experience and proven merit from their ranks. That, in effect, is what had happened when the previous four emperors had had to adopt their successors. The soldiers, however, always favored hereditary succession, and without dynastic loyalty it was all too easy for an ambitious general to use his army to contest the choice of a new emperor other than himself.[24]

The ancient reports that Marcus Aurelius feared Commodus to be an unsuitable candidate for emperor and that Commodus brought about Marcus' death are fictions designed to discredit Commodus and to justify his overthrow.[25] Marcus never left any doubt about his dynastic designs. In A.D. 166, when he and Verus celebrated their joint triumph over the Parthians, five-year-old Commodus and Marcus' other then-surviving son, three-year-old Annius Verus, were proclaimed Caesars, while some of Marcus' daughters rode in the triumphal procession.[26] Both Commodus and his father jointly received the title Germanicus on the northern front in A.D. 172.[27] In May of 175, Commodus again joined his father on the German frontier and received the *toga virilis* two months later.[28] Right after that, Marcus took Commodus on a trip to the east to ensure loyalty to his dynasty after Avidius Cassius' revolt.[29] After their return, Commodus received a grant of *imperium* and, in the subsequent triumph to celebrate Avidius Cassius' defeat, drove the triumphal chariot while Marcus humbly walked alongside.[30] A week later, on January 1, 177, Commodus, only four months past his fifteenth birthday, became the youngest consul in Roman history up to that time. Later that year he received the tribunician power, the name Augustus, and all other marks of imperial dignity except the title of Pontifex Maximus.[31] Contrary to the picture presented in *Gladiator*, Commodus was joint ruler with his father from the beginning of A.D. 177. After that, for example, imperial legal decisions were issued jointly in their names.[32] Finally, on August 3,

---

24   Cf. Birley, *Marcus Aurelius*, 224–5, and Michael Grant, *The Antonines: The Roman Empire in Transition* (London and New York: Routledge, 1994), 62–3.
25   *HA Marc.* 27.11–12, Dio 71/72.33.4–34.1 and 72/73.1, Herodian 1.3.1–4.6.
26   *HA Marc.* 12.7–10 and *Comm.* 11.13.
27   References in note 21, above.
28   *HA Marc.* 22.12 and *Comm.* 2.1–2 and 12.2.
29   *HA Comm.* 2.3. He also took some of his daughters and his wife Faustina, who died en route in Asia Minor (*HA Marc.* 26.49 and Dio 71/72.29.1). Cf. Birley, *Marcus Aurelius*, 286 note 20.
30   *HA Marc.* 16.2 and *Comm.* 2.4 and 12.4–5.
31   *HA Comm.* 2.4 and *Marc.* 27.5. Cf. Birley, *Marcus Aurelius*, 195–7.
32   Birley, *Marcus Aurelius*, 199.

178, they both left Rome to take command on the northern front, and they remained there until Marcus' death.[33]

Marcus was not quite fifty-nine when he died, perhaps of plague.[34] *Gladiator* does capture his kindly and philosophical nature, but Richard Harris's decrepit frailty, thin beard, and wispy hair bear little resemblance to Marcus' statues, portrait busts, and portraits on coins, even to one depicting him near the end of his life. Instead, they show him as a fairly vigorous man with a full beard and a thick curly head of hair.[35] Of course, official portraiture is not any more averse to improving on reality than are Hollywood make-up artists, and Marcus may have looked preternaturally aged by the time he died, especially if he had contracted the plague. He had been having problems with his health for a long time. In the mid-170s, he complained of chest and stomach pains and an inability to sleep. The famous physician Galen prescribed a compound of theriac that contained opium, and the historian Cassius Dio described him as very weak in body compared with the man that he had been in earlier days.[36] In his *Meditations*, Marcus remarks on his gray hair and refers to being on the threshold of death.[37] Indeed, rumors that he had died in A.D. 175 were believable enough to generate support for Avidius Cassius' abortive bid for power.[38]

Still, Dio and others may have taken too literally Marcus' gloomy view of his health. A man approaching sixty and seeing his gray hairs in the mirror may well feel the breeze of time's winged chariot and may exaggerate how much nearer he is to his last day than to his first, particularly if he is a man who is on active duty in a plague-ravaged war zone and who has already seen the deaths of his wife and at least eight of their children. Marcus seems to have suffered no ill effects from the rigors of the journey that undoubtedly hastened his wife's death in A.D. 175; he was able to accompany his triumphal chariot on foot in 176, and he set off for the rigors of a northern winter camp in 178.[39]

33 *HA Comm.* 2.5 and 12.7. Cf. Birley, *Marcus Aurelius*, 209–10.
34 Dio 71/72.33.4, *HA Marc.* 28.1–9, Herodian 3.1 and 4.7. Cf. Birley, *Marcus Aurelius*, 210.
35 See Birley, *Marcus Aurelius*, plates 16, 18 (coins), and 23 (the famous equestrian statue). Cf. Birley, 266–7.
36 Dio 71/72.6, 24.4, and 36.2. Cf. Birley, *Marcus Aurelius*, 179 and 285 note 41.
37 Marcus Aurelius, *Meditations* 2.2.
38 Dio 71/72.22.3–23.3.
39 Dio 71/72.27.3–32.3; *HA Marc.* 16.2 and 25.11–26.4, *Comm.* 2.3. Indeed, even Dio was compelled to comment that Marcus had trained his body in physical endurance (Dio 71/72.34.2).

There are no ancient portraits with which to compare the depiction of Maximus Decimus Meridius, because he never existed at all. He is a pastiche, a composite figure of the kind of able men from the provinces who were tangible proof of Marcus Aurelius' insistence on utilizing the talents of any man beneficial to the state.[40] Like Marcus himself and the earlier emperors Trajan and Hadrian, Maximus came from a provincial family in Spain. His longing for home and family echo sentiments that the historian Herodian attributes to Claudius Pompeianus, whose career as a military officer from the provinces resembled that of Maximus in many ways.[41] The man who actually held the supreme field command in the great battle of A.D. 179 on which the opening scene is probably based was Taruttienus Paternus, senior prefect of the Praetorian Guard, who was later executed for supposed involvement in the plot of 182.[42]

We might wish that the last character ever played by Oliver Reed, the gladiatorial impresario (*lanista*) Proximo, were a historical character, too. If he were, his name would be Proximus and not Proximo, which is a Latin dative or ablative and makes no sense as his name. Latin gets butchered even more when Proximo brings his troupe of gladiators to Rome, where they enter a building labeled LVDVS MAGNVS GLADIATORES instead of LVDVS MAGNVS GLADIATORVM.[43] Finally, Proximo wrongly claims that Marcus Aurelius had banned gladiatorial contests and thereby forced him to leave Rome to scratch out a living in hick towns such as Zucchabar, which really was a Roman colony in Mauretania.[44] Marcus had banned all games in Antioch to punish its citizens for supporting the rebel Avidius Cassius, but this would have had no impact on Rome or Proximo.[45]

However, Marcus had also created a serious shortage of gladiators throughout the empire in the early 170s by conscripting them for his northern wars. As a result, the cost of gladiatorial contests rose to ruinous levels for those wealthy citizens obligated to provide them.[46]

40   Dio 71/72.34.4.

41   Herodian 1.6.4.

42   *HA Comm.* 4.1 and 14.8. Cf. Birley, *Marcus Aurelius*, 207.

43   The *Ludus Magnus* did exist beside the Colosseum; see L. Richardson, Jr., *A New Topographical Dictionary of Ancient Rome* (Baltimore and London: Johns Hopkins University Press, 1992), 236–8.

44   *Barrington Atlas of the Greek and Roman World*, ed. Richard J. A. Talbert (Princeton: Princeton University Press, 2000), map 30 at D4.

45   *HA Marc.* 25.9.

46   *HA Marc.* 23.4–6. According to Dio 71/72.29.3–4, Marcus preferred to watch gladiators fight with blunted weapons to avoid bloodshed, which may have sparked the false rumor reported in *HA Marc.* 23.6 that he was going to ban gladiatorial combats.

If Proximo had possessed a supply of gladiators, he would have made windfall profits until Marcus and Commodus tried to remedy the situation in A.D. 177 by fixing the prices of gladiators throughout the empire and even permitting the use of condemned criminals at cheap rates in Gaul.[47]

The depiction of gladiatorial armor, weapons, and combat in *Gladiator* is riddled with inaccuracies. By the second century A.D., gladiators had become divided into a number of strict categories such as *eques* ("horseman"), *provocator* ("challenger"), *murmillo* (named after a Greek term for a kind of fish), *thraex* or *thrax* ("Thracian") and the similarly but not identically equipped *hoplomachus* ("heavily armed fighter"), *retiarius* ("net fighter"), and *secutor* or *contraretiarius*, each with specific armor, weapons, and styles of fighting.[48] Except for the fighters on horseback and the *provocatores*, gladiators of the same type were not paired together in fights, and a strict protocol determined which type was paired with which other.[49] For example, a *secutor* was invariably paired with a *retiarius*.

Commodus always fought as a *secutor*, so in the movie's climactic fight his head should have been completely enclosed in a bullet-shaped helmet with a small flared collar at the neck, a low metal crest running back to front on top, and only two round holes for the eyes. Except for a loincloth, tubular padding on his sword arm and shield-side leg, and a leather gaiter on the other leg, Commodus should have been naked, protected only by an oblong shield (*scutum*). He should have carried a *gladius*, the short thrusting sword that gave gladiators their name and the only thing that the movie had right. Maximus should have been a *retiarius*, naked except for a loincloth, gaiters on both legs, and a *manica*, a padded arm guard that ended with a high-swept metal shoulder guard. His weapons should have been a wide-meshed round net about ten feet in diameter, a trident, and a *gladius*.

47 Birley, *Marcus Aurelius*, 201.
48 Marcus Junkelmann, "*Familia Gladiatoria*: The Heroes of the Amphitheatre," in *Gladiators and Caesars: The Power of Spectacle in Ancient Rome*, ed. Eckart Köhne and Cornelia Ewigleben; English ed. by Ralph Jackson (Berkeley and Los Angeles: University of California Press, 2000), 31–74, provides a detailed outline of these matters, with illustrations, at 45–67. He gives information on all aspects of Roman gladiators, including the results of modern recreations of their outfit and combat, in *Das Spiel mit dem Tod: So kämpften Roms Gladiatoren* (Mainz: von Zabern, 2000). He discusses inaccuracies in *Gladiator* on several occasions.
49 Cf. Junkelmann, "*Familia Gladiatoria*," 51 and 57.

Not only did earlier gladiatorial combats in the movie fail to portray the standard combinations of armor and weaponry, but they also depicted them incorrectly. For the most part they are melees among a number of contestants, which in Rome were more characteristic of staged battles and criminal executions. True gladiatorial combats were limited to individual pairs who fought according to precise rules enforced by referees. They did not flail and hack at each other but fought like the highly trained professional duelists that they were.

Despite a plethora of factual errors, *Gladiator* vividly and convincingly portrays some important general truths about the Roman world in the late second century A.D. Many viewers found the movie violent and gory. Unfortunately, life in the ancient world was generally much more gruesome and bloody than life in modern industrial democracies. Marcus Aurelius spent most of his reign fighting wars. Despite the questionable use of fire-hurling catapults, the brutal hand-to-hand butchery of the opening battle gives us a good idea of the ugly side of legionary combat and the horrible ways in which one could be killed or wounded. Indeed, such scenes are graphically depicted on the famous column in Rome that commemorates Marcus Aurelius' northern wars.[50]

Not only on the battlefield but everywhere did people constantly confront sudden violent or painful death. Romans were acutely aware that we are, as Proximo said, "shadows and dust."[51] Murder was frequent in crowded and poorly policed cities, while brigands and raiders constantly harried the countryside. Early in Marcus Aurelius' reign, Britain was disturbed by raids and rebellions, Moorish tribesmen made frequent raids into Spain from northern Africa, and various Germanic tribes conducted severe raids from across the Rhine and the Danube into Roman territory and even penetrated Italy and Greece. Rome and Italy also suffered devastating floods and famine.[52] Politically, after the abortive plot of A.D. 182 the senatorial class again faced a murderous purge, such as had occurred earlier under Caligula, Nero, and Domitian.[53] The brutal murders of Maximus' wife and son in *Gladiator* mirror that reality. Marcus had avoided such extremes in dealing with opponents, but those who were loyal to him did not scruple to cut off the head of Avidius Cassius and send it to him.[54]

---

50   Birley, *Marcus Aurelius*, 178.
51   Proximo misquotes Horace, *Odes* 4.7.16.
52   Birley, *Marcus Aurelius*, 120–2.
53   Dio 72/73.5.1–7.3 and 9.1–14.3, *HA Comm.* 4.4–11, 5.7–8.4, and 14.8; Herodian 1.8.3–9.1.
54   Dio 71/72.27.3.

Plague had ravaged the Roman Empire since the return of Lucius Verus' army from Parthia in A.D. 166, and the lack of effective medicines rendered all diseases more deadly than they are now.[55] Death rates were very high, particularly for the young. For example, Marcus' beloved teacher Fronto lost five children, each before the next was born. Only the sixth lived to adulthood, and that one lost a three-year-old son before the disconsolate Fronto had had a chance to see him. Marcus himself had lost his father when he was three or four, at least four of his fourteen known children had died before their first birthdays, and in the case of four others probably only one had lived past his sixth birthday. His wife was dead at forty-five.[56]

With the grim reaper visible everywhere, people of all classes were preoccupied with the prospect of imminent death. That preoccupation permeates Marcus Aurelius' own *Meditations*. It is summed up in the movie in the words that Maximus ascribes to Marcus: "Death smiles at us all. All a man can do is smile back."[57] It is also behind the enormous growth of the medical profession in the first two centuries A.D., the proliferation of healing spas, outright quackery, and religious charlatans.

The perception of death lurking everywhere helps explain the popularity of gladiatorial shows all over the empire. As the movie's fictional senator Gracchus says of Commodus and his attempt to win the masses: "He will bring them death, and they will love him for it." Gladiatorial shows and related games like beast hunts and chariot races were religiously charged spectacles of Roman power and were used to maintain political and social control.[58] But the great popular enthusiasm they generated had nothing to do with any desire by the masses for Roman rituals and expressions of power and everything to do with the ancient warrior code that stressed overcoming death by achieving honor and undying fame through killing others or at least meeting a glorious death in battle. Gladiatorial combat paralleled the daily struggle with death faced by everyone and provided a model for how to confront it heroically.[59] As

55 *HA Marc.* 13.3–6, 14.5, 17.2 and 21.7–7; *HA Ver.* 8.1–4; Ammianus Marcellinus 31.6.24; Orosius 7.15.5–6 and 7.27.7; Dio 72/73.14.3–4.

56 Cf. Birley, *Marcus Aurelius*, 31 and 143.

57 These words may have been inspired by Marcus Aurelius' similar words at *Meditations* 9.3.

58 Cf. in general Alison Futrell, *Blood in the Arena: The Spectacle of Roman Power* (Austin: University of Texas Press, 1997; rpt. 2000).

59 Cf. in particular Thomas Wiedemann, *Emperors and Gladiators* (London and New York: Routledge, 1992; rpt. 1995), 34–9 and 92–7.

Juba, the black gladiator who healed Maximus' wound, tells him when he first refuses to play his new role as a gladiator: "Why don't you fight? We all have to fight!" By facing death heroically, one might actually overcome it for the present by defeating one's foe or, by fighting courageously even in the face of overwhelming odds, obtain a degree of heroic honor in defeat that transcended death. Proximo says it all: "Ultimately, we're all dead men. Sadly, we cannot choose how, *but* – we *can* decide how we *meet* that end in order that we are remembered as men."

The lesson of the arena was that by not giving up without a fight even someone who had suffered the all-too-common misfortune of enslavement could become a noble hero. To quote Proximo again: "When you die, and die you shall, your transition shall be to the sound of 'clap, clap.' Gladiators, I salute you." Maximus overcame his reversal of fortune and accomplished one of the deeds that brought the greatest heroic honor and fame: vengeance on his enemy. Thus he redeemed himself. When death had claimed him, Lucilla said: "He was a soldier of Rome. Honor him!" Many willing hands bore him off in triumph.

This powerful film has sparked enormous interest in the history behind it. Perhaps historians of ancient Rome should simply be grateful for its valid general insights and overlook its many factual errors. The *artiste* will say that concern with such details merely reflects the overly punctilious quibbles of pettifogging pedants who cannot appreciate the forest for the trees. Certainly creative artists must be granted some poetic license, but it is still disappointing that the scriptwriters of *Gladiator* did not show at least a little more intellectual discipline and respect for the historical record. Poetic license is not a carte blanche for the wholesale disregard of facts in historical fiction or films. In most cases, getting easily determined factual details correct is not incompatible with the drama and excitement needed for a best-selling book or a success at the box office.

In *Gladiator*, for example, the opening battle does not need either the anachronistic German shepherd or the questionable catapults to give us a visceral impression of war on Rome's northern frontier. A more accurate portrayal of gladiatorial arms and armor and their pairings in the arena would not have made the fighting less dramatic. A true portrayal of Marcus Aurelius' death and his relationship with Commodus would not have made it more difficult to make the latter a hated villain. An exciting plot and compelling characters along the movie's actual plot lines could easily have coexisted with recorded events and characters in the proper chronological framework.

First, the opening battle could have been the actual battle of A.D. 179. Then there could have been a quick segue to the death of Marcus Aurelius and to the succession of Commodus a few months later. During this sequence of events, the focus could have been on the historical Quintilii brothers, Condianus and Maximus, and their respective sons. These famous men were no friends of Commodus and, with the exception of Maximus' son, suffered execution at Commodus' command after the executions of Lucilla and Crispina. Historically, they could have been present as high-ranking officers and advisors at the battle of A.D. 179 and at Marcus' death, and they could have been sympathetic to Lucilla's plot. Dio's story of the surviving son's escape and disappearance has all the elements of a Hollywood script and could easily have fit the plot of *Gladiator*. When he found out that he was marked for death, he filled his mouth with the blood of a hare, spit it out while faking a fatal fall from his horse, had faithful servants substitute a dead ram for his body in the coffin on his funeral pyre, and disappeared, never to be found despite a massive manhunt.[60]

The scriptwriters could have made this man the hero of their film.[61] He could be wounded by pursuing assassins, fall into the hands of a *lanista*, and become a gladiator with the nickname "Narcissus," the name of the historical athlete who was part of the successful plot against Commodus that involved the emperor's mistress Marcia and others in A.D. 192.[62] Poetic license would allow the record to be altered somewhat to create a dramatic ending in the arena. Nevertheless, the end could be kept close to the historical record of Commodus' death. In this scenario, "Narcissus," whose true identity has been previously revealed to the audience, could fight as a *retiarius* in a classic match-up with Commodus as *secutor* and, after both lose their weapons, strangle Commodus with his last ounce of strength before dying from tiger-inflicted wounds in an unfair fight similar to the one that now occurs earlier in

---

60   Dio 72/73.5.3–6.5.
61   Dio makes it quite clear that the son of Maximus had the same name as Maximus' brother, Sextus Quintilius Condianus. One would expect that a son of that name belonged to Sextus, and that is how the later *Augustan History* identifies him. Dio, however, was a contemporary who had personal knowledge of these matters. Probably Maximus' naming a son after his brother was a sign of the brotherly affection for which they were famous (Dio 72/73.5.3–6.1, *HA Comm.* 5.9). In that case, it would not be too far-fetched to add "Maximus" to the son's name and keep it in the movie as the name of the hero.
62   Dio 72/73.22.6, Herodian 1.17.11.

the movie.[63] In this way, by a combination of rigorous attention to the historical record and creative imagination, *Gladiator* could have been much more historically valid and still have remained dramatically as exciting as it is.

CHAPTER FOUR

The Pedant Goes to Hollywood: The Role of the Academic Consultant

Kathleen M. Coleman

The job of the historian is to try to uncover the truth about the past.[1] This may sound straightforward, but in practice it is not. The historian has first to assemble the available sources; at this stage his enemy is the accident of transmission, since the survival of evidence is either distressingly random, as in the field of ancient history, or overwhelmingly inclusive, as in contemporary affairs. The next stage is to analyze this evidence in a manner so sophisticated as to present a coherent and compelling interpretation that takes account of gaps, bias, inconsistencies, falsifications, and all the other distortions attendant upon any event in which humans are involved. Part of the historian's method is akin to science, as in the painstaking reconstruction of a damaged inscription or the calculation of the time it would take an army of a certain size to march a certain distance under a variety of weather conditions. But another part of the historian's job is much closer to the creative arts than to science. This is the imaginative leap involved in any act of historical interpretation, however modest or limited.

What I have called the "imaginative leap" is usually closer to a series of cautious steps through a morass of uncertainty than to a bold jump

1 This essay is an expansion of an article that originally appeared in Swedish: "Pedanten åker till Hollywood: En rådgivande akademikers roll," *Filmhäftet*, 29.2 (2001), 4–6. I am grateful to Michael Tapper, the journal's editor, for having generously encouraged me to republish my essay in English.

across it onto the dry land of confident interpretation. Recently, however, the gulf between history and imaginative writing has been narrowed, most sensationally by the publication of a biography of Ronald Reagan in which the author claims the status of a first-hand witness by adopting the persona of an entirely fictitious character.[2] Ancient history, too, has seen the blurring of the boundary between fact and fiction. Keith Hopkins has recently published an analysis of the origins of Christianity which opens with the experiences of a pair of time-travelers transported from modern England to the Mediterranean world of the first century A. D.[3] In a work like this, history is intermittently cloaked as fiction, but the reverse is also perfectly respectable and familiar to all of us: fiction cloaked as history. The great historical novels of such authors as Mary Renault, bringing ancient Greece to life, or Rosemary Sutcliff, re-creating Roman, Viking, and Saxon Britain for an audience of young adults, are so exhaustively researched that they weave rich period detail into an atmosphere of seductive authenticity.[4] The convention that permits a work of fiction to be created around historical characters legitimizes and authenticates the historical novel as a proper literary pursuit. Do the same conventions apply to the historical film? Or, to put it another way, does the same responsibility for creating a historically authentic artifact apply to filmmakers as to novelists?

The factors that impinge upon historical authenticity on the screen are legion. Authenticity itself does not depend upon strict adherence to historical fact; a feature film is not a documentary. A fictitious plot involving historical characters can create a thoroughly authentic atmosphere,

2   Edmund Morris, *Dutch: A Memoir of Ronald Reagan* (New York: Random House, 1999).
3   Keith Hopkins, *A World Full of Gods: Pagans, Jews, and Christians in the Roman Empire* (1999; rpt. London: Phoenix, 2000), published in the United States as *A World Full of Gods: The Strange Triumph of Christianity* (2000; rpt. New York: Plume, 2001).
4   Mary Renault wrote eight novels set in ancient Greece: *The King Must Die* (1958) and *The Bull from the Sea* (1962) recount the adventures of Theseus; *The Praise Singer* (1978) is about the Greek lyric poet Simonides; *The Last of the Wine* (1956) is set in Athens during the Peloponnesian War; *The Mask of Apollo* (1966) deals with theatrical life in fourth-century Syracuse; *Fire from Heaven* (1969), *The Persian Boy* (1972), and *Funeral Games* (1981) comprise a trilogy about Alexander the Great. Renault also wrote *The Nature of Alexander* (1976), a biography. Rosemary Sutcliff's most famous novel set in the Roman period, *The Eagle of the Ninth* (1965), displays her special command of military detail. She also writes evocatively of the period of the Roman withdrawal from Britain in, for example, *The Lantern Bearers* (1959) and *Frontier Wolf* (1981). She is renowned for her Arthurian trilogy *The Sword and the Circle* (1981), *The Light Beyond the Forest* (1980), and *The Road to Camlann* (1981).

but it is very hard to achieve. In part, authenticity depends upon visual details such as artifacts, architecture, costumes, and the like. But in part it depends upon the ideology, outlook, and deportment of the characters. Hence the demands of the storyline will be incompatible with the goal of authenticity if the plot itself does not grow out of the historical context in which it purports to be placed. Grafting the plot onto a historical background is fraught with difficulty. Ideally, the scriptwriter who conceives the plot should be saturated in the study of the period. Even if this is so, however, the script itself remains only the skeleton; it is the acting, the sets, and the cinematography that put flesh on its bones. So the historical consultant should be a person who is intimately involved with the entire process of making the film, from its initial conception on the scriptwriter's keyboard to ultimate realization on the screen. To do the job thoroughly, such a person must be the close confidant of the director, a trusted and respected member of the creative team for the entire duration of the actual filming process. It is an utter fallacy to suppose that the consultant's role can be limited to a certain phase, such as the finalizing of the script prior to filming, not least because the script is never final until the last snippet of film has dropped onto the cutting-room floor.

It would be equally fallacious to treat the consultant's advice like a buffet supper from which one guest might select five dishes and someone else three entirely different confections. In responding to queries from different members of the production team, a consultant offers advice that is internally consistent. But if all of the consultant's responses and suggestions are not made available to the entire team, then nobody else sees these suggestions as a coherent whole, with the result that there is no coherence in the use to which they are put. In any case, the sheer range of issues that can impinge upon historical authenticity makes it almost inevitable that no single scholar could claim equal competence in them all. Consultants with specialized historical knowledge will certainly need to be involved, such as military historians for battle scenes. A chief consultant should be in an excellent position to recommend such specialists, and to coordinate their suggestions in the event that different specialists offer incompatible suggestions as a result of differing perspectives. But, as in any team endeavor, it is crucial for all the people involved to understand how the process is meant to work. A consultant who does not know whether specialized information is being sought from others runs the risk of expending enormous amounts of time and energy researching an area that may turn out to have been dealt with by somebody else. Alternatively, a consultant who has recommended a particular specialist is likely to refrain from commenting on any matter pertaining to the specialist's field, under the impression that the true expert is dealing with it, whereas no such person may in fact have been approached. As a result of such failures of communication, crucial items may escape scrutiny.

The issue of managing the consultant's role effectively is, of course, predicated upon the assumption that the director and the producers recognize historical authenticity as one of their top priorities. If it were their sole priority, they would presumably be making a documentary rather than a feature film. And so the consultant in turn has to recognize that historical authenticity must be made to harmonize with aesthetic and dramatic considerations, as well as much else. The more frankly producers and their director articulate their competing concerns, the more likely it is that a consultant will be able to suggest ways to accommodate them while remaining faithful to the overall historical context. Irreconcilable conflicts may ensue if authenticity is competing with a different intention that is both powerful and unstated, such as the desire to engage in intertextual dialogue with previous cinematic treatments of a similar theme. If the standard for authenticity is determined by what has already been monumentalized on screen, the consultant really has no role to play at all. Maybe there is a residual notion in the film industry that the hiring of a consultant is in itself sufficient to give a film a veneer of respectability. If that attitude exists, it is, to say the least, unethical, and it is predicated upon the assumption, undoubtedly correct, that the vast majority of cinemagoers have no way of judging the authenticity of a historical film and do not care at all whether it is authentic or not. The consultant, however, cares extremely, not only because concern for the past is what presumably got him (or her) into the professional study of history in the first place, but because inevitably he (or she) feels invested in the final product. What produces this sense of investment?

A scholar is used to taking authorial responsibility for his or her work, be it as sole author, co-author, or editor of a multi-authored volume or a series. In short, anyone who is named as part of the creation of a work of scholarship is implicated in responsibility for it. This is why authors who thank their mentors in fulsome prefaces take care to dissociate those mentors from any shortcomings in the work. It is common to see expressions of thanks to "X, who read the whole book in typescript and offered many useful suggestions, but who should not be held responsible for my obstinacy in ignoring some of his recommendations." No such disclaimer should of course be necessary in a film, since a consultant cannot be held responsible for the use that is made of his or her advice, least of all when there is no guarantee that the advice has got further than an assistant producer's IN tray. But a consultant's investment in a project is not just a matter of professional association, nor even of investment of time and expertise. It requires a unique effort of what might best be termed "lateral thinking." A consultant who simply castigates one error after another is not playing a constructive role and is liable to appear intellectually arrogant. It is obviously a help to the scriptwriter and producers to know why something flouts the conventions of authenticity. But equally the consultant needs to understand what the scriptwriter, director, and producer are trying to do; understanding the motivation for an error is the first step toward finding a solution to the problem. Then the consultant will be in a position to suggest alternative strategies. I use the plural "strategies" advisedly, since a choice of remedy is a luxury that preserves the defaulter's sense of self-respect. And this is a key concept: Respect on the part of consultant and production must be mutual, otherwise the relationship is not partnership but exploitation.

Scholars are, of course, notorious for being obsessed with detail. It could be argued that a consultant preoccupied with minutiae will inevitably fail to see "the big picture." But detail is the repository of authenticity. Much of the detail in a film is incidental to the plot, and so there is nothing to be gained by distorting it. But precisely because detail is incidental, a filmmaker may not see the necessity to submit it to review by a consultant – hence the manifold inaccuracies in, for example, the sword-and-sandals genre that has bred a snobbish contempt in educated cinemagoers. But if scholars are obsessed with detail, they are also relatively oblivious of the budgetary necessity of haste, the "time is money" imperative. Painstaking scholarship does not count the cost of days or weeks, let alone months or years. This is one area in which the principles of the academy and the film studio are likely to differ. A responsible consultant has to be aware of deadlines and the necessity of responding quickly to queries, so that there are no grounds for the objection "There wasn't time" to consult the consultant. If, as in my ideal scenario, a team of consultants is present throughout the entire process, every detail, at least in theory, will be smoothly integrated into the whole without hold-ups. Degrees of compromise, however, are inevitably involved, prompting the question: Can the end justify the means? When an individual detail is false but the overall atmosphere in a scene is authentic, is the falsification justified? How, indeed, does one define "authentic atmosphere"?

Consultancy is not a job for a doctrinaire purist, but it is a job for a rigorous scholar who is prepared to subject each element to a critical test. The test question is not "Did this happen?" but "Could this have happened?" Historians may instinctively shy away from hypothetical questions. Scholarship aspires to scientific objectivity, yet the act of imaginative re-creation involved in framing hypotheses is unmistakably subjective. This element of subjectivity is unsettling for anyone who has been trained to strive for certainty where it can be realized and to admit uncertainty where it cannot. The role of consultant can shake a scholar out of professional complacency because it reveals the limits of our historical knowledge. But there is also an ethical dimension that is more troubling still: Is it proper to let the cinema-going public think that the past looked like our cinematic conception of it? In a film that involves a fictitious plot employing real characters, is it legitimate to dispense with an epigraph or postscript stating the bald historical facts? Is such an omission justifiable simply for the sake of preserving dramatic illusion? Will generations to come persist in believing that the cinematic fiction is what "really happened"? If so – and this is the really worrying question, especially on the lips of those whose bank balances are swelled by the takings at the box office – does it matter?

Undeniably, the public appetite for history is vastly stimulated by historical cinema, and once people have become interested in the past they are at liberty to acquaint themselves with the facts via the appropriate authorities. Cinematic versions of history, however, generate their own momentum. The self-referential aspect of historical cinema may be conditioned not so much by narcissism as by the perception that the past has to be presented in a recognizable package. Sir Lawrence Alma-Tadema, for instance, conceived of the Romans in Pre-Raphaelite mode; his legacy as "the painter who inspired Hollywood" determines the look that makes the Romans familiar even today.[5] The wardrobe department on the set of

5   Lawrence (born Laurens) Alma-Tadema (1836–1912) was an Anglo-Dutch painter who left Holland for England in 1873, acquiring a knighthood in 1899. His soubriquet "the painter who inspired Hollywood" was the title of an article about him by Mario Amaya in the London *Sunday Times* of February 18, 1968. In the words of Russell Ash in the unpaginated introduction to his book, *Sir Lawrence Alma-Tadema* (New York: Abrams, 1990), Alma-Tadema's sweeping canvases depicting crowd scenes from the ancient world anticipated "the grandeur of the wide-screen Hollywood epic." Reproductions of his paintings, specifically *Spring* and *The Finding of Moses*, influenced the set decorators and costume designers of such pioneering classics as D. W. Griffith's *Intolerance* (1916), Fred Niblo's *Ben-Hur: A Tale of the Christ* (1925), and Cecil B. DeMille's *Cleopatra* (1934) and *The Ten*

Ridley Scott's *Gladiator* could just as easily have modeled their costumes on Roman statuary in the Metropolitan Museum or the Louvre. But the bared shoulders and revealing garments sported by Lucilla and her entourage come ultimately from the canvases of Alma-Tadema, whose rendering of Roman luxury and decadence was bequeathed to the cinema in the silent era by Italian and American directors of epics set in ancient Rome. If the producers of *Gladiator* consulted an expert in Roman clothing, that process has left no trace; the costumes are simultaneously a tribute to the Rome created by Hollywood and an acknowledgment that the Rome that Hollywood created is now the only Rome that is universally familiar. But those who see clothing as the outer manifestation of the principles that inform a society will uncompromisingly reject such license. The Roman upper classes kept up appearances that are utterly at variance with Alma-Tadema's seductive portrayal. Yet for those viewers whose reception of history begins and ends with the version presented on screen, Hollywood's Rome is not a palimpsest but an original and ineradicable document.

The power of the Hollywood stereotype would be of scant concern if we did not look to the past for guidance. One of the many virtues of studying history is that it trains us to recognize human failings and the strategies that Man has adopted to cope with perennial problems in the human condition. It is natural and valuable for us to hold up the mirror of history and see ourselves in it. But here we are on the edge of another moral quagmire: Is it legitimate to make a film that is ostensibly about historical events but is fundamentally conceived as a critique of contemporary society? Does that falsify the past? Historians are, of course, fooling themselves if they imagine that they are free from the preconceptions imposed by their own time and culture. But frank awareness of this tendency is not the same as tacit exploitation of it. A respect for historical authenticity is a type of scholarly humility, just as a cavalier disregard for it arises from a combination of ignorance and intellectual arrogance. But most of the historical distortions in cinema are probably not the result of such ignorance or arrogance. They are much more likely to be conscious decisions based upon esthetics, pragmatism, or an estimation of the public appetite. Meanwhile the academy, too skittish (or too circumspect) to admit to re-creating the past, snorts and stamps at

Commandments (1956). See also Vern G. Swanson, *Sir Lawrence Alma-Tadema: The Painter of the Victorian Vision of the Ancient World* (London: Ash and Grant, 1977), 43. R. J. Barrow, *Lawrence Alma-Tadema* (London and New York: Phaidon, 2001), reproduces and discusses the painter's entire body of work.

the falsification. The academy's outrage may be fueled by a territorial imperative. But the real reason for the skirmish is ideological: Is the responsibility of relaying history compatible with an act of imaginative reconstruction? Sophisticated collaboration between film director and historical consultant could provide a positive answer to that question.

CHAPTER FIVE

Commodus and the Limits of the Roman Empire

Arthur M. Eckstein

Why did the Roman Empire stop expanding? For 500 years informal Roman influence over foreign peoples and states and direct Roman administration and rule over others consistently increased. The Romans' growing ambition to exert international control kept pace with their equally growing military and diplomatic capabilities to effect that control. The period from the mid-fourth century B.C. to the reign of Augustus, the first emperor (31 B.C. to A.D. 14), is marked by continuous and spectacular military success and territorial expansion. The city-states of Latium had been subjected and gradually assimilated, as had the Etruscans, Samnites, Greeks, and many other peoples who inhabited Italy from the Apennines to the straits of Messina. Sicily, Sardinia, and Corsica had been taken from the Greeks and Carthaginians. The Po Valley in northern Italy had been wrested from wild Celtic tribes. The powerful states of the Hellenistic east had come under Roman sway and in some cases under direct Roman administration; the last of those subjected was Cleopatra's Egypt. Control of Spain had been taken from Carthage and Spain's indigenous Celtiberian inhabitants, a conquest of many campaigns but complete by 20 B.C. The frontiers of Roman power had expanded especially quickly in the first century B.C., driven by the energies of a series of great generals. Pompey had pushed Roman power as far east as the Euphrates, Caesar as far north as the Rhine, Augustus all the way to the Danube.

But the pace of conquest slowed dramatically after Augustus, when a more monarchical-style government had replaced the republic. Although the conquest of Britain began in the 40s A.D. under Emperor Claudius and was essentially complete a generation later, on the continent German tribes thwarted sporadic Roman attempts to extend their influence north and east of the Rhine. The great indigenous kingdom of Dacia – roughly, modern Romania – had fallen to Emperor Trajan by A.D. 110, but after this there was little Roman movement north of the Danube. Roman attempts to extend control east of the Euphrates were sporadic, too, and met with little permanent success.

Both Anthony Mann's *The Fall of the Roman Empire* (1964) and Ridley Scott's *Gladiator* confront us early in their stories with savage fighting to bring the Germans north of the Danube into the Roman Empire. The campaign depicted in these films was begun by Emperor Marcus Aurelius (A.D. 161–80) but was abandoned by his son and successor Commodus (A.D. 180–92). Commodus is the villain in both films. They present his decision to forgo the conquest or assimilation of the Germans as a strong indication of his corrupt personal character. And more: The films also present Commodus' decision as a signal of the eventual end of Rome itself. Hence *The Fall of the Roman Empire* opens with slow, even funereal, music played by organ and strings under the credits and with dark and depressing images of Roman fortifications set amid the snowy forests and hills of the north, as a narrator's voice proclaims the coming end. In *Gladiator*, too, Commodus' decision to abandon Marcus' conquest is wrong and dangerous from a military perspective. More to the dramatic point, it is also morally outrageous within the terms of the Roman ideals presented to the viewer, which in turn become the viewer's ideals. In the earlier film, his insanity and megalomania make Commodus give up the wise policies of his father; in *Gladiator*, it is sheer love of luxury paired with sexual debauchery. (Commodus lusts after his sister Lucilla and threatens to seduce her young son.)

It is my purpose to show that neither of these portrayals is true to the facts. The decision of the historical Commodus to abandon his father's campaigns on the middle and upper Danube was well within Roman cultural and geo-political traditions. It was part of the Roman government's haphazard series of attempts to deal with problems on a frontier held against the constant pressure of the Germanic peoples. Moreover, Commodus' decision had nothing to do with the eventual end of Roman power. That occurred 300 years later, as the voice-over at the beginning of Mann's film admits, thereby undermining the whole point of the introduction. The best way to understand Commodus' decision of A.D. 180 is to place it within the framework of the broader and more important problem of the end of Roman expansion under the emperors.

Many scholars view the Roman republic as a state which came to possess exceptional bellicosity, a military machine that lived by constant predatory aggression. The main "foreign policy" task of the senate under the republic was the assignment, every spring, of army commands against enemies established or potential; the Roman state assumed that some war would occur somewhere each year. The aristocrats who sat in the senate, deliberated on war and peace, and handed out commands were a militarized elite deeply imbued with a warrior ethos in which success in warfare was the main road to power, influence, glory, and, not least, wealth, the last through systematic looting of enemies. Roman merchants prospered by selling army supplies to the state and profited from the extension of Roman political influence overseas: Roman trade did follow Roman legions. The general populace benefited from booty won and especially from land confiscated from defeated enemies and then parceled out to needy Romans; social problems, such as land maldistribution, were often solved at others' expense. In the words of Joseph Schumpeter, the sociologist of modern imperialism, about ancient Egypt: "*Created by wars that required it, the machine now created the wars it required.*"[1]

This view is now dominant among modern scholars of Roman history, too.[2] On this assumption, however, the end of Roman imperial

1   Joseph A. Schumpeter, "The Sociology of Imperialisms," in *Imperialism and Social Classes*, ed. Paul M. Sweezy; tr. Heinz Norden (1951; rpt. Philadelphia: Orion, 1991), 1–130; quotation at 33. Schumpeter's work was first published in German in 1919.

2   Schumpeter's vision was taken up in the groundbreaking work of William V. Harris, *War and Imperialism in Republican Rome 327–70 B.C.* (Oxford: Clarendon Press, 1979; rpt. 1992). See also, among many other studies, Ernst Badian, *Roman Imperialism in the Late Republic*, 2nd edn (Ithaca and London: Cornell University Press, 1968; rpt. 1981), and, more recently, Tim Cornell, "The End of Roman Imperial Expansion," in *War and Society in the Roman World*, ed. John Rich and Graham Shipley (London and New York: Routledge, 1993; rpt. 1995), 139–70, especially 140–2; and Nathan Rosenstein, "Republican Rome," in *War and Society in the Ancient and Medieval Worlds: Asia, the Mediterranean, and Mesoamerica*, ed. Kurt Raaflaub and Nathan Rosenstein (Cambridge and London: Harvard University Press, 1999), 193–216, especially 196–205. Cf. further Edward N. Luttwak, *The Grand Strategy of the Roman Empire: From the First Century A. D. to the Third* (Baltimore and London: Johns Hopkins University Press, 1976; rpt. 1979). The charge that Romans had an imperial master plan to obtain world power is quite old. An eloquent early statement is chapter 6 ("The Conduct the Romans Used to Subjugate All Peoples") of Montesquieu's *Considerations on the Causes of the Greatness of the Romans and Their Decline*, first published in 1734 and revised in 1748. It is easily accessible under the title quoted above in the translation by David Lowenthal (1965; rpt., with corrections, Indianapolis and Cambridge: Hackett, 1999).

expansion in the first and second centuries A.D. becomes extremely mysterious. If the Roman state and Roman society and culture under the republic had been a military machine not only geared for war but ever in need of it, what brought the machine – if we assume for the moment that there actually was such a machine – to a stop?

The traditional argument had been that Roman power, upon reaching the Rhine, Danube, and Euphrates rivers, had finally found secure frontiers beyond which expansion was unnecessary for reasons of security. But although the Rhine makes a fine defensive barrier – it is both deep and swift – this is not true of either the Danube or the Euphrates. These two rivers are not very defensible and are odd places at which to stop expansion. Moreover, in antiquity these rivers were not frontiers separating ethnic groups and therefore were not natural boundaries, either. Rather, ethnic groups spanned both sides of all three rivers. For instance, Germanic peoples lived on both sides of the Rhine.[3] The traditional idea that the three rivers formed natural boundaries in antiquity is therefore false, and the Rome-of-the-river-lines that we see on modern maps only looks like a "natural" empire to us in hindsight.[4] But most importantly, the entire idea of the rivers as strong natural defenses at which Roman government would choose to stop disintegrates if it can be demonstrated that the Romans were not primarily interested in security and defense.[5]

Scholars have also pointed to the tradition that Augustus on his deathbed in A.D. 14 instructed his successors to keep the empire within its existing borders, which by this time had reached the Rhine, Danube, and Euphrates. The story is found in both Tacitus and Cassius Dio.[6] As founder of the principate, the new semi-monarchical order, Augustus enjoyed enormous prestige both in his own time and later. But if the Roman state was indeed a military machine thriving on conquest, it is hard to see why the words of one old man could have brought imperial expansion pretty much to a halt or, just as importantly, why any Roman, for example a politically sophisticated and cynical historian like Tacitus, should have believed that Augustus' advice was at all important.[7]

---

3   On the ethnic and cultural complexities of the Rhine frontier see now Peter Wells, *The Barbarians Speak: How the Conquered Peoples Shaped Roman Europe* (Princeton: Princeton University Press, 1999; rpt. 2001).

4   See, e.g., J. C. Mann, "Power, Force and the Frontiers of the Empire" (review of Luttwak's book), *Journal of Roman Studies*, 69 (1979), 175–83, at 176.

5   See Cornell, "The End of Roman Imperial Expansion," 141–3.

6   Tacitus, *Annals* 1.11.4; Dio 56.33.5–6.

7   Hence the puzzlement by Cornell, "The End of Roman Imperial Expansion," 149.

Edward Luttwak has offered a third explanation: that the Romans stopped their imperial expansion at the rivers not necessarily for defensive reasons but because further expansion was impractical. Their heavy infantry force, the heart of the Roman army, had been designed primarily for war between city-states or at least between civilized regimes which possessed cities. The basic Roman strategy was to advance their infantry towards important targets such as towns or cities, to force the enemy to come out and defend those targets, and then to beat them in set battle. Such an enemy, once defeated, would submit to Roman dominance or control rather than risk their cities being sacked and pillaged. But north of the Rhine and the Danube there were no cities, only primeval forests inhabited by semi-nomadic populations who at best lived in villages and possessed nothing they had to defend in set battles. Such populations could melt into the surrounding woods and swamps at the first approach of the Roman legions and wage a guerrilla war on them from their vantage points. The most famous example of the effectiveness of such tactics is the utter destruction of three legions under Publius Quinctilius Varus in the Teutoburg Forest north-east of the Rhine in A.D. 9. To deal with such a highly flexible enemy, Rome had only the option of attempting an out-and-out war of extermination, but such operations were not only difficult to accomplish, given the state of ancient technology, but would also leave the Romans in control of nothing much worth controlling. The bitter remark made by Scottish chief Calgacus, that the Romans make a wasteland and call it peace, is instructive on this point.[8]

The same lack of tempting targets existed for Rome in the south, among the troublesome nomads of the north African semi-desert who constantly raided the settled and civilized Mediterranean coast, and in the east, where the kingdom of Parthia, a Persian state much more powerful than any of the tribes Rome faced elsewhere, lay in the arid and inaccessible plateau of modern Iran. So what was there to be gained beyond the rivers? As the historian Appian wrote ca. A.D. 140: "Possessing the best parts of the earth and sea they [the Romans] have, on the whole, aimed to preserve their empire by the exercise of prudence, rather than to extend their sway indefinitely over poverty-stricken and profitless tribes of barbarians."[9] Or as the British chieftain Carata-

---

8   Tacitus, *Agricola* 30.4.

9   Appian, *Roman History*, Preface 7.3, quoted from *Appian's Roman History in Four Volumes*, tr. Horace White, vol. 1 (New York: MacMillan; London: Heinemann, 1928; several rpts.), 11; cf. Florus 2.29, on the land of the Sarmatians. See also Luttwak, *The Grand Strategy of the Roman Empire*, 45–6.

cus is supposed to have said upon being brought to Rome as a prisoner around A.D. 45: "You Romans possess things of such magnificent scale and beauty, and so much of it – and yet you lust after us in our little tents?"[10]

Luttwak offers valuable thoughts about the geo-strategic situation which Rome had come to confront by the age of Augustus and was still confronting under Marcus Aurelius and Commodus about 150–200 years later. But scholars who believe that Rome was intensely motivated by its culture of exceptionally bellicose and violent aggression developed over long centuries of war are forced to reject much of Luttwak because the obstacles to expansion to which he points would not have been insuperable. The Romans, after all, had conquered the high Alps, the Pyrenees, and the forests of Gaul, and the legions had found little trouble in the first century A.D. in bringing under control the relatively primitive Celtic peoples of southern and central Britain, making sure that the province eventually ran at a profit. Why then should the forests of Germany or the hills of the Black Forest or of the Carpathians have deterred them? And immediately eastward of the Euphrates frontier lay the rich cities of agricultural Mesopotamia, tempting targets, which Alexander the Great had found no great trouble in bringing under his sway. (For Alexander, the same had been true of Iran.) None of this geography would have stopped a state highly motivated to aggression and conquest.[11]

Wars, it is true, were expensive, and as in all pre-modern states, the Roman treasury must often have been in a rather chaotic condition – accurate records were difficult to keep – while the difficulties of projecting one's power under ancient technological conditions were substantial, especially over land and even with the famous Roman road system in place.[12] But Rome had fought wars continually under such difficult conditions for centuries; moreover, those conditions did not keep emperors from conducting large-scale wars of conquest whenever they wished. The most obvious example of this is Trajan, who pushed Roman conquest far beyond both the Danube and the Euphrates, though the eastern conquests were only temporary. And it is true, as shown in both *The Fall of the Roman Empire* and *Gladiator*, that Marcus Aurelius spent the last

---

10   Dio 61.33.3, quoted from *Dio's Roman History in Nine Volumes*, tr. Earnest Cary, vol. 8 (Cambridge: Harvard University Press; London: Heinemann, 1925; several rpts.), 23.

11   Cornell, "The End of Roman Imperial Expansion," 145–6.

12   On the inherent weaknesses of all pre-modern empires in both these respects see now Greg Woolf, "Inventing Empire in Ancient Rome," in *Empires: Perspectives from Archaeology and History*, ed. Susan Alcock, Terence N. D'Altroy, Kathleen D. Morrison, and Carla M. Sinopoli (Cambridge: Cambridge University Press, 2001), 311–22, especially 311–13.

years of his reign in a war on the Danube against the Germanic Quadi and Marcomanni that was at least in part a war of conquest. But despite Hollywood films, it is actually Trajan and Marcus who stand out as exceptions from the general run of Roman emperors and not Commodus, who ended by following the precepts of Augustus. The financial, technological, and military resources of the Roman Empire would have been adequate for wars of conquest if the emperors had wished to launch them, but the fact is that most emperors chose not to do so. Once again the question arises: Why not?[13]

Scholars have put forward the personal predilections of some emperors as a reason: Tiberius and Vespasian, who had long experience as generals on the imperial frontiers and whose military reputations were well established, came to the throne as middle-aged men and preferred the pleasant life of Italy. Nero was simply a sybarite. Institutionally, as Susan Mattern has pointed out, it is also the case that under the principate major wars came increasingly to be launched by no one except the emperor, usually present himself on the battlefield. The most telling example of this is the physically decrepit Emperor Claudius, who was in personal command of the Roman invasion of Britain. It was politically too dangerous for the emperor to allow anyone else, especially prominent provincial governors who belonged to the elite and who commanded legions, to engage in any large-scale military offenses. If successful, they stood to gain too much prestige, thereby endangering the emperor's position and rule.[14]

The fact that major warfare was increasingly at the discretion and in the hands of the emperors restricted all possibilities for military activity, since only the central government and not the provincial commanders could engage in it.[15] Yet most of the men who did become emperor were men of considerable energy and wide military experience. So, if the trend in Roman warfare is clearly away from expansion except with Claudius

13   This is the plaintive question of Cornell, "The End of Roman Imperial Expansion," 149, who believes in Roman republican society as a war-machine. Tacitus, for one, perceived that a change had occurred: The world was more peaceful under the principate and his history therefore ran the risk of dullness (*Annals* 4.32).

14   Susan Mattern, *Rome and the Enemy: Imperial Strategy in the Principate* (Berkeley and Los Angeles: University of California Press, 1999), 8–14. Cf. Fergus Millar, "Government and Diplomacy in the Roman Empire during the First Three Centuries," *International History Review*, 10 (1988), 345–77, especially 374–5.

15   It is even possible that the division of the crucial frontier provinces of Germania, Pannonia, and Moesia each into two parts was done to prevent large Roman armies from falling into the hands of potential rivals to the emperor, even though the result was strategic inefficiency along the river lines. On this see Mattern, *Rome and the Enemy*, 202.

and Trajan, something else must be involved beyond mere chance personality.

To imagine that the emperor and his advisors sat around devising long-range policy, whether for offense or defense, is anachronistic. Modern governments do this; ancient states did not. The central bureaucracy of the principate was tiny; its expertise and reliable information to act on were very limited. Moreover, the entire tradition of Roman government was passive, with the organs of the state responding in an ad-hoc manner to crises as they emerged, rather than actively devising policies. Administrative myopia of dealing just with day-to-day events was a strong obstacle to deliberate imperial planning of any sort, especially long-range planning. Such lack of planning had been even more pervasive under the republic.[16] Given administrative traditions in which the primary function of government was response to pressing circumstances, not initiation of action from above, the deliberate planning of large-scale conquest such as that undertaken by Claudius and Trajan was unusual, for it went against the entire Roman administrative history. In that sense, too, Commodus' decision to abandon the deliberate advance across the upper and middle Danube and instead to rely for frontier security on ad-hoc military responses to German attacks, should they occur, was a return to tradition, despite the depictions of his decision in *The Fall of the Roman Empire* and *Gladiator* as irresponsible or even treasonous.

Indeed, it has been argued that under the republic and even under the principate Roman government was so disorganized and averse to long-range planning that it is a mistake for us to conceive of the Roman frontiers as a conscious or coherent system. Rather, the frontier emerged haphazardly, geographic section by geographic section, out of a jumble of ad-hoc decisions, arrangements, and military failures. It was not at all the result of planning. To put it bluntly, the Roman frontiers just happened.[17] In the Roman conception, the very idea of the frontier was vague. Wars which we think of as provincial rebellions within the empire – Pannonia in A.D. 6–9, Judaea in A.D. 66–70 – Romans viewed as

16   On the generally passive stance of the emperor's administration see especially Fergus Millar, *The Emperor in the Roman World 31 BC–AD 337*, 2nd edn (Ithaca and London: Cornell University Press, 1992), especially chapters 3 and 5. On the passive attitude of central government under the republic see my *Senate and General: Individual Decision Making and Roman Foreign Relations, 264–194 B.C.* (Berkeley, Los Angeles, and London: University of California Press, 1987), 319–24.

17   Cf. Cornell, "The End of Roman Imperial Expansion," 150, and Fergus Millar, "Emperors, Frontiers and Foreign Relations, 31 BC to AD 378," *Britannia*, 13 (1982), 1–23.

foreign wars.[18] But if Rome had operated in the almost unconscious or shortsighted manner described above and simultaneously had been pushed toward military expansion that lasted for centuries, the change under the principate is all the more striking. Again the unavoidable question: Why did the wars stop?

They did not stop completely, of course, as Tim Cornell has rightly pointed out. Even under the principate the legions were often engaged in low-level conflict along the frontiers. These were "ordinary" military actions – either defensive actions against raiders or punitive expeditions across the rivers – which are probably under-recorded, because the elite historians on whom we depend for our information tend to focus on high drama on the frontiers and at the imperial court. In addition, there were true large-scale fights in seven major provincial rebellions in the first century A.D., major campaigns against the Parthians, and the conquest of Britain. The principate of the first century A.D. was not an age of total peace in sharp contrast to the previous republican age of war. The same is true for the second century, in which we find more provincial rebellion, e.g., in Judaea, and major foreign wars on the Euphrates and in the north, the latter including the conquest of Dacia.[19]

More importantly, although the textbook dates for the *pax Romana* are traditionally set as 31 B.C. to A.D. 250, the Roman peace was already emerging in significant areas of the Mediterranean at a fairly early date even under the republic. This is true for Italy after 200 B.C., for the Po Valley after 190 B.C. – even though half of it remained populated by Celtic peoples, who over the next century became peaceably Romanized – for most of Spain after 133 B.C., for north Africa after 100 B.C., and for ever longer stretches of time in the Greek east.[20] But this raises a new conundrum for us. How can the *pax Romana* have emerged in significant regions of the Mediterranean at quite an early period under the republic if the Roman state was a war machine not merely geared for war but dependent upon war in order to prosper? On this, John Rich has demonstrated that Roman republican warfare, even during the age of great expansion in the Mediterranean, roughly from 264 to 148 B.C., was not at all regular in its intensity; rather, it varied widely according to the nature of the external crises being faced. The very period of this great imperial expansion saw warfare becoming intermittent rather than regular, and many of the annually elected chief magistrates, the consuls,

18   Mattern, *Rome and the Enemy*, 4–5 and 193.
19   Cornell, "The End of Roman Imperial Expansion," 152–3.
20   Cornell, "The End of Roman Imperial Expansion," 157–60.

served as administrators of settled and relatively peaceful provinces rather than as generals committed to large-scale fighting.[21]

The more striking phenomenon then is not that war continued under the principate but that peace had already begun to emerge under the republic. In addition, to understand what happened during and after the great period of Roman expansion it is not enough to concentrate attention on Rome alone. However brutal and aggressive it could be and often was, Rome was also confronted with other brutal and aggressive states. The main targets of Roman imperialism were other imperialists in a world almost completely unregulated by international law.[22] Every militaristic feature and custom that can be attributed to the Romans can be paralleled among Rome's competitors for power in Italy or the Mediterranean, sometimes at even greater intensity. Every ancient Mediterranean state, not only great ones but also second-rank and even minor states, had to become highly militaristic in order to survive in that harsh environment.[23] But this means that Rome, however bellicose, was not exceptional. Bellicosity may explain Rome's survival but cannot explain its rise to power since all Mediterranean states were bellicose. Despite modern misconceptions, a major indication of the actual harsh situation in which Rome existed is that for the Romans war was never an easy road to victory. On the contrary: Rome suffered 90 major defeats on the battlefield during the republic alone, with 40 commanding generals dying on the battlefield, and such defeats continued under the empire.[24] The reasons why Rome won out in the ferocious international competition for power had more to do with its exceptional ability to mobilize its internal resources and to manage alliances and assimilate outsiders than with sheer aggression. The consequence of the harsh reality of a world in which Rome struggled with competent and ambitious enemies and learned its lessons from glorious but also very bitter warfare was that, when serious threats had finally been dealt with, when control was

21   John Rich, "Fear, Greed and Glory: The Causes of Roman War-Making in the Middle Republic," in *War and Society in the Roman World*, 38–68.

22   Rightly noted by Adrian Goldsworthy, *The Punic Wars* (London: Cassell, 2000; rpt. 2001), 71.

23   On this see John Ma, "Fighting Poleis of the Hellenistic Age," in *War and Violence in Ancient Greece*, ed. Hans van Wees (London: Duckworth; Classical Press of Wales, 2000), 337–76.

24   For the startlingly long list of severe Roman defeats during the republic see Nathan Rosenstein, *Imperatores Victi: Military Defeat and Aristocratic Competition in the Middle and Late Republic* (Berkeley and Los Angeles: University of California Press, 1990), 179–203.

established where the Romans needed or wanted it, Roman warfare sensibly and noticeably diminished.[25]

By the late republic, peaceable interludes in Roman relations with the external world were becoming longer and more frequent, while major imperialistic adventures, although famous and spectacular under such men as Pompey and Caesar, became rarer. This does not mean that Roman armies were demobilized; rather, as would later be the case under the emperors, the legions were being increasingly converted to garrison duty, just as their commanders turned more and more from fighting generals into administrators. This is the familiar "peaceful" Roman Empire of Edward Gibbon, already emerging under the republic. So perhaps we should place Pompey's conquests in the East (67–63 B.C.), Caesar's campaigns in Gaul (60–52 B.C.), Claudius' invasion of Britain (A.D. 43), Trajan's invasion of Dacia (A.D. 106–10), and the Marcomannic wars of Marcus Aurelius under one category, that of being unusual events set in motion by great dynasts and interrupting an increasingly prevailing peace.[26]

The reasons for the end of Roman imperial expansion under the principate are now clearer. Expansion had been coming to an end under the republic as serious enemies disappeared. But if so, then Commodus' decision to forgo his father's aggressive campaign of conquest against the Marcomanni and Quadi once more looks different to us from the simplistic villainy that appears in *The Fall of the Roman Empire* and *Gladiator*. So we should not be misled by actors, directors, and screenwriters, who are chiefly interested, quite legitimately, in telling a good story that also makes money. In terms of our understanding of Commodus and the limits of empire, especially as portrayed in the two films, the main question is not whether the decision of the real Commodus to abandon his father's Marcomannic war was strategically correct. (It could have been strategically unwise but still reasonable and also have remained within the parameters of Roman custom, as outlined above.) More important from a historical point of view is the question if Commodus' decision was strategically wrong. It may come as a surprise to us to realize that the record does not make it clear that his decision was indeed wrong.

After a long period of quiet, the tribes on the upper and middle Danube had exploded into action under Marcus Aurelius. This was the

---

25 Cf. Rich, "Fear, Greed and Glory," 44–55. I examine the harsh nature of the international environment and the internal reasons for Roman success in that environment in "Brigands, Emperors, and Anarchy," *International History Review*, 22 (2000), 862–79.
26 Cf. Cornell, "The End of Roman Imperial Expansion," 158.

region from which Italy was most vulnerable to direct invasion. The cause of the troubles in this area may have been the Goths' continuing migration southeast. They were moving behind the Germanic peoples who lived along the Roman frontier and were putting violent pressure on them. Marcus had gone north from A.D. 168 on to deal with the problem, at first together with his co-emperor Lucius Verus. At the time, the Roman army's strength in trained military manpower was being significantly damaged by a severe plague which had arisen in the eastern Mediterranean and had now struck in the Balkans and Italy. Thousands of legionaries, along with important officers, including eventually Marcus' co-emperor, died from the disease. An invasion Marcus led across the Danube ended in disaster, followed by an invasion of Italy by the Quadi and Marcomanni across the eastern Alps probably in A.D. 170, the first time such an event had occurred in almost 300 years. By A.D. 172, this invasion had been defeated, and Marcus had pursued the Germans back across the Danube, defeating them again after difficult fighting. At this point he took the title "Germanicus" to commemorate his success. Despite such proclamations of victory, the fighting continued for another eight years. It is likely but not quite certain that Marcus intended to solve the problem on the upper and middle Danube by conquering and gaining firm control over the immediate region across the river and turning it into two new Roman provinces, roughly modern Bohemia, Moravia, and Slovakia. The only source to say this explicitly is the not always trustworthy biography of Marcus in the fourth-century *Augustan History*, but scholars have tended to accept it.[27] Tiberius had thought of doing the same thing in response to problems on the upper and middle Danube about 150 years before, but nothing had actually been done at that time.[28] By A.D. 180, Marcus' plans were significantly advanced but not complete, with perhaps 20,000 Roman soldiers garrisoned year-round at strategic locales in Marcomannic territory, a situation known to us from modern archeological discoveries. Simultaneously, Marcus agreed to the requests of some German tribes to settle within the empire, including Italy itself, from which, however, they were soon expelled as being too violent.[29] From A.D. 175 on, Commodus, then fifteen years old, was an occasional witness to this fighting and eventually a commander in it. In a medallion from Cyprus dating from about A.D. 178, portraits of Commodus and Marcus appear

---

27   *HA Marc.* 27.10.
28   Cf. Velleius Paterculus 2.110.
29   Dio 72.11.4–5.

on one side; its inscription on the other side reads *propagatoribus imperii* ("to the enlargers of the empire"), within a laurel wreath symbolizing victory. This appears to associate Commodus and Marcus with an attempt at Roman expansion north of the Danube. Yet Cassius Dio implies that Marcus' goal was not the establishment of new provinces but simply the destruction of the Marcomanni.[30]

Commodus is said to have thought originally of attempting the completion of Marcus' plans, whatever they were.[31] In *Gladiator*, Senator Gracchus sneers during Commodus' triumphal entry into Rome: "But what has he conquered?" And the answer is "Nothing," for this Commodus intends to substitute gladiatorial spectacles for the hard work of conquest in the north. The historian's answer, however, is "The Quadi," for evidence is strong that Commodus engaged in successful fighting against them in the initial months of his reign.[32] But we are told that, despite the opposition of the friends and counselors of his father, Commodus then gave up Marcus' plans.[33] Given the institutional trend in the principate toward concentrating the conduct of any major war in the hands of the emperor alone, Commodus' return to Rome thus meant that no major offensive on the Danube would now occur. So why did Commodus come to this decision?

In *The Fall of the Roman Empire*, we see friends of Commodus murdering Marcus by poisoning him; in *Gladiator*, evil Commodus smothers him to death in his embrace. This is fiction. According to a prevalent ancient tradition, Commodus feared that if he stayed on the Danube he and his army would catch the plague that may well have killed the old emperor. There is no reason to doubt that such a concern was an important factor.[34] We have four sources on Marcus' death, of which not one

---

30   Dio 72.20.1. On the current state of scholarly debate over Marcus' intention to create new provinces north of the Danube see Olivier Hekster, *Commodus: An Emperor at the Crossroads* (Amsterdam: Gieben, 2002), 40–2; he concludes that Marcus had this intention. Anthony R. Birley, *Marcus Aurelius: A Biography*, 2nd edn, rev. (1993; rpt. London and New York: Routledge, 2000), 208–9, examines the province issue, including a Roman inscription about army winter quarters at modern Trencin, 80 miles north of the Danube. Dio 72.20.2 implies that Marcus' goal was not the establishment of new provinces but simply the destruction of the Marcomanni. Herodian 1.2–7 is unclear. Birley, *Marcus Aurelius*, chapters 7–9 and appendix 3, gives a general history of the Marcomannic wars.

31   Herodian 1.5.6.

32   Aurelius Victor, *On the Caesars* 17.2, and Eutropius, *History* 8.15, praise the campaign; cf. the general statement at Herodian 1.6.1. Recent scholarship accepts the historicity of the campaign; cf. Hekster, *Commodus*, 48 and note 50.

33   Herodian 1.6.5.

34   Hekster, *Commodus*, 43–4, discusses the possible impact of the plague on Commodus' campaign.

has Commodus personally murdering his father. Cassius Dio, one of these sources, reports a rumor that Marcus' doctors poisoned him in the hope of winning favor with the new emperor. The others are satisfied with reporting that Marcus died of an illness of some sort, probably the plague.[35] Given the eventual unpopularity of Commodus among the senatorial elite who wrote the histories on which we depend, the very absence of an accusation of murder by Commodus forces us to conclude that he was innocent of such a crime.[36] Indeed, there are more stories that Marcus himself had murdered his co-emperor Lucius Verus in A.D. 168 than there are stories that Commodus murdered Marcus. The stories about Verus' death even include one version in which Marcus used a serving knife coated with poison on one side. In *The Fall of the Roman Empire*, such a knife appears as the weapon that dispatches noble Marcus himself.[37]

To the danger of plague we must add the difficulties inherent in any permanent exertion of control over the Quadi and Marcomanni in their forests, difficulties that Commodus had personally experienced by the time he made his decision. We may also add that Marcus Aurelius' plans, if the *Augustan History* is correct, would have created an enormous and perhaps unstable Roman territory jutting out north from the Danube, one exceeding Dacia much farther east and requiring the imposition of a larger Roman garrison on a longer frontier. Such an area might have collapsed under barbarian pressure, or it might have necessitated a new large-scale movement forward elsewhere for its protection, across the Rhine toward the Elbe – an enormous military undertaking whose difficulties were well known. Commodus' decision to abandon Marcus' plans may have been strategically correct or incorrect, but in either case its military logic is evident. It was not an irrational decision.[38]

Moreover, despite the worries of Marcus Aurelius' old counselors mentioned by Herodian, there were no immediate negative consequences to

---

35   So especially *HA Marc.* 27.11–12.

36   *HA Marc.* 27.11–12; Dio 71.33–4; Aurelius Victor, *On the Caesars* 16.4; *Epitome de Caesaribus* 17.2 (a work that has come down to us under Victor's name but by an unknown author). See further Birley, *Marcus Aurelius*, 209–10.

37   *HA Verus* 10.1–5 and *Marc.* 15.5–6; Dio 71.3.1. Not that any of this gossip should be believed, either; cf. Birley, *Marcus Aurelius*, 158. On the poisoned knife in *The Fall of the Roman Empire* see Martin M. Winkler, "Cinema and the Fall of Rome," *Transactions of the American Philological Association*, 125 (1995), 135–54, at 139.

38   On the strategic problems with Marcus' proposed new provinces see C. R. Whittaker on Herodian 1.5.6 in *Herodian in Two Volumes*, tr. Whittaker, vol. 1 (Cambridge: Harvard University Press; London: Heinemann, 1969), 26–7 note 2. See also Michael P. Speidel, "Commodus and the King of the Quadi," *Germania*, 78 (2000), 193–7.

Commodus' decision. On the contrary, the Danube frontier was mostly quiet during the entire thirteen years of Commodus' reign and continued to remain so during the entire reign of Emperor Septimius Severus. Indeed, we have no reports of the Marcomanni and the Quadi giving serious trouble until the calamitous reigns of the emperors Valerian and Gallienus, in A.D. 253–60. This amounts to more than seventy years of comparative peace on the upper and middle Danube, most surprising after the enormous turmoil the Danube Germans had caused under Marcus. It is a very significant achievement.[39] Herodian himself, who disapproves of Commodus' decision, admits that Commodus acted responsibly when departing for Rome and appointing experienced commanders who continued to act very effectively against the Danube tribes.[40]

Despite the depiction of Commodus in the two films as a debauched monster, there is significant evidence that the real Commodus often worked hard and dutifully at the imperial administration which was an emperor's main task. No doubt he was an unpleasant person to know and dangerous to be around, a man obsessed, among other things, with gladiatorial games. But we have evidence that he continued to take personal interest in the Danube defenses, that he authorized the building of large-scale fortifications along the river, and that he maintained serious concern about the Rhine as well. We know that he even read petitions from humble peasants complaining about the unfairness of government exactions and personally signed replies to them.[41] None of this daily routine of responsible bureaucratic work can be shown in Hollywood films; they would be much too dull. When Septimius Severus became emperor after the civil war following Commodus' murder, he had the senate deify Commodus and proclaimed himself son of the deified Marcus and brother of Commodus. These propaganda moves make no sense unless Commodus, despite the bile of senatorial historians, had enjoyed the respect of much of the population in the empire.[42]

39 Cf. Hekster, *Commodus*, 46–7.
40 Herodian 1.6.1–8.
41 On the fortifications along the Danube see the *Corpus Inscriptionum Latinarum* 3.3385, with Mattern, *Rome and the Enemy*, 113. On the Rhine: *HA Comm.* 12.8 and Whittaker on Herodian 1.6.8 at *Herodian*, vol. 1, 35 note 2. On the peasants' petitions: *Inscriptiones Latinae Selectae* 6870 and Millar, *The Emperor in the Roman World*, 246. Not even Caligula escaped administrative work, sometimes doing two tasks at once according to the eyewitness Philo of Alexandria, *Embassy to Gaius* 44.351–45.367; cf. Millar, 22–3.
42 See Dio 76.7.4. Cf. Anthony R. Birley, *Septimius Severus: The African Emperor*, 2nd edn, rev. (London and New York: Routledge, 1999), 118. Dio, however, notes in the same sentence that Severus had previously taken a far dimmer view of Commodus. Cf. also Dio 77.14.7.

If a case can be made for the historical Commodus' decision in the north on grounds of geo-politics, did it violate Roman cultural norms? The answer to this question can tell us much about the nature of Roman imperial expansion.

In Herodian, Marcus Aurelius' old friends and counselors argue that Commodus, if he gave up Marcus' campaigns, would only encourage the Germans toward aggressive action and that Roman honor required that he stay the course set by his father. Perhaps something like this was indeed said, for it fits with the importance which Roman culture assigned to maintaining and enforcing Roman honor in the face of hostile foreign polities.[43] But as we have seen, the advisors of Marcus, at least as far as their arguments go in Herodian, were wrong about the military danger. Were they correct on the issue of the empire's honor?

One conclusion to be drawn from our discussion of the history and character of Roman expansionism is that Rome, while exceptionally aggressive and militaristic in modern terms, was not exceptionally aggressive within its own contemporary environment. Rome tended to fight wars, sometimes aggressive wars, against serious enemies in a harsh and unforgiving world. But the Romans did not invent their enemies, who were real enough.[44] When those enemies were defeated or no longer considered a threat, the Romans' wars stopped. This is why the *pax Romana* was coming into existence in important regions of the Mediterranean as early as about 150 B.C.

This is the background important for Commodus' judgment of the situation on the Danube. The war to conquer the Marcomanni and the Quadi was a large-scale and unnecessary expenditure of lives, money, and effort. The Marcomanni and their allies had been beaten up enough by the legions to have learned the lesson of Roman superiority. Cassius Dio, who was himself an experienced general, later criticized Septimius Severus for wishing to extend Roman control across the Euphrates into Mesopotamia.[45] Dio did not mention or believe that Roman honor was at stake.

Commodus' decision was well within the Roman tradition not only of geo-politics but also of personal and state honor, no matter how Hollywood later chose to tell the story. Augustus' decision in A.D. 9 to

43   See especially Mattern, *Rome and the Enemy*, chapters 1 and 5.
44   Despite extreme statements such as that of Stephen Oakley, "The Roman Conquest of Italy," in *War and Society in the Roman World*, 9–37, at 16: The Romans were so aggressive that they "looked for war when none was ready at hand." Similarly Harris, *War and Imperialism in Republican Rome*, chapter 5, on the entire history of Roman wars.
45   Dio 73.3.3–4.

abandon all attempts to move the imperial frontier across the Rhine to the Elbe was far more problematic in terms of maintaining Roman honor because it was a decision taken in the face of a devastating defeat.[46] The same was true of the decision of Nero's general Gnaeus Domitius Corbulo, a hero of Tacitus, to accept a compromise peace with Parthia over the issue of Armenia without first avenging the serious defeat which the Parthians had inflicted upon Lucius Caesennius Paetus, his predecessor.[47] Nero accepted Corbulo's treaty.

In contrast to both of these cases, Marcus Aurelius' legions had not suffered any defeat by the Marcomanni and Quadi when Commodus made his decision to return the Roman army to the Danube. On the contrary, Rome had ultimately been victorious against the Germans although the fighting had, as usual, been very tough. The proof is in the terms of peace laid down by Commodus to the Marcomanni and the Quadi in A.D. 180. Roman troops were to leave the areas they had occupied north of the Danube. In return, the tribes had to turn over all Roman prisoners and deserters and provide a total of 23,000 forced recruits to the Roman army. They also had to give up a portion of their weapons and all their boats which could be used to cross the Danube, and they were forbidden to build new ones. They were also forbidden to come within ten Roman miles of the north bank of the river, they were to pay Rome an annual tribute in grain, and their popular assemblies were to be held no more than once a month and only under the supervision of a Roman centurion. Finally, the tribes were forbidden to wage war on specified Roman allies north of the river and forbidden to support enemies of Rome in any way. This was a treaty much to Rome's advantage. As scholars agree, the terms of the treaty show that the victories of Marcus and Commodus had proven too much for the tribes.[48]

---

46 In the period after Varus' defeat, Roman armies continued to launch large-scale punitive expeditions across the Rhine, whose purpose, as was typical, was to punish the Germans for their victory. This might have been transformed into a second serious attempt at conquest, but Tiberius, the most experienced general of the empire, put an entire stop to the effort in A.D. 17. See Erich S. Gruen, "The Expansion of the Empire under Augustus," in *The Cambridge Ancient History*, 2nd edn, vol. 10: *The Augustan Empire, 43 B.C.–A.D. 69*, ed. Alan K. Bowman, Edward Champlin, and Andrew Lintott (Cambridge: Cambridge University Press, 1996), 147–97.

47 Discussion in Mattern, *Rome and the Enemy*, 177–8.

48 Dio 73.3.3 gives the treaty terms. On the treaty as indication of a significant Roman victory see now Hekster, *Commodus*, 48-49, with notes 51–3 on earlier scholarship. A detailed study is Géza Alföldi, "Der Friedensschluß des Kaisers Commodus mit den Germanen" (1971), now updated in his *Die Krise des römischen Reiches: Geschichte, Geschichtsschreibung und Geschichtsbetrachtung: Ausgewählte Beiträge* (Stuttgart: Steiner, 1989), 25–68.

Treaties such as this fit into the larger Roman cultural and geo-
political context. The fundamental Roman stance on the frontiers was
not one of straightforward or passive defense or, conversely, outright
conquest and expansion but rather an evident readiness to take violent
revenge for attacks. Despite the images we have of Roman walls, most
famously Hadrian's Wall in Britain, as the markers of imperial boundary and conquest, it was in fact difficult for Rome to stop all invasions
across its river frontiers. The river lines were long, and the Roman troops
garrisoned there were limited in numbers and mobility. (In large part,
they were infantry troops.) The rivers, especially the Danube and
Euphrates, were always permeable in spots, as the invasion of Italy by
the Marcomanni and Quadi about A.D. 170 had shown only too
well. The message that Rome sent across the frontiers in repeated military actions was that serious trouble would be followed sooner or later
by the arrival of the emperor in person with a large field army and that
when he arrived punishment of malefactors would be terrible.[49]

This was a stance of deterrence by means of revenge, carried out
in punitive expeditions across a permeable frontier. The goal of such
deterrence was not primarily the punishment meted out to trouble-
makers, although this certainly weakened the enemy. Rather, victorious
vengeance by the emperor and his army was important in itself, for it
restored or preserved Roman honor diminished by invasion and damage.
This concept of honor is somewhat foreign to modern states, but in the
ancient world vengeance was a widely accepted and practiced motive for
state action. Nor was this a quaint or primitive custom, for revenge had
a grim and practical point. As mentioned, the ancient Mediterranean
was a harsh environment without international law, in which every state
had to depend for protection and self-preservation upon itself alone. In
such an environment the restoration of state honor and status through
vengeful violence helped establish reliable security because it made
unmistakably clear to all and sundry that it was very dangerous to con-
travene a certain state's interests. This was the fundamental reason why
the maintenance of honor and status was important. We may compare
what Seneca, the Roman philosopher and high government official
under Nero, reports on the general belief about anger after an injury
suffered: It is useful because we do not become contemptible and can
frighten off bad people.[50]

49   Mattern, *Rome and the Enemy*, 184–94.
50   Seneca, *On Anger* 2.11.1. On the role of revenge among classical Greek city-states see
now J. E. Lendon, "Homeric Vengeance and the Outbreak of Greek Wars," in *War and
Violence in Ancient Greece*, 1–30.

This was the Roman stance on the frontiers for much of the period of the *pax Romana*. Caesar reports that the arrogance of the Helvetii, who invaded Gaul in 59 B.C. from what is now Switzerland, had been caused by an unavenged Roman defeat decades before and that they prided themselves on inflicting such harm on the Romans with impunity.[51] Caesar taught the Helvetii the proper lesson – by annihilating two-thirds of them. Tacitus indicates that the Roman expeditions across the Rhine after A.D. 9 were launched to abolish the infamy of the army lost under Varus.[52] Emperor Domitian considered revenge against border barbarians as an absolute necessity, should they be victorious over local provincial garrisons.[53] The monument built by Trajan in celebration of his victory over the Dacians at what is today Adamklissi in Bulgaria was dedicated to the god Mars the Avenger, for the Dacians had inflicted defeats on Roman frontier governors. And according to Cassius Dio, even Marcus Aurelius' campaigns against the Marcomanni and Quadi were conducted not to acquire their land but to inflict vengeance upon them for their aggressions against Rome.[54]

Scholars are uncertain how truthful such texts are about Roman motives. Some assert that Rome acted on coldly rational grounds, such as desire for control of natural resources, including manpower, through outright conquest.[55] But for us the point is that this ideology of revenge, and the ideology of victory that accompanied it even if no practical results but the restoration of Roman honor were achieved, was an acceptable and indeed the predominant public face of Roman imperial ideology.

What follows from this finding is that the historical Commodus could easily have argued that Roman honor had been well satisfied by Marcus' great victories across the Danube over the German peoples who had invaded Italy and that further expensive efforts were unnecessary. Marcus' victories were already being celebrated in Rome by a monumental column that matched in scale and in the brutal triumphalism of its images of his campaigns against the barbarians the famous column of Trajan which celebrated the conquest of Dacia. Moreover, Commodus had apparently won his own victories against the Quadi before he departed. The treaty that Commodus imposed on the Germans was much

51   Caesar, *The Gallic War* 1.14.
52   Tacitus, *Annals* 1.3.6.
53   Suetonius, *Domitian* 6.1, on the campaign against the Sarmatians. Domitian did not need to explain to the senate why.
54   Dio 72.20.1. On all these cases see Mattern, *Rome and the Enemy*, 184–91.
55   See, e.g., Birley, *Marcus Aurelius*, 208–9.

to Rome's advantage, and was an explicit expression of Roman superiority in both power and status. In such a situation, the withdrawal of the legions to south of the Danube would by no means diminish the strong message of Roman power which had been sent, in the traditional Roman language of violence, to the Marcomanni and the Quadi. Revenge and victory had been achieved. And the evidence of the next 70 years of relative peace on the middle and upper Danube suggests that the two tribes had received and understood the message. Commodus was the first Roman emperor to take the title *Invictus* ("Invincible").[56] *The Fall of the Roman Empire* and *Gladiator* would make such a title seem a joke to us – not that the films even mention it – but the Marcomanni and Quadi did not think it a joke.

It has not been my intention to castigate the films' directors and screenwriters for presenting their mass audiences with a distorted version of Roman history. Such distortion, even if very gross, is only to be expected, so what does it matter if in *Gladiator* Commodus rules for about thirteen months instead of for thirteen years? (The real Commodus must have been doing something right; Caligula lasted only four years.) But the goals of historians and the goals of those who read essays by historians are not the same as the goals of Hollywood. They are different and more serious: to try to ascertain, as nearly as we can, the complex truth of the actions of a different culture in a vastly different world of the past. Knowing how complex the truth was in turn only enhances our appreciation of the visual and dramatic pleasures which Hollywood puts on the screen for us – as long as we keep in mind that pleasures are about all they are intended to be.

---

56   Mattern, *Rome and the Enemy*, 197 note 117.

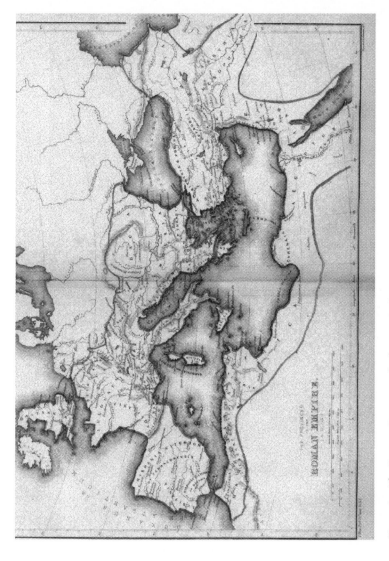

Figure 1   The Roman Empire in the late second century A.D.

Figure 2 The Emperor Commodus. Roman marble bust dating to his reign.
Museo Archeologico Venice Bridgeman Art Library.

Figure 3   The Roman Emperor Commodus Fires an Arrow to Subdue a Leopard which has Escaped from its Cage in the Arena. Sixteeenth-century hand-colored engraving after Jan van der Straet. The Stapleton Collection Bridgeman Art Library.

Figure 4 Edwin Howland Blashfield, *Commodus, Dressed as Hercules, Leaves the Amphitheater at the Head of the Gladiators* (1878). Hermitage Foundation Museum, Norfolk, Virginia.

Figure 5   Edwin Howland Blashfield, *Commodus as Hercules, Leaves the Amphitheater at the Head of the Gladiators* (1878, detail of Figure 4). Hermitage Foundation Museum, Norfolk, Virginia.

Figure 6 Gladiatorial scenes with *retiarii* and *secutores*. Roman mosaic from the early fourth century A.D. now in the Galleria Borghese, Rome. Photo Bridgeman Art Library/Alinari.

Figure 7   Victory of *retiarius* over *secutor* (detail of Figure 6). Galleria Borghese,
Rome/photo Bridgeman Art Library/Alinari.

Figure 8   Retiarius and fallen *secutor*, with one victorious and one dying *retiarius* at right (detail of Figure 6). Galleria Borghese, Rome/photo Bridgeman Art Library/Alinari.

Figure 9   Pietro Santi Bartoli. *Gladiators* (1674). Watercolor. Glasgow University Library/photo Bridgeman Art Library.

Figure 10 The Colosseum in a nineteenth-century Italian engraving. The
Stapleton Collection/Bridgeman Art Library.

Figure 11   View of the Colosseum in an early-twentieth-century photograph.

Figure 12 The computer-generated Colosseum of Ridley Scott's *Gladiator*.

Figure 13 The Colosseum as religious site with cross and altars for the Stations of the Cross. Nineteenth-century photograph taken before the 1874 excavations of the arena floor.

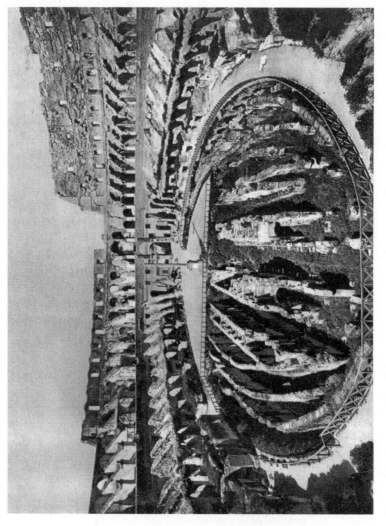

Figure 14   Interior of the Colosseum in a nineteenth-century photograph.

Figure 15 Stanley Kubrick's *Spartacus*. Gladiatorial combat between Spartacus (Kirk Douglas) and Draba (Woody Strode).

Figure 16 Anthony Mann's *The Fall of the Roman Empire*. Commodus (Christopher Plummer) during his triumphal parade through the Roman Forum.

Figure 17   Gladiator. Commodus (Joaquin Phoenix) on his triumphal entry into Cyber-Rome.

Figure 18 Leni Riefenstahl's *Triumph of the Will*. Hitler's cavalcade entering Nuremberg for the 1934 Nazi Party rally.

Figure 19   *Gladiator*. Commodus in the senate.

Figure 20   The Fall of the Roman Empire. Commodus practicing his gladiatorial skills.

Figure 21 Gladiator. "Are you not entertained?" Maximus (Russell Crowe) in the arena at Zucchabar.

Figure 22   *Gladiator.* A moment in the Battle of Carthage, with *metae* in the background.

Figure 23   *Gladiator*. Maximus facing two tigers. one of them human (Tigris of Gaul).

Figure 24 *Gladiator*. Lobby card with advertising slogan: "A Hero Will Rise."

Figure 25   Gladiator. Maximus, surrounded by Praetorians, before his duel with Commodus.

Figure 26   The Fall of the Roman Empire. The duel between Livius (Stephen Boyd) and Commodus inside an extemporized arena of shields.

CHAPTER SIX

Gladiators and Blood Sport

David S. Potter

The city population was a spectator to the combatants, as if at some public
entertainment, favoring first one side, then the other, with applause.
Whenever one of the sides gave way, they demanded that those hidden
in taverns or who had fled into some house be dragged out and killed . . .
Horrible and dreadful sights filled the city: In places there were battles
and wounds, in others baths and bars; there was blood, there were piles of
bodies next to prostitutes and those who were like them. There was
the debauchery that takes place in luxurious peace, there was the crime
that takes place in a savage conquest, so that you might well think
that the city was at the same time mad with rage and running riot with
pleasure.[1]

Tacitus' description of the capture of Rome by Vespasian's army in A.D.
69 underlines the fascination with radical contrast that is key to our
understanding of the place of arena spectacles in Roman life. The professional combatants – gladiators, beast hunters, or beast handlers – per-
sonified this contrast, for they were despised and exalted at the same
time. The arena spectacles in which they participated could reinforce or
undermine the social order. The men who sponsored such combats pro-
fessed to despise the events for which they paid but celebrated them on
the mosaics that decorated the public areas of their houses or with
monuments in the public areas of their cities. The people who might form
a gladiatorial fan club such as the "Lovers of the Vedii" at Ephesus could
be enthralled by the peril into which their heroes were thrust for their
entertainment.[2] The Roman senate might declare that people of high
status would lose their social standing for having disgraced the elite by
appearing in the amphitheater or on the stage, but they admitted that

---

1   Tacitus, *Histories* 3.83.1–2. This and subsequent translations are my own.
2   Louis Robert, *Les gladiateurs dans l'orient grec* (1940; rpt. Amsterdam: Hakkert, 1971),
25–7.

people would do just this.[3] Members of the senate would deplore the fact that Emperor Commodus had appeared as a gladiator and beast hunter while they themselves engaged in mock arena combats in the demi-monde of the city and bid up the prices for Commodus' equipment.[4] In later centuries, Christians would profess disgust for blood sport while exalting as martyrs members of their faith who had allowed themselves to be executed in those same spectacles and carefully recording all the grisly details.

The games would continue to be central to Roman life for centuries. Their inherent contradictions would become even more pronounced in the fourth century with the arrival of Christian emperors, who had doctrinal reasons to oppose the games. But if they let doctrine influence their decisions, they rarely resorted to direct action, as did Constantine with his ban on the delivery of prisoners to *lanistae* (gladiatorial trainers) in A.D. 325.[5] While he said that he deplored gladiatorial combats, he did not stop them. His son, Constantius II, issued an order in A.D. 357 to prevent people who were putting on games from recruiting members of the imperial guard to be gladiators.[6] Fourth-century emperors who did try to discourage arena entertainments simply ceased to act as sponsors; and this strategy led to a gradual decline in gladiatorial combat. But their distaste for gladiatorial events did not extend to public executions and beast hunts. No matter who was on the throne, imperial justice needed to be horrific, and control of the natural world implicit in the ability to slaughter animals needed to be demonstrated.

The fate of the games under Christian emperors reminds us that we must keep these different sorts of entertainment separate. While modern

---

3   Barbara M. Levick, "The *Senatus Consultum* from Larinum," *Journal of Roman Studies*, 73 (1983), 97–115. I discuss this decree below. It survives on the Tabula Larinas, a bronze tablet found in Larino, Italy.

4   This is only one reflection of an amphitheatrical subculture revealed at telling moments throughout the imperial period. Cf. Suetonius, *Caligula* 32.2, on Caligula stabbing a gladiator in a training session. It is not the session that arouses Suetonius' comment but Caligula's conduct.

5   *Codex Theodosianus* 15.12.1. This may have represented a change of heart, since Constantine had ordered in A.D. 315 that someone convicted of kidnapping should be given to the beasts if he were a slave or to a gladiatorial trainer if free-born, with strict instructions that he be sent to fight in the arena before he had learned how to fight and that he should be killed within a year (*damnatio ad gladium*). Cf. *Codex Theodosianus* 9.18.1, although it is arguable that *Codex Theodosianus* 15.12.1 refers only to the penalty of *damnatio ad ludum*, by which a man was condemned to fight in duels to the death, with the implication that he might survive and be freed.

6   *Codex Theodosianus* 15.12.2. Members of the imperial guard, it may be presumed, saw this as a way to supplement their income.

sensibilities might be as horrified by penalties that involved a bear or lion mauling a human being as they are by those that forced trained men to fight each other to the death, ancient sensibilities were not so finely tuned. Executions involving two men in mortal combat were not the same thing as the duels of gladiators. The soldiers who agreed to fight did so for the money and, we may suspect, the desire for applause. They did not do so because they expected to be killed.

1. Death in the Amphitheater

When we separate events in which death was an almost invariable outcome for one or both contestants in gladiatorial combat, we are left with the task to understand what the games were actually about in the eyes of ancient spectators. To do this, we may turn first to the decree of the senate that became law in A.D. 19. The crucial passage on the Tabula Larinas reads:

> And with regard to what was written and provided for under the decree of the senate that was passed when Manius Lepidus and Statilius Taurus were consuls [A.D. 11], namely that it should be permitted to no free-born woman younger than the age of twenty nor to any free-born man younger than the age of twenty-five to offer himself or herself as a gladiator or hire out his or her service on the stage, except those consigned [to those statuses] by the Divine Augustus or by Tiberius Caesar Augustus . . .

The decree dealt specifically with young men and women of high status who were appearing on the stage; it stripped them of their class privileges. The decree of A.D. 11 relates to a broader issue: the decision of young men and women who were Roman citizens of any class to enter these professions. Plainly, the senate at the time of Emperor Augustus had forbidden any Roman citizen from doing this, as part of an effort to draw a distinction between what was regarded as a proper activity for a Roman as opposed to someone free-born who was not a Roman. Acting and gladiatorial combat were professions for the young; they were what we would call "career choices" today. It is also plain that, despite their disapproval, the senate and the emperors were willing to make exceptions. In the case of gladiatorial combat sponsored by him, the emperor could accept the statement of people who appeared before a magistrate and said that this was what they wanted to do. The same was probably true for potential stage performers. The decree of A.D. 19 was passed because Tiberius, who had strong feelings about the dignity of the upper classes, was concerned about people making decisions that, he felt, "contravened the dignity of their order."[7]

To us, the pairing of gladiatorial combat with acting might appear odd. It is less odd if we realize that aristocratic Romans and, indeed, Romans of all stations in life were passionate about the stage and that this decree is concerned with people following their pleasure. Just as Romans could, in private, practice swordplay, many Roman aristocrats trained with actors for careers as public speakers – even Cicero did this – and delighted in amateur dramatics. Acting on a public stage, however, was always regarded as a profession for people of servile or foreign background; so was gladiatorial combat. No such restriction could be imposed on chariot racing, a sport run by members of the Roman elite. Emperor Nero was not the only high-status Roman to train as a driver; Caligula is alleged to have presided over a race in which every charioteer was of senatorial status.[8] Indeed, jurists of the first century explicitly maintained that "theater musicians, athletes, charioteers, those who sprinkle horses with water, and all the men who work in contests run by the state should not be held to incur loss of status (*infamia*)."[9] This distinction depends on the idea that charioteers and athletes appeared in *ludi* ("games"), which were state-sponsored festivals, while gladiators appeared in *munera*, which were, technically, "gifts" offered by individuals in their own name.

Even if gladiatorial combat and acting were considered professions for non-Romans, we might still wonder why they could be put on a par with each other. The problem is actually smaller than it seems. Despite common modern perceptions, gladiators rarely found themselves in a situation in which death was likely. There was a rule, imposed by Augustus, that no one could put on a *munus sine missione*, an exhibition of gladiators fighting to a definite conclusion.[10] There was enough danger if gladiators fought until one wounded another or was compelled to surrender, which he did by taking the shield off his arm and raising the first finger of the principal hand with which he fought. It was even

7   Quotation from the Tabula Larinas.

8   Suetonius, *Caligula* 18.3.

9   Ulpian, *Digest* 3.1.4.1. Ulpian cites the jurists Sabinus and Cassius.

10   Suetonius, *Augustus* 45.3. On the meaning of *sine missione* see Robert, *Les gladiateurs dans l'orient grec*, 258–61, and Georges Ville, *La gladiature en occident des origines à la mort de Domitien* (Rome: Ecole française de Rome, 1981), 403–5. In general, cf. my "Entertainers in the Roman Empire," in *Life, Death, and Entertainment in the Roman Empire*, ed. D. S. Potter and D. J. Mattingly (Ann Arbor: University of Michigan Press, 1999), 256–325.

more dangerous if gladiators fought with sharp weapons. In the provinces, special dispensation had to be obtained for this from some imperial authority, probably the emperor himself.[11] Ordinarily, as the third-century historian Cassius Dio makes plain, gladiators fought with dull weapons.[12] Most dangerous of all, of course, was the fight to the death, a contest for which we have direct attestation only in two Greek texts and, possibly, in a Latin rhetorical work of the early first century A.D.[13] The author of the Latin text quotes an orator saying that "among gladiators the harshest condition of victory involves the death of a fighter."[14] One of the Greek texts records that permission was sought from Emperor Gordian III to have three fights to the death on each day of a three-day festival rather than the usual two.[15]

The rules were different for games which the emperor put on at Rome. He could hold games *sine missione*, and the contests usually seem to have been with sharp weapons. We know, for instance, that this was the case when Titus held huge games to celebrate the opening of the Colosseum. Our source is the contemporary poet Martial:

> When Priscus and Varus each extended the struggle and there was equal prowess on both sides for a long time, release (*missio*) was sought for the men with great clamor, but Caesar obeyed his own rule; the rule was that they fight until the finger was raised and the shield set aside; he did what was permitted, and he often gave lances and gifts. Nonetheless an end was found to the equal fight: they fought on a par, and they surrendered on a par. Caesar sent the wooden swords and palms of victory to both: ingenious virtue discovered this reward. This happened only under your rule, Caesar: when two men fought, each one was the victor.[16]

Martial's statement that two men won only under Titus may be no more than flattery, but it suggests that imperial fights *sine missione* were rare. Other aspects of this poem are also significant: the crowd demanding that the emperor stop the fight before one man had to concede defeat and the reference to the rewards. The lances were perhaps modeled on rewards given to brave soldiers, and the wooden sword indicated that the

11   Cf. Robert, *Les gladiateurs dans l'orient grec*, 63, 97, and 139.
12   Dio 71(72).29.3.
13   On them cf. Robert, *Les gladiateurs dans l'orient grec*, 255–6.
14   Seneca the Elder, *Controversies* 9.6.1. I am indebted to John Lobur for calling this passage to my attention.
15   *L'année épigraphique* (1971), no. 431.
16   Martial, *On the Spectacles* 29. I read *parma* ("shield") for *palma* ("palm") in line 5.

recipient was free from the obligation to fight.[17] If he was a slave, he would now become a free man. The palms of victory, which appear on many gladiatorial monuments, were also offered to athletes and charioteers. Finally, there is the moment when the men ended their fight. Evidently, they both agreed to stop at the same time, a decision which suggests a great deal of trust between them.

Titus' behavior is a sign of his good character. Far grimmer stories are told about other emperors. Suetonius, the early second-century biographer of the Caesars, gives us an example of the bloodthirsty conduct of Claudius:

> At any gladiatorial show, whether his own or another's, he ordered that even gladiators who had fallen by accident be killed, especially *retiarii* [gladiators who fought with a trident and net and did not wear helmets] so that he could see their faces as they died.[18]

In the reign of Caligula, Suetonius reports, five *retiarii* were matched against five *secutores*, a very unusual event since gladiators ordinarily fought only one on one. When the *retiarii* refused to engage, an order was given that they all be killed.[19] Centuries later, Emperor Caracalla compelled a famous gladiator to fight three opponents in a row. The third one killed him.[20] But not only emperors could behave brutally or with poor taste. On a monument from northern Turkey a man who had sponsored a gladiatorial combat makes it plain that half of his gladiators had died.[21] Other such monuments record a far lower death rate – around ten per cent.[22] Not surprisingly, gladiators could be brutal as well. On an inscription from Milan, the wife of a deceased gladiator, who had fought thirteen times, tells us that he killed whomever he defeated.[23]

Death was an obvious danger for inadequate performance, but it was not a necessary result. We know of instances when gladiators who lost their nerve and ran away were flogged in the arena. Flogging was a penalty for poor performance in artistic and athletic contests alike and

---

17   Ville, *La gladiature en occident des origines à la mort de Domitien*, 325–9.
18   Suetonius, *Claudius* 34.1.
19   Suetonius, *Caligula* 30.3.
20   Dio 77(78).6.2.
21   See *Inscriptiones Latinae Selectae* 5062 for a *munus* in Campania during the third century A.D. with a death rate of fifty percent and the *Supplementum Epigraphicum Graecum*, 39 no. 1339, for an extremely bloody exhibition at Claudiopolis in Bithynia, at which the death rate may have approached fifty percent.
22   Ville, *La gladiature en occident des origines à la mort de Domitien*, 318–19.
23   *Inscriptiones Latinae Selectae* 5115.

should not be regarded as a consequence of the fact that many gladiators were slaves; athletes and other performers in the Greek world, where the habit of flogging bad performers is well attested, were free.[24] Moreover, in combats sponsored by private individuals, there were strong financial incentives to make sure that as many gladiators as possible survived. Gladiators were acquired in one of three ways. They were purchased, rented, or hired for the occasion. The gladiators who were bought or rented were slaves, while those who were hired, the *auctorati*, were free men. These could charge very high rates. Tiberius is said to have paid the staggering sum of 100,000 sesterces to men who were to fight in the games he offered in memory of his brother Drusus. He later imposed price controls.[25] Later yet, Marcus Aurelius set the maximum sum that an *auctoratus* could charge at 12,000 sesterces.[26] Rental of gladiators involved severe restrictions on what could be done with them. There was a very steep fine of fifty times the rental price if a gladiator was killed or so seriously injured that he could not fight again.[27] Those who rented a gladiator could not free him even if the crowd demanded it.[28] Someone who purchased gladiators obviously had more freedom to determine what would happen, although such people were often stretched to the limit of their financial capacity by the requirement to put on gladiatorial exhibitions, and they would only be able to recover some of their costs if they were able afterwards to sell the gladiators they had purchased. Imperial restrictions on dangerous combats seem to have been intended to protect such people from being considered miserly if they did not put on games resulting in bloodshed.

Despite such restrictions on the danger of gladiatorial combat, people still died in the amphitheater. The way their deaths are presented on their funerary monuments is revealing. These people never blame the crowd – they might say that they were victims of Nemesis, the goddess of revenge, that they were deceived, or that their opponent cheated. In death, gladiators wish to appear to have been masters of their fate and not to have been victims of the crowd or of the cruelty of whoever had put on the games.[29]

---

24 Cf., e.g., *Codex Inscriptionum Latinarum* 4.2351 and 5214; Petronius, *Satyricon* 45.12.
25 Suetonius, *Tiberius* 7.1 and 34.1.
26 *HA Marc.* 11.4. Cf. also, e.g., Tacitus, *Annals* 13.49.1, on limitation of cost by limitation of the number of fighting pairs.
27 Gaius, *Institutes* 3.146.
28 Ulpian, *Digest* 40.9.17; *Codex Juris* 7.11.3.
29 Cf. my "Entertainers in the Roman Empire," 315–16.

People went to the amphitheater and other public venues not only to be entertained but also to make themselves heard. Their heroes were people like themselves: of poor background, slaves, or men who had foresworn high rank in displays of solidarity with the crowd. That the leaders of Roman society saw the places of public entertainment in this way is illustrated by the example that Emperor Severus provided. He decreed to ban women from public contests after some had so much roused the passions of the crowd that the spectators called for women of high rank to join them.[30]

2. Gladiatorial Combat and Beast Hunts Prior to Augustus

Gladiatorial combat arrived relatively late on the scene of Roman public entertainment. The first recorded exhibition was at the funeral games of a man named Junius Brutus in 264 B.C. The association of gladiatorial combat with funeral games derived from the original home of gladiatorial spectacle, the warrior society of Samnium, whose funeral games were intended to illustrate the virtues held dear by that society.[31] Combats in funerary contexts are also attested for archaic Greece, although they did not employ people of low status, as was the tradition within Italian societies. Fights at Greek funerals would only be to first blood, and there is no reason to think that the situation was different in archaic Italy. A painting found in a tomb near Paestum in southern Italy shows a bout in which one combatant has been wounded in the leg; this is probably the decisive moment in the fight.[32]

In the middle of the second century B.C., the ruler of the Greek kingdom that dominated Syria and the Middle East included gladiatorial combats in a display to celebrate his royal power. He thought – correctly, according to our sources – that the sight of gladiators would enflame his people with a desire for military glory. Gladiatorial games rapidly gained in popularity; the Roman ones soon became closely associated with traditional Roman virtues. In the course of the first century B.C., gladiatorial exhibitions came to be part of the Roman electoral system. Candidates for political office appear to have believed that an impressive display of gladiators

30   Dio 75(76).16.1.
31   Cf. my "Entertainers in the Roman Empire," 305–6.
32   For archaic Greece cf. the example at *Iliad* 23. 798–825, on which see Michael Poliakoff, *Combat Sports in the Ancient World: Competition, Violence, and Culture* (New Haven: Yale University Press, 1987), 154. On the tomb paintings near Paestum see Ville, *La gladiature en occident des origines à la mort de Domitien*, 1.

before an election would enhance their chances, so much so that the young Julius Caesar staged games in honor of various family members well after their deaths. It is unlikely that he was the only person to do this, although he seems to have taken things further than others. His practice led to the first attested decree of the senate limiting the number of pairs that a politician could put on. Various efforts to stem electoral corruption were also passed; these included limits on how close to the year in which someone would seek office he could put on games. But none of this seems to have worked. Some politicians employed individual gladiators and even troupes of gladiators as bodyguards. Caesar's own collection of gladiators was so vast that special efforts were made to disperse them when civil war broke out in 49 B.C. so that they would not be a threat to public order.[33]

Caesar's gladiators were thought to be loyal to Caesar; this suggests that they were treated well. Others were less fortunate. Spartacus and his immediate followers are specifically said to have been kept in close confinement "through the injustice of their owner," which may have inspired them to rebel.[34] After their escape, Spartacus' band gathered an enormous army from among slaves and the rural poor of Italy. Some, if not many, seem to have been veterans of the civil wars that had ended in 82 B.C., since they are described as being able to fight as legionaries.[35] Spartacus was finally defeated and killed in 71 B.C. The mass crucifixion of 6,000 of his followers along the Appian Way was the final act of brutality in a war that was marked with great cruelty on both sides – Spartacus himself is said to have sacrificed 300 prisoners.[36] The revolt of Spartacus did not inspire any effort to reform the system of gladiatorial combat; it was by then too deeply embedded in the Roman political system.

While the city of Rome would have none until the reign of Augustus, permanent amphitheaters were now being built throughout Italy, usually in cities that had the status of Roman colonies and in places with a special attachment to the city or, in the wake of the civil wars of the 80s B.C., dominated by veterans of Sulla's victorious army. These veterans, it seems, regarded the stone amphitheaters in their cities as a

---

33   Caesar, *The Civil War* 1.14.4–5; Cicero, *Letters to Atticus* 7.15(14).2, says that there was a rumor that they would break out.

34   Plutarch, *Crassus* 8.2.

35   Appian, *Civil Wars* 1.116 (free men joining Spartacus); Plutarch, *Crassus* 9.1 (preference for legionary arms), 9.3 (men armed as legionaries), and 11.3 (possibly a reference to set formations).

36   Appian, *Civil Wars* 1.120 (mass execution) and 1.117 (human sacrifices).

symbol of their link to the ruling faction in Rome and the fights of gladiators as reminders of the martial glory to which they laid claim themselves.[37]

Beast hunts have a different history at Rome, for their origins lie not in the conquest of Italy but in the defeat of Carthage. The first recorded instance occurred in 250 B.C. at the triumph of a Roman magistrate who had defeated the Carthaginians in Sicily. The Carthaginians used elephants in battle, and the magistrate appears to have acquired a large number of them for exhibition and slaughter in a hunting display at his triumph.[38] The defeat of Carthage in the Second Punic War (218–201 B.C.) made possible a larger supply of exotic animals, so that in 186 B.C. we find another Roman magistrate celebrating a triumph with an exhibition of animal hunting, among other things, which caused enough of a stir to have the practice briefly banned. After the ban was lifted, the exhibition of animals was no longer limited to triumphs. Beast hunts now joined gladiatorial combats on a more regular basis in the games given by magistrates. By the end of the second century B.C., with much of North Africa under Roman control, more and more beast hunts took place. As other parts of the Mediterranean world came under Roman power, their animals, too, became fodder for the arena. Thus, from 51 B.C. on, we have a remarkable series of letters from the Roman official Caelius Rufus to Cicero, who was then governing a Roman province that consisted of much of southern Turkey. Once, for example, Caelius asks Cicero to make sure to get panthers for the games he is planning to put on.[39]

Animals and status soon became inextricably linked. In the empire, the ability to bring animals before the Roman people was a symbol of the emperor's power. Emperors restricted the rights of others to put on exhibitions, especially fights involving dangerous animals. This restriction was, however, often lifted, and people could hire animals to fight each other, to fight men, or to execute criminals sentenced to the beasts. (These they might purchase from the imperial authorities for this very purpose.) When animals fought with each other, they were often forced

37   On the importance of Roman arenas of that time cf. Katherine Welch, "The Roman Arena in Late-Republican Italy: A New Interpretation," *Journal of Roman Archaeology*, 7 (1994), 79–80.

38   Livy, *perioche* 19 (= summary of lost Book 19); Florus 1.18.27–8; Pliny the Elder, *Natural History* 7.139. At 8.16–22, Pliny gives a detailed account of elephant fights in the arena. Cf. also Livy 44.18.8 on elephants at games held in 169 B.C.

39   Ville, *La gladiature en occident des origines à la mort de Domitien*, 92–3, provides the references.

to do so by being chained together. The men involved in this very dangerous work, the *bestiarii* (beast handlers), were considered inferior to the *venatores*, those who actually hunted the animals. The training of the *bestiarius*, however, who would also manage condemned prisoners, must have been particularly intense. It would be no mean feat, for example, to hook up a bull to a bear without being killed. Animal battles suggest that even animals could participate in the star system. They are sometimes named on mosaics and inscriptions that record their presence at an entertainment. Beast hunts and the execution of criminals by wild animals survived even after gladiatorial combats had ceased.

3. Emperors and the Arena

In his study of a praetor's edict that can be dated to the reign of Septimius Severus, the third-century jurist Ulpian discusses the sort of people a magistrate could admit as witnesses for legal actions. In comparison with someone convicted of bringing vexatious litigation, Ulpian writes:

> So, too, the man who has hired out his services to fight with beasts. But we ought to interpret the term beasts with reference to the animal's ferocity rather than according to its species. For what if it be a lion, but a tame one, or some other tame carnivore? Is it then only the man who hired out his services who suffers *infamia*, whether he ends up fighting or not? For if he did not hire out his services, he should not suffer *infamia*. For it is not the man who fought against beasts who will be liable, but only the man who has hired out his services for this purpose. Accordingly the ancients say that they will not suffer *infamia* who have done this for the sake of demonstrating their courage, without pay, unless they have allowed themselves to be honored in the arena: I think that these men do not escape *infamia*. But anyone who hires out his services to hunt wild beasts or to fight one which is damaging the district outside the arena does not suffer *infamia*.[40]

Ulpian's appeal to the ancients was specious. The issue of a free man appearing to fight beasts was of contemporary significance. Notoriously, Commodus had appeared in the arena in A.D. 192 as both *venator* and gladiator. A major feature of Commodus' self-display was to look like

40   Ulpian, *Digest* 3.1.1.6.

Hercules. According to Cassius Dio, Commodus sought to re-create at least some of the labors of Hercules in the amphitheater.[41]

The use of the amphitheater as a place to re-create myth was not without precedent.[42] Since the time of Augustus, public executions had often been dressed up as mythological moments. A "new Orpheus," for instance, might be given a lyre and put into the arena surrounded by beasts. The purpose of this was not that he should charm them with the power of his song, as the mythical Orpheus had done, but rather that he should fail. A man who had stolen an apple from an orchard that belonged to Nero's Golden House was dressed as Hercules and placed upon a pyre with the announcement that the victim had imitated Hercules' labor of attaining an apple of the Hesperides and would now imitate Hercules' death by incineration. In Commodus' case, Hercules' role in the defeat of the Earthborn, the enemies of Jupiter, was re-enacted with cripples brought onto the floor of the amphitheater. The abuse of the disabled was nothing new; Caligula is said to have compelled old or decrepit people to fight, albeit with wooden swords.[43] Those victimized by Commodus were less fortunate, since he appears to have mounted a podium in the amphitheater from which he could attack them with a club. Suetonius includes Caligula's actions among his deeds as a "monster," so members of the crowd may well have been disgusted by what Commodus did. But Commodus did not stop there. He even introduced ostriches into the amphitheater and killed them with arrows. His arrows had a special head that would decapitate the animals as they ran. On one occasion, Commodus descended onto the floor of the arena with his sword to cut off the head of a fallen ostrich and waved it at the senators, indicating his desire to do something dire to them. Dio, who was there, claims that he could barely restrain his laughter at the absurdity of the scene.[44]

Following his demonstration that he had Hercules' skill as a hunter, Commodus also showed that he had Hercules' skill as a warrior. He fought a series of duels against gladiators who had to use wooden swords.[45] Commodus was, unsurprisingly, victorious and had himself proclaimed a *secutor* of the first rank.[46] But all this did not make a good

41   Dio 72(73).20.3.
42   Kathleen M. Coleman, "Fatal Charades: Roman Executions Staged as Mythological Enactments," *Journal of Roman Studies*, 80 (1990), 44–73, is the standard account of this.
43   Suetonius, *Caligula* 26.5.
44   Dio 72(73).21.1–2 and Herodian 1.15.5 describe Commodus' ostrich hunt.
45   Dio 72(73).19.2.
46   Dio 72(73).22.3; *HA Comm.* 15.8.

impression on the Romans. One of the reasons that the senate gave for its *damnatio memoriae*, its public damnation of Commodus after his death, was that he had fought in the arena.

Commodus was not the last emperor to appear in the arena. Septimius Severus' son Caracalla did so as well, both as a charioteer and as a beast hunter.[47] He, too, seems to have wanted to assimilate himself to Hercules through display of his deeds as a hunter, but he went out of his way to avoid any direct comparison with Commodus. Caracalla seems to have been less than successful because people thought that chariot races were fixed so that his favorites would win, a problem in other sports venues as well. Some athletes claimed as a mark of distinction that they had won without imperial favor. More significantly, people simply seemed not to have liked what they saw after the novelty value of Commodus' performance had worn off. And the Roman people expected the emperor to show respect for their heroes. Caracalla won himself no friends when he forced the gladiator Bato to fight to his death, because people thought he was being unfair. He did not show Bato the respect to which his deeds entitled him. So, too, Caracalla broke the rules when he told a gladiator that he did not have the power to spare him, for that power resided with his opponent. The victorious gladiator would have spared his rival. But when the emperor refused to do this, he thought that he could not do so, either.[48]

Gladiators and beast hunters rose through their abilities. They beat the odds that were stacked against them by their station in life and by the danger inherent in combat. The gladiator was a hero because he embodied the courage that people believed to be essentially Roman and because he achieved fame although he was outside polite society. The contrast between the gladiator's fame and his social status made him a popular hero. That gladiators were aware of this fact is illustrated most clearly by an incident in A.D. 238, when the Praetorian Guard advanced into Rome to suppress a senate revolt against Emperor Maximinus, who was on the Danube at that time. The guard failed, and gladiators from the *ludus magnus*, the main gladiatorial school, led the resistance. They even led the people in an attack on the Praetorians' camp itself.[49]

Members of the aristocracy who played at hunting beasts or being gladiators also wanted to receive the accolades given beast hunters and gladiators. That is why they played at such games in private, for instance

47 Dio 77(78).10.1–3.
48 Dio 77(78).19.3–4.
49 Herodian 7.11.7–9.

with prostitutes dressed as leopards or with tame beasts like the lion mentioned by Ulpian. But unless they were willing to forgo the privileges of their rank, they could not be participants in public blood sports. Instead, they could decorate their houses with images of the games they had put on, re-creating events when they had heard the applause of the crowd for their generosity, or they could exhibit entertainers, for example at a festival marking the completion of a public monument in commemoration of their earlier generosity, but this was about all they could do.

Not the least of Ridley Scott's achievements in *Gladiator* is to draw a modern audience into the emotions of an ancient Roman crowd. While very little in his scenes of gladiatorial combat resembles what actually happened in the amphitheater, he succeeds, as no one else has succeeded, in bringing the experience of spectatorship alive. His Maximus is a gladiator in the Roman tradition in that he becomes a hero in the arena and, at the same time, in a kind of theater. The spectacle of a man inverting the social and political order through his own courage – that is what the Romans went to see. And it is what Scott makes it possible for us to see and to feel.

CHAPTER SEVEN

Gladiator and the Colosseum: Ambiguities of Spectacle

Martin M. Winkler

The Colosseum is remarkable for the complexity of meanings that reveal its cultural significance as a place of fascination, of simultaneous attraction and repulsion. Roman blood sports, especially gladiatorial combat, have modern analogies in professional sports events and other spectacles, less deadly as these are than their predecessors. Our popular media can now imitate bloodshed and death to such a degree of verisimilitude as to make distinctions between the real and the fake impossible. In this, the cinema has led the way for over a century. As Alex, the anti-hero of Anthony Burgess's novel *A Clockwork Orange* (1962), put it memorably: "It's funny how the colours of the like real world only seem really real when you viddy them on the screen."[1] Stanley Kubrick's 1971 film version preserves the statement; indeed, the film itself exemplifies it. So does Ridley Scott's *Gladiator*.

The main place for spectacle in *Gladiator* is the Colosseum, which can itself be a symbol for the cinema theater. In *The Sign of the Cross* (1932), Cecil B. DeMille presented the greatest Roman show on earth at that time in an arena modeled on the Colosseum, although the story takes place during the reign of Nero, some sixteen years before the Colosseum opened.[2] DeMille's film ends with an arena sequence of such intense

1   Anthony Burgess, *A Clockwork Orange* (New York and London: Norton, 1963; several rpts.), 103.
2   DeMille had an enormous set for his arena that was modeled on the Colosseum. Cf. on this Charles Higham, *Cecil B. DeMille* (1973; rpt. New York: DaCapo, n.d.), 216. Mervyn

power as to hold cinemagoers in its grip more than seventy years later. DeMille shows us not only deadly spectacles but also a young Roman couple who are more interested in each other than in the bloody games they came to see. We also observe an older married couple, whose bickering reveals that before their marriage they, too, had come to the Colosseum for the same purpose as the young couple have. These Romans see in the Colosseum the same attractive environment to "make out" as modern teenagers may be tempted to do in the back rows of a dark cinema. DeMille's older couple still sit high up in the cheap seats, as they had done as youngsters. Now, however, they come only to watch the games. So it is entirely fitting that since the days of silent cinema metropolitan film palaces should have been named after the Colosseum. One of them, the Colisée on the Champs Elysées in Paris, even received its own cinematic homage. The protagonists of Jean-Luc Godard's *Breathless* (1960) are shown coming out of this Colisée. They have just watched an example of the quintessential genre of spectacle film, Budd Boetticher's Western *Westbound* (1959).

Like the Colosseum spectators in *Gladiator* and in a number of its cinematic predecessors, we, too, belong to a society that watches. Even more than sports events that we attend and at which we watch real people, film, television, and now computers have come to be our daily companions that provide us with vicarious visual thrills. At least since the war in Vietnam, politics and contemporary history, too, have turned into a ceaseless barrage of images, with the unavoidable effect that these images have become predominant over and outclass reality.[3] Alex was right.

The double-edged fascination that images of violence, war, and death exert on us is nowhere better seen than in the cinema. Films set in ancient Rome have held a prominent place in this tradition that, until now, has culminated with *Gladiator*. With ever increasing degrees of mayhem and realism, such epics have delivered the goods since the

LeRoy's 1951 version of *Quo Vadis*, also taking place in Nero's reign, is a comparable case. The cover picture of the DVD issue of Delmer Daves's *Demetrius and the Gladiators* (1954), which depicts the rule of Caligula, also wrongly shows the Colosseum, although the film does not.

3   Cf. on this the now classic accounts by Michael J. Arlen, *Living-Room War* (1969; rpt. Syracuse: Syracuse University Press, 1997) and *The Camera Age: Essays on Television* (1981; rpt. New York: Penguin, 1982), and Neil Postman, *Amusing Ourselves to Death: Public Discourse in the Age of Show Business* (1985; rpt. New York: Penguin, 1986). Postman's title is from Aldous Huxley's *Brave New World*. Cf. further Jonathan Rosenbaum, *Movies as Politics* (Berkeley, Los Angeles, and London: University of California Press, 1997).

earliest days of cinema. Regarding the ambivalence of spectacle, *Gladiator* is a particularly suitable object of study. Even its plot, set at a turning point in the history of the Roman Empire, conveys a certain duality: nostalgia for an old and noble Rome on the one hand, fascination with decadence and death on the other. Marcus Aurelius, the philosopher-emperor, and his son Commodus, an evil ruler, personify the two sides. So Olivier Hekster rightly calls Commodus an emperor at the crossroads of history.[4] This expression reminds us of two classic opinions on the age of the Antonine emperors and its end. One of these was voiced by ancient historian Cassius Dio, a contemporary of Commodus, the other by Edward Gibbon, the most famous modern historian of imperial Rome. Gibbon wrote about the period from A.D. 96 to 180:

> If a man were called to fix the period in the history of the world, during which the condition of the human race was most happy and prosperous, he would, without hesitation, name that which elapsed from the death of Domitian to the accession of Commodus. The vast extent of the Roman empire was governed by absolute power, under the guidance of virtue and wisdom.[5]

Commodus' accession was the moment when Rome arrived at the crossroads. Dio, who experienced Commodus' rule as a Roman senator, characterizes the change in a memorable phrase: "our history now descends from a kingdom of gold to one of iron and rust, as affairs did for the Romans of the day."[6]

So the question arises: How does *Gladiator* portray this descent? Moreover, is the film not itself an indication that cinematic spectacle has reached a turning point? On the one hand, *Gladiator* is the first big-screen ancient epic in thirty-five years, heavily indebted to cultural and filmic traditions of spectacle; on the other, it is a new epic, displaying in its computer-generated images a kind of Cyber-Rome. The ambivalences inherent in *Gladiator* are best seen in how it presents the Colosseum and the combat that takes place there. Rome's most famous landmark has appeared in a number of films, even in some which are set in a time long before it was built. George Sidney's musical romance about Hannibal, *Jupiter's Darling* (1955), is the most egregious example, with a Colosseum

4 Olivier Hekster, *Commodus: An Emperor at the Crossroads* (Amsterdam: Gieben, 2002).
5 Edward Gibbon, *The History of the Decline and Fall of the Roman Empire* (New York and Toronto: Knopf, 1994), vol. 1, 90. This volume first appeared in 1776.
6 Dio 72(73).36.4, quoted from *Dio's Roman History in Nine Volumes*, tr. Earnest Cary, vol. 9 (Cambridge: Harvard University Press; London: Heinemann, 1927; several rpts.), 69.

on view almost 300 years too early. Riccardo Freda's *Spartaco* (*Spartacus the Gladiator* or *Sins of Rome*, 1954) is off by only half that time. It gives us a good impression of what the famous *naumachiae* (sea battles) in the flooded Colosseum may have looked like.[7] But the Colosseum has never played as prominent a part as it was to do in *Gladiator*. Its importance as the place of crucial story points even exceeds that of the Circus in the two *Ben-Hur* films, Fred Niblo's version of 1925 and William Wyler's of 1959. The Colosseum in *Gladiator* characterizes the very nature of the Roman Empire as the film presents it. As such it serves a major thematic function, which we can better grasp if we consider how the Colosseum has come to be regarded over the course of time: "This long-explored but still exhaustless mine/Of contemplation." These words of Byron's about the Colosseum still apply.[8]

1. The Colosseum as Ambiguous Symbol

In A.D. 80, Emperor Titus dedicated what Romans called the Flavian Amphitheater with the first of countless games held in its oval arena. The contemporary poet Martial recorded and immortalized the event in a book of epigrams entitled *On the Spectacles*. In the first of these, Martial dismisses other wondrous buildings of the ancient world – the Pyramids, the walls of Babylon, the temple of Diana at Ephesus, the altar built by Apollo on Delos, and the Mausoleum – as inferior to "Caesar's amphitheater." From now on, "Fame will proclaim only one work in place of all others."[9] This is "the awe-inspiring mass of the amphitheater, visible from afar," as he says in the next poem.[10] About two centuries later, the historian Ammianus Marcellinus describes the first visit to Rome of Emperor Constantius II in A.D. 357 and testifies to the stupendous impression that the sights of the Eternal City made on the emperor, not least among them "the huge mass of the Amphitheater . . . to whose

7   Frank F. Sear, *Roman Architecture* (1982; rpt. Ithaca: Cornell University Press, 1983), 141, is cautious about the tradition that *naumachiae* took place in the Colosseum. Cf. Marcus Junkelmann, "*Familia Gladiatoria*: The Heroes of the Amphitheatre," in *Gladiators and Caesars: The Power of Spectacle in Ancient Rome*, ed. Eckart Köhne and Cornelia Ewigleben; tr. Anthea Bell (Berkeley and Los Angeles: University of California Press, 2000), 31–74, at 74.

8   *Childe Harold's Pilgrimage* IV.1150–1 (stanza 128). Quotation from *Lord Byron: The Complete Poetical Works*, ed. Jerome J. McGann, vol. 2 (Oxford: Clarendon Press, 1980), 167.

9   Martial, *On the Spectacles* 1.7–8; my translation.

10   Martial, *On the Spectacles* 2.5–6; my translation.

very top human sight ascends only with difficulty."[11] In modern literature, Byron begins a long passage on the Colosseum in Canto IV of *Childe
Harold's Pilgrimage* (1812) with this ovation:

> Arches on arches! as it were that Rome
> Collecting the chief trophies of her line,
> Would build up all her triumphs in one dome,
> Her Coliseum stands.[12]

In line with such praise, the Colosseum has come to be regarded as "the
most magnificent expression of the Roman character."[13] Until this day,
it has preserved its reputation as "the most renowned of Roman buildings."[14] It is "not just an architectural masterpiece, but in terms of planning, engineering and organization it must rank as one of the most
astonishing achievements of antiquity."[15] The Colosseum is a symbol not
only of the Eternal City but also of its empire and, by extension, of all of
Western culture and civilization, indeed of the entire world. A passage
in the concluding chapter of Gibbon's history makes this evident:

> the amphitheatre of Titus . . . has obtained the name of the COLISEUM,
> either from its magnitude, or from Nero's colossal statue: an edifice, had it
> been left to time and nature, which might perhaps have claimed an eternal
> duration . . . Reduced to its naked majesty, the Flavian amphitheatre was
> contemplated with awe and admiration . . . [as] in a sublime proverbial
> expression, which is recorded in the eighth century . . .: "As long as the
> Coliseum stands, Rome shall stand; when the Coliseum falls, Rome will fall;
> when Rome falls, the world will fall."[16]

Byron quotes this saying in his concluding stanza on the Colosseum:

11   Ammianus Marcellinus, *History* 16.10.14; my translation.
12   *Childe Harold's Pilgrimage* IV.1144–7 (stanza 128). Quotation from *Lord Byron: The
Complete Poetical Works*, vol. 2, 166–7.
13   So Ludwig Curtius in Ludwig Curtius and Alfred Nawrath, *Das antike Rom*, 4th edn,
rev. and ed. Ernest Nash (Vienna and Munich: Schroll, 1957), 194: "der großartigste Aus-
druck römischen Wesens."
14   Will Durant, *Caesar and Christ: A History of Roman Civilization and of Christianity from
Their Beginnings to A.D. 325* (New York: Simon and Schuster, 1944; several rpts.), 287. This
was the third volume in Durant's *The Story of Civilization*.
15   Sear, *Roman Architecture*, 144.
16   Gibbon, *The History of the Decline and Fall of the Roman Empire*, vol. 6, 633–4. This
volume was first published in 1788. Gibbon's quotation is from the Latin of the Venerable
Bede: *Quamdiu stabit Colyseus, stabit et Roma; quando cadet Colyseus, cadet Roma; quando cadet
Roma, cadet et mundus.*

'While stands the Coliseum, Rome shall stand;
When falls the Coliseum, Rome shall fall;
And when Rome falls – the World.'[17]

Since the Middle Ages, the Colosseum has represented what William Vance aptly calls the ambiguities of empire.[18] On the positive side, it is an architectural marvel, an unparalleled feat of engineering, an esthetically and intellectually pleasing structure which displays beauty through the symmetry of its shape and the different orders of its arched tiers, decorated with statuary. On the inside, it is a place of heroism, where brave gladiators and beast hunters display either their death-defying skills or their noble suffering of death to the cheering of enormous crowds. (The Colosseum is estimated to have held around 50,000 spectators.) The philosopher Seneca, for example, takes the occasion of gladiators' deaths to make a general point about the human spirit. His description, although written before the Colosseum was built, indicates the heroism of fighters fallen in any arena:

> For death, when it is close, gives even inexperienced people the courage not to avoid what is unavoidable; so the gladiator, who during his entire fight has been utterly afraid, offers his throat to his opponent and directs the wavering sword right into it.[19]

But the deadly games and the martyrdom of the Christians point up the Colosseum's negative side, with jaded crowds lusting for ever more blood and death and with an evil or megalomaniac emperor presiding over refined tortures or, like Commodus, making a spectacle of himself by fighting and killing in the arena. From this perspective, the Colosseum's very size and height are proof of Roman hubris. Even today it may evoke the biblical myth of the Tower of Babel, as it did to Pieter Brueghel the Elder, who modeled the tower on the Colosseum in his famous painting *Building the Tower of Babel* (1563).[20] So the

17   *Childe Harold's Pilgrimage* IV.1297–9 (stanza 145); quotation from *Lord Byron: The Complete Poetical Works*, vol. 2, 173.
18   William L. Vance, *America's Rome*, vol. 1: *Classical Rome* (New Haven and London: Yale University Press, 1989), 43–67 and 395–6 (notes), a chapter entitled "The Colosseum: Ambiguities of Empire." Peter Quennell, *The Colosseum* (New York: Newsweek, 1971; several rpts.), gives an illustrated outline of the Colosseum's history and its influence on Western culture down to the nineteenth century. See also Christopher Woodward, *In Ruins* (New York: Pantheon, 2001), 11–31.
19   Seneca, *Moral Epistles* 30.8; my translation.
20   The painting may conveniently be found in Quennell, *The Colosseum*, 110–11.

ruins of the Colosseum have long been regarded as a symbol for the fall of Rome.

Since the nineteenth century, the Colosseum has cast a particular spell over Americans, citizens of a modern powerful country modeled in several important ways on ancient Rome.[21] As Vance has observed, adducing an apt analogy to American literature, the Colosseum yields

> a cumulative American image . . . that in its complexity expresses an ambivalent attitude toward imperial power, its rise, its glories and terrors, and its fall. The Colosseum becomes the Moby-Dick of architecture, a sublimely multivalent symbol sacred yet malignant, alien and dreadful yet magnificent, ravaged yet enduring.[22]

A popular American historian expressed this traditional view of the Colosseum in the twentieth century. In his history of Rome called, revealingly, *Caesar and Christ* and first published when Americans were fighting a new would-be Roman Empire in World War II, Will Durant assesses the Colosseum as follows:

> The Colosseum is not a beautiful building, and its very immensity reveals a certain coarseness, as well as grandeur, in the Roman character. It is only the most imposing of all the ruins left by the classic world. The Romans built like giants; it would have been too much to ask that they should finish like jewelers.[23]

While we may disagree with parts of this verdict, Durant's comparison of Romans to giants is apt for an American writer. As builders on a gigantic scale, Americans are the Romans' natural successors with their sports arenas and skyscrapers. So it is appropriate that a modern translator of Martial should use the phrase "highrise skyline" for the walls of Babylon mentioned by Martial, whose height, Martial says, the Colosseum exceeds.[24] American skyscrapers may strike many as modern

---

21   Meyer Reinhold, *Classica Americana: The Greek and Roman Heritage in the United States* (Detroit: Wayne State University Press, 1984), and Carl J. Richard, *The Founders and the Classics: Greece, Rome, and the American Enlightenment* (Cambridge: Harvard University Press, 1994; rpt. 1995), deal with this large subject, among numerous other works.

22   Vance, *America's Rome*, vol. 1, 45.

23   Durant, *Caesar and Christ*, 361.

24   Peter Whigham, "Caesar's Ring" (i.e., the oval of the Colosseum), in *Martial in English*, ed. J. P. Sullivan and A. J. Boyle (London: Penguin, 1996), 367. Whigham's version earlier appeared in his *Letter to Juvenal: 101 Epigrams from Martial* (London: Anvil Press Poetry, 1985), 27, and in *Epigrams of Martial Englished by Divers Hands*, ed. J. P. Sullivan and Peter Whigham (Berkeley, Los Angeles, and London: University of California Press, 1987), 51.

versions of Babel Tower or the Colosseum. So the destruction of two of them in 2001 may have looked like an ominous sign of doom. If the Twin Towers can fall, can America fall? Its fall has been predicted since 1778.[25] If America falls, will the world, or at least the West as we know it, also fall? To put it in *Gladiator* terms: Who is the Maximus to defeat the barbarians? Does such a savior even exist? From this point of view, a 2002 cartoon by David Levine showing President George W. Bush as a Roman warrior dressed in the breast plate and military "skirt" familiar from Hollywood epics is telling. Behind his shield, on which the presidential seal is displayed, the tips of assorted rockets and other hi-tech weaponry are visible.[26] Is Bush the real Maximus?

In this context it is worth considering some science-fiction films which, taken together, comment on the analogy of the fall of Rome and America. That science-fiction empires may be modeled on the Roman Empire is a familiar American phenomenon.[27] The fall of Rome is the end of an ancient civilization. The fall of America as imagined in science fiction is a modern analogy; both are usually meant as warnings about the present. A familiar example of the latter is Franklin J. Schaffner's *Planet of the Apes* (1968), in which the fallen Statue of Liberty is the only remnant of human culture after a nuclear holocaust.[28] That tall buildings in science-fiction films can signify human hubris is most obvious from Fritz Lang's *Metropolis* (1927). This film opens with a prologue showing the biblical Tower of Babel story as an analogy to the futuristic city. The dominant skyscraper of Metropolis is accordingly named the new Tower of Babel. Metropolis is modeled on both ancient Rome and

25   Cf. Karl Galinsky, *Classical and Modern Interactions: Postmodern Architecture, Multiculturalism, Decline, and Other Issues* (Austin: University of Texas Press, 1992), 54 and 174 note 3 (in a chapter entitled "The Decline and Fall of the Roman Empire: Are There Modern Parallels?").

26   The drawing was first published in *The New York Review of Books* (February 28, 2002), 44. Shortly before, *The Washington Post* (February 8, 2002), section A, page 30, had published a comparable one (with the byline "By Horsey for the Seattle *Post-Intelligencer*"). These two examples are representative. More recently, a large full-color cartoon by Barry Blitt of Paul D. Wolfowitz, Bush's Deputy Defense Secretary, as a Roman warrior preceded the article by James Atlas, "Leo-Con: A Classicist's Legacy: New Empire Builders," *The New York Times* (May 4, 2003), section 4, pages 1 and 4. The classicist is Leo Strauss.

27   I have dealt with this topic in "*Star Wars* and the Roman Empire," in *Classical Myth and Culture in the Cinema*, ed. Martin M. Winkler (New York: Oxford University Press, 2001), 272–90.

28   Woodward, *In Ruins*, 196, mentions this film in a chapter entitled "The Ozymandias Complex" (177–204); he quotes Shelley's "Ozymandias" at 204.

twentieth-century New York, the latter an inspiration for its architectural design.[29] The new Babel Tower of Metropolis remains standing. But in Fred F. Sears's *Earth vs. the Flying Saucers* (1956), alien spacecraft demolish several symbols of American government and liberty. They damage the dome of the Capitol and topple the Washington Monument (and set a precedent for the aliens who would later blow up the White House in Roland Emmerich's *Independence Day* of 1996). As with other science fiction from the Cold War era, the aliens stand in for godless Communists; they may also represent any un-American barbarians. A year after Sears's film, in Nathan Juran's *Twenty Million Miles to Earth*, a monster from outer space takes refuge on top of the Roman Colosseum – "COLOSSUS ASTRIDE COLISEUM" proclaimed a headline in the film's trailer – from where it falls to its death. This ending is an intentional reprise of the climax of Merian C. Cooper and Ernest B. Schoedsack's *King Kong* (1933) atop the Empire State Building. The films by Sears and Juran had the same producer and studio, some actors were in both casts, and both films are memorable for their special effects by Ray Harryhausen. The latter was filmed in Italy only for economic reasons; the original story had been set in Chicago. On its rampage through the Roman Forum, the monster destroys the Temple of Saturn, originally built in 498 B.C. and one of the Eternal City's most venerable and imposing ruins. The Colosseum fortunately survives the creature and the army's missiles fired at it with minimal damage. Hollywood destroyed it only in 2003 in Jon Amiel's science-fiction spectacle *The Core*.

In 1961, Lewis Mumford drew a line of continuity from ancient to modern architecture and from Roman to American mass society. He did so with an indignation reminiscent of the Roman satirist Juvenal, who had delivered a tirade on the horrors of the city of Rome in his Third Satire. Mumford advanced perhaps the most condemnatory case against the Colosseum and what it stands for, with clear analogies to modern atrocities:

---

29 Lang had visited New York City in 1924, when the screenplay for *Metropolis* was already being written. On the sources for the film's architectural designs see Patrick McGilligan, *Fritz Lang: The Nature of the Beast* (New York: St. Martin's, 1997), 110–13. The Roman side of Metropolis appears most clearly in its subterranean catacombs and in the classicizing architecture of its stadium, replete with neo-classical colossal statuary. Lang and his set designers had only the lower parts of their skyscrapers built for filming; the upper parts were photographed from painted images added by mirror. For *Gladiator*, Scott followed the same principle for the on-screen images of the Colosseum, except that its upper parts were computer-generated images.

Roman life, for all its claims of peace, centered more and more on the imposing rituals of extermination . . . But sensations need constant whipping as people become inured to them: so the whole effort reached a pinnacle in the gladiatorial spectacles, where the agents of this regime applied a diabolic inventiveness to human torture and human extermination.

The inhabitants of modern metropolises are not psychologically too remote from Rome to be unable to appreciate this new form . . . Every day, in the arena, the Romans witnessed in person acts of vicious torture and wholesale extermination, such as those that Hitler and his agents later devised and vicariously participated in – but apparently lacked the stomach to enjoy regularly in person.[30]

Mumford's comparison of Roman gladiatorial games and the Holocaust may strike some as bordering on the tasteless. But it is in keeping with his assessment of imperial Rome as "the city in its characteristic degeneracy." Mumford intends us to understand "American" alongside "Roman" and "Manhattan" alongside "Rome" when he observes a little later:

It was here that the Roman mastery of engineering problems perhaps reached its height: it was here that the Roman delight in quantitative achievement conceived an architectural form whose very success depends upon mass and scale . . . Rome had become the arena of arenas, where the usual activities of a city were subordinated to the mass production of violent sensations derived from lust, torture, and murder.[31]

Fortunately, we have more balanced assessments of the Colosseum as an expression of imperial Roman architecture and culture. Under the heading "Imperial Civilization and Architecture," William MacDonald discusses the vaulted style characteristic of large-scale Roman buildings as an expression of Roman civilization during the empire and notes: "It

30   Lewis Mumford, *The City in History: Its Origins, Its Transformations, and Its Prospects* (New York: Harcourt, Brace and World, 1961), 229–30 (in a chapter section entitled, after Hemingway, "Death in the Afternoon"). He contradicts his own exaggeration about daily gladiatorial games on the following page. His earlier discussion (224) of the Colosseum and the Baths of Caracalla as public *vomitoria* is also hyperbolic; it derives from a misunderstanding of the Latin term.

31   Both passages are at Mumford, *The City in History*, 232. The beginning of the longer quotation refers to the Colosseum, although Mumford makes this statement in a discussion of "a new urban form, the circus." The Circus Maximus is, however, something else. It is regrettable that Vance, *America's Rome*, vol. 1, 48, quotes this passage without comment.

is unlikely that the style was an autonomous artistic phenomenon, unrelated to the culture of its time." Rather, through features such as "axis, symmetry, and the properties of concavity," this style was

> a mimesis of the state, a metaphor in tangible form upon its traditions and its claims to all-embracing sovereignty . . . Roman architecture might be defined as a body of law in masonry, governing human responses by didactic forms whose expressive force was intended to be recognized or apprehended immediately by the sensory faculties.[32]

MacDonald's conclusions apply specifically to the Colosseum, which has a "multitude of functions and social values attached to it." As another scholar has stated, "the Colosseum was a conservative monument extolling the traditional male virtues of courage (*virtus*), discipline (*disciplina*) and skill at arms (*ars militaris*) . . . The Colosseum was not a monument to depravity and vice; it was a testimony to the power and stability of the social order of Roman society and the cardinal position of traditional military virtues within that society."[33]

2. The Fascination of Spectacle

Mumford's phrase "lust, torture, and murder" summarizes the negative view of the Colosseum as place of gladiatorial games, animal hunts, and Christian martyrdom. Especially with regard to the latter, the Colosseum has come to exemplify to modern stage and screen audiences a particularly curious site. Torture and death are not what good people should enjoy, but when they are presented as part of uplifting moral lessons about the evils of paganism and the goodness of the righteous, they become not only acceptable but even desirable to watch. Stage plays such as *Ben-Hur* or Wilson Barrett's *The Sign of the Cross* (1895), the source for DeMille's film, are symptomatic of this. Given the immediacy of a spectacle observed first-hand, they exceed popular novels, their precursors, in audience appeal. What Vance has noted about novels and plays is true for films, too: "the popular romances and stage productions have it both ways: they combine self-righteous indignation with the thrill of

---

32   William L. MacDonald, *The Architecture of the Roman Empire*, vol. 1: *An Introductory Study*, rev. edn (New Haven and London: Yale University Press, 1982), 179–83; quotations at 180–1.

33   The quotations are from D. L. Bomgardner, *The Story of the Roman Amphitheatre* (London and New York: Routledge, 2000), 31.

vicariously witnessing the bestiality and suffering they deplore, while taking satisfaction in painless identification with steadfast martyrs or rebellious slaves."[34] Much of nineteenth-century painting depicting ancient Rome serves the same purpose, combining the lurid with the edifying. Of special significance in this regard is Jean-Léon Gérôme with his paintings *Ave Caesar, Morituri Te Salutant* (1859) and *Pollice Verso* (1874), both set in the Colosseum. They are the more effective in that they put the spectator right into the sand of the arena, in close-up proximity to fighting or dying gladiators. Mainly through the technological advances that made mass reproduction possible, Gérôme's gladiator paintings "furnished America in the second half of the nineteenth century with its popular image of ancient Rome."[35] Gérôme was outdone in vividness and immediacy only by the cinema. Films set in the arena tended to imitate his canvases. These films also demonstrated the ambiguity of fascination. A case in point is *The Sign of the Cross*, which culminates in one of the most ferocious arena sequences ever put on screen before *Gladiator*. The latter film virtually owes its making to Gérôme, for a copy of *Pollice Verso* convinced Ridley Scott to take on the project.[36] Both DeMille and Scott manage to catch the steamy, fetid, and bizarrely erotic afternoon atmosphere of the Colosseum which Gérôme had made standard. DeMille shows the traditional American approach to such subjects. His Roman and biblical spectacles are characterized by sex, sadism, and sanctimoniousness, a potent formula that still works, as *Gladiator* makes evident. Both films illustrate what a film historian said about *The Sign of the Cross*: "the film . . . combined sadism, religious elements, and an agreeably sophisticated distortion of history with immense flair."[37]

More than Scott, DeMille reveals the ambiguity of fascination through a number of close-ups on the reactions of spectators, especially women. A late ancient description provides us with a vivid verbal example. St. Augustine gives the following account of the corrupting effect the games could have even on a morally steadfast young man. In Rome, Augustine's student Alypius, a devout Christian,

34   Vance, *America's Rome*, vol. 1, 52.
35   On Gérôme's paintings and their connection to popular novels cf. Vance, *America's Rome*, vol. 1, 48–9; quotation from 48.
36   Cf. *Gladiator: The Making of the Ridley Scott Epic*, ed. Diana Landau (New York: Newmarket, 2000), 22–6 and 88; cf. 80–9 on the film's Colosseum. Among painters, it is especially Sir Lawrence Alma-Tadema who has exerted lasting influence on modern views of antiquity. In the case of Scott's film, cf. *Gladiator*, 64, 66, 93, and 95.
37   Higham, *Cecil B. DeMille*, 220.

was carried away by a well-nigh incredible hunger for the gladiatorial games, and in a way that almost defied belief. Although he regarded such games with loathing and abomination, some of his friends and fellow-students took him with good-natured force into the amphitheatre . . . He protested vehemently . . . When they arrived and had sat down in what seats they could, the whole place was boiling with pleasures of the most savage kind. Alypius closed the doors of his eyes, and forbade his mind to pay any attention to all this wickedness. Would that he had stopped his ears! For at one moment in the fight, a gladiator fell, and a great clamour arose from the whole populace, and beat against him; and, overcome by curiosity and ready, as it were, to despise whatever the cause, even when he had seen it, and to prove stronger, he opened his eyes, and was more severely wounded in his soul than the gladiator whom he longed to see had been in his body, and suffered a more pitiable fall than his whose fall had been the cause of all the clamour. The noise had entered his ears and unlocked his eyes, to make a path by which his mind could be assailed and overthrown . . . When it saw the blood, it drank in the savagery; nor did it turn away, but fixed its gaze and glutted itself on the fury, unknowingly taking pleasure in the wickedness of the fight, and becoming drunk on its bloody pleasure. He was no longer the man he had come, a true companion of those who had brought him. What more is there to say? He watched, he cheered, he burnt; he took his madness away with him, to stir him up to come again – not just with the friends who had dragged him there previously, but more enthusiastically than they, even dragging others along with him.[38]

In one of his letters, Seneca made a related point: Avoid crowds and masses. Spectacles are more ruinous to good character than anything else, and vice insinuates itself through such pleasures.[39] Traditionally, Seneca has been thought to be against the games, but recent scholarship has refuted this view.[40] Augustine's passage is a vivid and gripping example of the hostility of early Christians to Roman culture: "The principal charge levelled against all spectacles was that they were pagan, idolatrous and demonic rituals"; the Colosseum was "the haunt of howling mobs of the unemployed urban masses of Rome drinking in debauchery

38   Augustine, *Confessions* 6.8.13; quoted from Augustine, *The Confessions*, tr. and ed. Philip Burton (New York and Toronto: Knopf, 2001), 120–1. Cf. Bomgardner, *The Story of the Roman Amphitheatre*, 202–4 ("The Christian Reaction" to the games).
39   Seneca, *Moral Epistles* 7.
40   See Magnus Wistrand, "Violence and Entertainment in Seneca the Younger," *Eranos*, 88 (1990), 3–46. Wistrand expanded on this in *Entertainment and Violence in Ancient Rome: The Attitudes of Roman Writers of the First Century A.D.* (Göteborg: Acta Universitatis Gothoburgensis, 1992).

and lewdness with their eyes and ears as they watched the spectacles in the arena below them."[41] This perspective is one-sided but comprehensible on a visceral level. Modern Christian culture has preserved and revived it in the cinema. American films even outdo European ones in this regard, not least because of the country's Puritan tradition.[42]

The psychological effect of the games on an impressionable youngster finds its modern analogy in that of special-effects mayhem in Hollywood spectacles or, for instance, in Spanish bullfighting.[43] The Colosseum design for *Gladiator* was even based on that of a bull ring.[44] The following description of the matador fits the Roman gladiator and his cinematic reincarnation in equal parts:

> Appealing to aggression and sexuality as human impulses, the matador is a warrior, a taboo-breaker, and a risk-taker who puts honor above life. The masses revere him for his demonstration of *majismo* in manner, body language, dress, honor, and morality . . . Just as the bullfight is inherently erotic because of its passion and emotionalism and the physiological arousal of the spectators, Roman spectacles were erotic, intoxicating, and voyeuristic. Like matadors, gladiators appealed to spectators as forbidden, déclassé killers.[45]

The death of matador Manuel Vare (or Varé, nicknamed Varelito) in 1922 reinforces the analogy. The death of a Roman gladiator was often accompanied by cries of *"Habet!"* ("He's got it!"). Vare had been taunted by the crowd, took too great a risk, and died from a fatal goring. As he was being carried out of the arena, he kept saying: "Now you've given it to me. Now I've got it. Now you've given it to me. Now you've got what you wanted. Now I've got it. Now you've given it to me. Now I've got it. Now I've got it. I've got it."[46]

41   Bomgardner, *The Story of the Roman Amphitheatre*, 31.

42   I have addressed this subject in more detail in "The Roman Empire in American Cinema After 1945," *The Classical Journal*, 93 (1998), 167–96; slightly revised in *Imperial Projections: Ancient Rome in Modern Popular Culture*, ed. Sandra R. Joshel, Margaret Malamud, and Donald T. McGuire, Jr. (Baltimore and London: Johns Hopkins University Press, 2001), 50–76.

43   Cf. Marcus Junkelmann, *Das Spiel mit dem Tod: So kämpften Roms Gladiatoren* (Mainz: von Zabern, 2000), 12–18, on post-classical sports and games.

44   *Gladiator*, 87 and 89.

45   Donald G. Kyle, *Spectacles of Death in Ancient Rome* (London and New York: Routledge, 1998), 85.

46   Ernest Hemingway, *Death in the Afternoon* (New York: Scribner, 1932), 253–4. Hemingway, 253, calls Varelito "probably the best killer of my generation." On him see Miriam B. Mandel, *Hemingway's* Death in the Afternoon: *The Complete Annotations* (Lanham and London: Scarecrow Press, 2002), 441–3.

3. The Technology of Spectacle

The fascination of spectacle in *Gladiator* depends primarily on the technological fireworks on display in the film, on its state-of-the-art computer images. These turn it into a new kind of epic that is appealing to youthful audiences, but at the same time they, too, reveal an inherent dichotomy. What art historian Erwin Panofsky observed long ago about early Walt Disney cartoons is applicable to much of popular cinema in general and to *Gladiator* in particular:

> They retain the most important folkloristic elements – sadism, pornography, the humor engendered by both, and moral justice – almost without dilution and often fuse these elements into a variation on the primitive and inexhaustible David-and-Goliath motif, the triumph of the seemingly weak over the seemingly strong; and their fantastic independence of the natural laws gives them the power to integrate space with time to such perfection that the spatial and temporal experiences of sight and hearing come to be almost incontrovertible.[47]

The sadism of *Gladiator* is the explicit visual and aural violence of its battle and arena sequences. Its pornography is not so much the titillation presented in the depiction of a sexual deviant – Commodus' incestuous longings for his sister Lucilla and the sexual threat he poses to his pre-teen nephew – but the pornography of violence, highly detailed as it is on the screen and on the soundtrack. It precipitates visceral and often vociferous enjoyment of the spectacle in the viewers, related to the reactions caused by violent cartoons. Moral justice is served up with a vengeance at the conclusion of *Gladiator*, again with a high degree of the pornographic kind of violence which is now expected. When Maximus pushes Commodus' dagger through his throat, the blade's slicing through flesh is accompanied by a pumped-up sound effect, sickening to the squeamish but highly satisfying to the aroused. The independence from natural laws that occurs in cartoons, as when characters defy the force of gravity, can have no literal equivalent in a live-action film, but through its computer-generated images, for instance, *Gladiator* can also boast of being able to show its viewers what in reality would be impossible to see. This, too, borders on the fantastic, as the film's action sequences prove. In particular, the Battle of Carthage and Maximus'

---

47   Erwin Panofsky, "Style and Medium in the Motion Pictures" (1947); rpt. in Panofsky, *Three Essays on Style*, ed. Irving Lavin (Cambridge and London: MIT Press, 1995), 91–125 and 210 (notes); quotation at 104. A shorter version of Panofsky's essay had appeared in 1936 under the title "On Movies."

simultaneous fight against tigers and Tigris of Gaul overcome all semblance of, or dependence on, reality through extremely rapid cutting, slow motion at climactic moments, close-ups on bodies or body parts, and an increased sound volume at crashes, woundings, and killings. (The voices of, for instance, Cassius, the announcer of the games, and Tigris are amplified.)

During the filming of the Colosseum sequences, only a small part of the people visible on the screen were real; most are digital images. The 2,000 spectators present on the set were later joined by 33,000 computer-generated ones.[48] The shouts and cries of the mob had to be amplified electronically to simulate the likely reactions of the thousands whom we see but who were not there. So the result is a curious transfer of audience reaction. The only audience that responds instinctively and viscerally to the show in the Colosseum is that in the cinema. The film's effectiveness in manipulating this audience is evinced by the fact that the artificial aural reactions from the Roman spectators are echoed by the real reactions from the modern spectators. Anybody who has watched *Gladiator* sitting in an excited crowd will readily attest that the reactions coming from the loudspeakers are identical to those coming from all around. The yells of the modern viewers may even drown out those of the Romans. Film theaters are the equivalents of the Colosseum.

More than the spectators in the ancient Colosseum, who would have watched the arena fights in real time and without an omnipotent director enhancing their thrills, those in the film theater now witness a perfect condensation – or better: compression – of space and time, one no less effective than the one Panofsky postulated for cartoons. That these experiences are irresistible is borne out by the film's success in manipulating its viewers' emotions. The audience in the Colosseum reacted to the reality of what they saw. Today, the lack of such reality must be countered by close-ups, fast editing, and cranked-up sound; otherwise modern audiences, especially young ones, would be considerably less involved. The action scenes in *Gladiator* are consequently MTV-era filmmaking; their style reflects Scott's early experiences with television commercials.

4. *Spectacle, Power, and the Power of Spectacle*

Wider analogies between imperial Roman society and our own may be drawn in connection with games and spectacles: "The spectacle is the

48   *Gladiator*, 89.

self-portrait of power in the age of power's totalitarian rule over the conditions of existence."[49] Although public spectacles play important political parts in democratic or benignly autocratic forms of government, too, spectacles in twentieth-century totalitarian states revealed the need of the ruling elite for pomp and circumstance. Fascist, National-Socialist, and Communist mass rallies held in stadiums and sports arenas are cases in point and may have been patterned on the ancient games held in the Colosseum or Circus Maximus. All, ancient and modern, were presided over by the man in absolute power. Leni Riefenstahl's *Triumph of the Will* (1935), a propaganda film about the 1934 Nazi party rally at Nuremberg, plays a major role in the iconography of Commodus' Rome in *Gladiator*.[50] The image of the absolute ruler who is also the ruler of the games reveals the political importance of mass shows. In the words of Guy Debord:

> In all its specific manifestations – news or propaganda, advertising or actual consumption of entertainment – the spectacle epitomizes the prevailing model of social life . . . In form as in content the spectacle serves as total justification for the conditions and aims of the existing system. It further ensures the *permanent presence* of that justification.[51]

In an outtake included in the DVD edition of *Gladiator*, Proximo says to Maximus before a fight: "Remember you are an entertainer – *so entertain!*" Maximus does. So does Scott, whose perspective on *Gladiator* well fits Proximo's exhortation:

> Entertainment has frequently been used by leaders as a means to distract an abused citizenry. The most tyrannical ruler must still beguile his people even as he brutalizes them. The gladiatorial games were such a distrac-

---

49   Guy Debord, *The Society of the Spectacle*, tr. Donald Nicholson-Smith (New York: Zone Books, 1994), 19. Cf. Keith Hopkins, *Death and Renewal* (Cambridge: Cambridge University Press, 1983; rpt. 1985), 14–20 ("Gladiatorial Shows as Political Theatre"), especially 18: "The emperor was the centre of everyone's attention . . . This dramatic enactment of imperial power . . . before a mass audience of citizens, conquerors of the world, helped legitimate the emperor's position." See further Paul Plass, *The Game of Death in Ancient Rome: Arena Sport and Political Suicide* (Madison: University of Wisconsin Press, 1995), and Karl-Wilhelm Weeber, *Panem et circenses: Massenunterhaltung als Politik im antiken Rom*, 2nd edn (Mainz: von Zabern, 2000), on the connections between Roman spectacle and ancient and modern politics.

50   Cf. *Gladiator*, 78 and 120, and in particular the contribution by Arthur Pomeroy in the present volume.

51   Debord, *The Society of the Spectacle*, 13.

tion. Our story suggests that, should a hero arise out of the carnage of the arena, his popularity would give him tremendous power . . . and were he a genuine champion of the people, he might threaten even the most absolute tyrant.[52]

Scott's conclusions are an exaggeration about Roman history, but they illustrate his film's modern nature in terms of politics and mass spectacles. Juvenal's famous phrase characterizing the Roman crowd as wanting *panem et circenses* ("bread and games") points to the fact that mass entertainments, not least those of the cinema today, are potent social and political factors.[53] Debord comments on the spectacle:

> It is the sun that never sets on the empire of passivity. It covers the entire globe, basking in the perpetual warmth of its own glory. The spectacle, being the reigning social organization of a paralyzed history, of a paralyzed memory, of an abandonment of any history founded in historical time, is in effect a *false consciousness of time*.[54]

Small wonder that *Gladiator* should have found such worldwide resonance. The film attests to the truth of Debord's view. "Ridley definitely wanted to capture a concept of Rome as the New York City of its day," observes a member of the director's technical crew.[55] *Gladiator* is symptomatic of our own lack of historical knowledge or consciousness. So it does not matter much whether the violent celluloid sports we watch have ancient, contemporary, or futuristic settings. The Colosseum and the arena in films like Norman Jewison's *Rollerball* (1975) or its 2002 remake by John McTiernan are, in effect, one and the same place.[56] Scott's understanding of himself as film director applies here: "In interviews, Scott has taken the position that he is primarily an entertainer,

---

52　Quoted from *Gladiator*, 32.

53　Juvenal, *Satires* 10.81. This famous phrase led to the inclusion of a scene in *Gladiator* in which loaves of bread are being distributed before the Colosseum games begin.

54　Debord, *The Society of the Spectacle*, 15 and 114.

55　Quoted from *Gladiator*, 78. On the Rome–New York analogy cf. the following description of Martin Scorsese's *Gangs of New York* (2002) by David Denby, "For the Love of Fighting," *The New Yorker* (December 23 and 30, 2002), 166–9, at 167: "at times it has the depressive feverishness of Fellini's film [*Fellini Satyricon*, 1970] – the jeering spectators mounted in multitiered sets, the furtive life of the crime-ridden metropolis, with its hapless poverty, its barbaric entertainments, its obscure and unredeemed suffering."

56　A little-known short film by Ed Apfel on the earlier *Rollerball* is therefore aptly entitled *From Rome to Rollerball: The Full Circle* (1975). Cf. also Paul Michael Glaser's *The Running Man* (1987), a film comparable to *Rollerball*.

not a social critic. But like Proximus [*sic*] in *Gladiator*, who also claims to be just an entertainer, Scott knows that entertainment is a form of power."[57]

Such power, innocuous as it may appear at first sight, carries its own ambivalence. From Scott's gladiators to the American soldiers in his *Black Hawk Down* a year and a half later there is only a small step. The display of killing even in serious-minded films is calculated to arouse the audience's curiosity and fascination with what they are watching, else there would be no audience and no box-office return. Steven Spielberg's *Saving Private Ryan* (1998) is a telling example. Its long opening slaughter sequence was its biggest selling point, despite the director's and star's eager protestations that they wanted to show the horrors of war realistically. The battle with the Germans that opens *Gladiator* is a parallel case; this sequence, too, has become famous. Explicit violence is now an effective means to hook an audience from the very beginning, and the examples of Spielberg's and Scott's films have been followed even by Martin Scorsese in *Gangs of New York*. But even anti-war films are war films. Only very few manage to transcend the attractiveness of violence and gore in their portrayals of battle; Lewis Milestone's *All Quiet on the Western Front* (1930) is the most honorable case. But Scott's action and war cinema is not on this level. Rather, his two films just mentioned only express the spirit of their time, although *Gladiator*, which was released shortly before a turning point in American politics, anticipates the renewed martial spirit of the country in the second Bush administration. A comparison of Scott's two films with Antoine Fuqua's *Tears of the Sun* (2003), a war film with obvious plot parallels to *Black Hawk Down* and with thematic affinities to *Gladiator*, will corroborate this point. What critic David Denby has said about Fuqua's film applies to Scott's films: Each is "a celebration of improvisation under fire and of self-sacrifice." The two films set in twentieth-century wars in Africa allow "Americans to demonstrate their honor while fighting and killing a great many nasty Africans."[58] Substitute Roman legionaries or good gladiators for American soldiers and Germans or enemy gladiators for Africans, and you have a description of *Gladiator*. Denby's conclusion about *Tears of the Sun* also fits *Gladiator*: "when future historians want to understand the lock-and-load moralism of the Bush Administration at the time of the second Gulf

---

57   Schwartz, *The Films of Ridley Scott*, xi. His next sentence ("He uses his power to liberate us from preconceived restrictions") is an exaggeration. Cf. also the contribution by Peter Rose in the present volume.
58   David Denby, "Riding into Battle," *The New Yorker* (March 17, 2003), 152–3; both quotations at 152.

War, they will look to this simple-minded but rousing celebration of the American warrior as an inescapable guide."[59] From Maximus' "Strength and Honor!" to Bush's "Shock and Awe" – a seamless transition.

5. *Spectacle and History*

Gladiator confirms the psychological, political, and sociological implications of spectacle. For this reason the Colosseum is the film's most important setting in regard to spectacle as a display of power and the power of display. Emperor Commodus fights in the arena, although *Gladiator* downplays the extent and the nature of the historical Commodus' fixation on gladiatorial combat. As Cassius Dio and the biographer of Commodus in the *Augustan History* make abundantly clear, Commodus was obsessed with gladiatorial games to the extent of styling himself after Hercules, son of Jupiter and mightiest of ancient mythical heroes. This obsession was the main cause of his assassination.

Following the ancient historiographical tradition, Gibbon put the case against Commodus most eloquently: "every sentiment of virtue and humanity was extinct in the mind of Commodus . . . he valued nothing in sovereign power, except the unbounded licence of indulging his sensual appetites."[60] Gibbon rises to a rhetorical climax when he turns to Commodus the gladiator:

> But the meanest of the populace were affected with shame and indignation when they beheld their sovereign enter the lists as a gladiator, and glory in a profession which the laws and manners of the Romans had branded with the justest note of infamy . . . Commodus had now attained the summit of vice and infamy. Amidst the acclamations of a flattering court, he was unable to disguise, from himself, that he had deserved the contempt and hatred of every man of sense and virtue in the empire. His ferocious spirit was irritated by the consciousness of that hatred, by the envy of every kind of merit, by the just apprehension of danger, and by the habit of slaughter, which he contracted in his daily amusements.[61]

Classical and modern authors have generally considered Commodus' self-display in the arena as an irredeemably shameful and immoral

---

59   Denby, "Riding into Battle," 153. These words were written before the second Gulf War began.
60   Gibbon, *The History of the Decline and Fall of the Roman Empire*, vol. 1, 105.
61   Gibbon, *The History of the Decline and Fall of the Roman Empire*, vol. 1, 107 and 108–9.

disregard of expected standards of behavior and as the ultimate symptom of his moral depravity. So has painting. The emphasis of Edwin Howland Blashfield's *Commodus, Dressed as Hercules, Leaves the Amphitheater at the Head of the Gladiators* (1878) is "purely on the decadence of the Empire, for which the spectacular architecture provides a congruently luxurious setting instead of a grandly ennobling theater."[62] Blashfield was strongly influenced by Gérôme; he, too, takes the viewer to the floor of the Colosseum.[63] The 2.1:1 horizontal format of Blashfield's huge canvas is nearly identical to the standard widescreen format of epic films (2.35:1), including *Gladiator*. Hekster aptly observes on his very first page: "The emperor Commodus was the first purple-born Roman emperor, and according to our literary sources an evil tyrant – Hollywood style."[64] The heroine of Henry Koster's *The Robe* (1953), the first of the 2.35:1 widescreen epics, voices the traditional view of evil emperors in her denunciation of Caligula, which also fits Commodus: "Once the Caesars of Rome were noble. But in you noble blood has turned to poison. You corrupt Rome with your spite and malice . . . Vicious, treacherous, drunk with power, and evil . . ."

The tone of her indictment is not far from the Roman senate's condemnation of the historical Commodus after his death. The senators placed heavy emphasis on his gladiatorial activities. But recent scholarship recognizes much greater complexity in Commodus, who was not as irresponsible or cowardly as hostile ancient sources and many modern authors have portrayed him.[65] Hekster in particular has shown that Commodus' activities in the arena exerted a socially stabilizing influence.[66]

Gladiator displays Commodus as a "bad guy," a villain in the tradition of Dio, Gibbon, and Hollywood spectacle. This Commodus is depraved, but he is also humanized by his loneliness, lack of paternal affection, and the complete absence of a mother. This latter side is relentlessly modern

---

62   Vance, *America's Rome*, vol. 1, 49.

63   See Vance, *America's Rome*, vol. 1, 49–50, on Blashfield's Roman paintings and the influence of Gérôme. Vance, 50, errs, however, in his description of Commodus' death.

64   Hekster, *Commodus*, i.

65   Contrast the traditional image of Commodus as evil and incompetent ruler with the observations by Barry Baldwin, "Commodus the Good Poet and Good Emperor: Explaining the Inexplicable," *Gymnasium*, 97 (1990), 224–31, especially 229–31, with brief discussion of later ancient sources on Commodus and further references to scholarship. Cf. also the contribution of Arthur Eckstein in this volume.

66   Hekster, *Commodus*, especially 137–62 on Commodus as gladiator (a chapter entitled "An Emperor on Display").

in its reflection of today's obsession with dysfunctional families and nostalgia for traditional family values. The misunderstood youngster alienated from everybody turns into a rebel with a bad cause. Absolute power becomes Commodus' ultimate goal, meant to fill the void of family affection and to counteract universal rejection. Ironically, none other than Gibbon foreshadowed such a conception of Commodus when he observed about Commodus' crimes and ambition: "Of all our passions and appetites, the love of power is of the most imperious and unsociable nature, since the pride of one man requires the submission of the multitude."[67]

That such an inexperienced and confused young man should also alienate the senate, his governing body, is unavoidable. This makes for a more effective struggle between the forces of good and evil. Despite treachery and collaboration with Commodus in the senatorial ranks, the senate as a whole is meant to represent traditional, i.e., good, government. This is a necessity for a film like *Gladiator* because in American history the senate has stood for democratic government in the face of monarchical abuses of power since the days of the Founding Fathers. So does the Roman senate in the cinema. Americans have always felt a close affinity for the Roman republic, perceived as pure, unspoiled, and the opposite of the corrupt and decadent empire: "Americans were especially well placed to understand the early Romans of the republic, because they were kindred spirits" and "the antecedents of American liberalism." So "the Romans (like Americans) acted out their love of freedom during the republic."[68] Gibbon sums up the common view of the Roman senate in the empire: "That assembly, whom Marcus [Aurelius] had ever considered as the great council of the nation, was composed of the most distinguished of the Romans."[69] Stanley Kubrick's *Spartacus* (1960) and Anthony Mann's *The Fall of the Roman Empire* (1964) are the most obvious models for *Gladiator* in this regard.

But this cinematic tradition goes back further and is not exclusively American. In *The Robe*, Senator Gallio rebukes his son for antagonizing Caligula, heir to Emperor Tiberius, in modern terms: "I lead the senators who oppose him [Caligula]. I'm fighting for what's left of the republic

---

67   Gibbon, *The History of the Decline and Fall of the Roman Empire*, vol. 1, 97.
68   Richard Saller, "American Classical Historiography," in *Imagined Histories: American Historians Interpret the Past*, ed. Anthony Molho and Gordon S. Wood (Princeton: Princeton University Press, 1998), 222–37, at 224–5. His first two quotations summarize the views of Tenney Frank, the third that of Lily Ross Taylor. Cf. Quennell, *The Colosseum*, 135.
69   Gibbon, *The History of the Decline and Fall of the Roman Empire*, vol. 1, 99.

against the growing tyranny of the emperors." Umberto Lenzi's *L'ultimo gladiatore* (1964) restates this position.[70] Emperor Caligula falls victim to a senatorial conspiracy; while he is being stabbed to death, there are shouts of "Death to all tyrants! Long live the republic!" and "Justice for all!" Leading conspirator Cassius Chaerea then summarizes the senators' goal: "Whoever shouted 'Death to tyrants!' was expressing all our opinion. We want to re-establish the ancient republic." The film follows Suetonius' report that after Caligula's assassination and in the absence of a successor the senate unanimously decided to return to the republic, an explanation or pretext for political action that appeared several times in early imperial Roman history.[71] The film changes the social status of the historical Cassius Chaerea, prefect of the Praetorians, from *eques* (knight) to senator to strengthen the contrast between the good republic and the evil empire.[72] The topic occurs even in thinly disguised analogies to Roman history. In George Lucas's *Star Wars* trilogy (1977–83), the Rebel Alliance overthrows the Evil Empire and restores the republic.[73] *Gladiator* revives this anachronistic concept and makes it an integral part of its plot.

That history does not bear out the facile dichotomy between republic and empire is self-evident. Gibbon's praise of the Antonine age is a useful corrective.[74] Nevertheless, the American view of the Roman republic as restated in *Gladiator* owes much to Gibbon, too. In the same paragraph in which he extols the age of the Antonines, he goes on to observe: "Such princes deserved the honour of restoring the republic had the Romans of their days been capable of enjoying a rational

---

70   Lenzi's film has several alternative titles: *Gladiatore di Messalina* and, in the English-language version, *Messalina, Messalina Against the Son of Hercules, Messalina Vs. the Son of Hercules,* and *Empress Messalina Meets the Son of Hercules.*

71   Suetonius, *Caligula* 60. The senate's intentions were thwarted when the Praetorians proclaimed Claudius the new emperor. Earlier, Augustus had begun the account of his achievements with the statement that he restored the free republic (*Res Gestae* 1.1), and Tiberius' brother Drusus had discussed the restoration of the republic in a letter to Tiberius (Suetonius, *Tiberius* 50.1). Later, Galba preferred the republic to empire (Tacitus, *Histories* 1.16), and Otho was said to have overthrown Galba to restore freedom and the republic (Suetonius, *Otho* 12.2).

72   Cf. Suetonius, *Caligula* 58.2–3, on the emperor's death.

73   Cf. my "Star Wars and the Roman Empire," 285–6, on the conclusion of *Return of the Jedi.*

74   Those who consider Gibbon's view exaggerated may consult, e.g., Chester G. Starr, Jr., "The Perfect Democracy of the Roman Empire," *The American Historical Review,* 68 (1952), 1–16.

freedom."[75] This did not occur in history, nor does it in *Gladiator*. The film has resurrected long-standing traditions of historical and cinematic spectacles. Despite all its historical inauthenticities and its strong emphasis on spectacle, it even bears witness to the enduring influence of Gibbon.

---

75   Gibbon, *The History of the Decline and Fall of the Roman Empire*, vol. 1, 90.

CHAPTER EIGHT

The Vision of a Fascist Rome in *Gladiator*

Arthur J. Pomeroy

DreamWorks heralded Ridley Scott's *Gladiator* as featuring a modern kind of heroism to suit the new millennium. Posters with Russell Crowe in gladiatorial dress in front of the Colosseum announced "A Hero Will Rise" in "May 2000 A.D." Still, critics inevitably regarded the film as just the latest in a long line of Hollywood sword-and-sandal epics. Such a reaction was to be expected since numerous deliberate echoes of earlier treatments of imperial Rome recur in the film's narrative. At the same time, borrowings from other cinematic genres in *Gladiator* serve to emphasize its divergences from the standard epic tradition. In particular, the film explores the nature of power in its critique of imperialism and of the Roman political system, playing with images that in later European history would be associated with Fascism. The film's Colosseum scenes display both the most advanced technology of today and the primal emotional reactions of the crowds of the past. So the Colosseum is an appropriate symbol for the depiction of ancient Rome as simultaneously civilized and savage. This paradox seems to be resolved at the film's conclusion, when the camera cranes up to reveal a radiant dawn rising over the city from the Colosseum, heralding a Rome that is politically and, by implication, spiritually new. However, an examination of the moral values that underlie the plot of *Gladiator* and of the images of Rome it presents on the screen makes this straightforward interpretation questionable. Instead of celebrating freedom, the film reinforces reactionary social attitudes through its confused linkage of conservative morality, advanced technology, and a nearly superhuman hero. Unwittingly, *Gladiator* may be re-creating the Fascist values it appears to condemn.

The film shows Maximus, its hero, as a capable general, brave soldier, resourceful antagonist, and loving husband and father. He has other positive character traits that we expect from ideal cinematic identification figures, not least a deep love for his country. Altogether he is a man who lives up to his watchword, "Strength and Honor!" But this is a soldier's code not all that far from the Hitler Youth's motto *Blut und Ehre* ("Blood and Honor"), if without the latter's racial overtones. If Maximus appears to be a true patriot, as he does, it must be asked what this patriotism represents. In a significant scene after the battle with the Germans that opens the film, Marcus Aurelius asks his general why he thinks the Romans are in Germany. Maximus' response that they have come for the glory of the empire is countered by Marcus' observation that the expansion of Rome's boundaries has merely led to endless bloodshed. Maximus, however, cannot accept that many of his men have perished in vain; to him, they have died for their emperor and for Rome. The following dialog is revealing:

> Marcus: And what is Rome, Maximus?
> Maximus: I have seen much of the rest of the world. It is brutal and cruel and dark. Rome is the light.

The conquering general, who has never been to Rome, is bound to an ideal that is quite different from the reality of the great city, as his emperor reveals and as he will find out for himself. Marcus Aurelius extracts from Maximus the promise "to give power back to the people of Rome and end the corruption that has crippled it" and in the process to restore the Roman state to its true self. Yet even this "true" state is hardly more than an ideal, "a fragile dream which could only be whispered." Such a treatment of Rome as an ideal is based on the early history of the city as a republic, free from political strife and corruption. This view is much closer to Maximus' simple way of life on his Spanish farm than to the reality of the imperial city. Rome, once restored to the people, will not be the capital of an empire but of a republic in which the senate as the people's chief governing body must have power. The conversation of Commodus, senators Gaius and Falco, and Maximus makes this clear, although Gaius' claim that "Rome *was* founded as a republic" will surprise anybody who remembers that Romulus, its founder, was the first of seven kings.

As we, the viewers, find out together with Maximus, this ideal city is a far cry from the reality of Rome in the late second century A.D. In the first depiction of Rome in *Gladiator*, the camera descends through the clouds to display a city of grandiose buildings. Actually, what we see is patterned on the model of Rome in the Museo della Civiltà Romana that had been commissioned by Benito Mussolini for an exhibition intended to celebrate the twentieth anniversary of the Fascist march on Rome in 1922. The scene in *Gladiator* then segues into Commodus' triumphal entry into his capital, accompanied by his sister. His chariot makes its way along a grand avenue packed with crowds that are being held back by Praetorian Guards. Some of the spectators cheer, a few shout abuse. Finally Commodus arrives at a great square outside the senate building, dismounts, and ascends the steps. Once inside the senate, Commodus quickly shows his impatience with the advice the senators give him. Dismissing the claim that "the senate is the people . . . chosen from the people, to speak for the people," a phrase with obvious connotations for American audiences, Commodus announces his intention to court the populace, whom he describes as his children, by direct appeal. Rather than observing old traditions which he regards as mere illusions, Commodus will provide Rome with a new vision, that of the arena. It is left to Senator Gracchus to inform us about the full implications of Commodus' plan:

> Rome is the mob. He will conjure magic for them, and they will be distracted. He will take away their freedom, and still they will roar. The beating heart of Rome is not the marble of the Senate. It is the sand of the Colosseum. He will give them death, and they will love him for it.

A later scene reinforces this depiction of a Rome of violence and of the fickleness of the crowd when gladiatorial trainer Proximo makes the following prophecy to his new star Maximus:

> We shall go to Rome together and have bloody adventures, and the great whore will suckle us until we are fat and happy and can suckle no more. And then, when enough men have died, perhaps you will have your freedom.

Soon after he says this, the gladiators arrive in Rome and, as they climb out of their wagon, look up in amazement at the enormous size of the Colosseum. This awe-inspiring building will be the site of the struggle between Commodus and Maximus, first for the favor of the people, then for life itself. In the end, along with Proximo and most of the gladiators, Maximus sacrifices himself for Marcus Aurelius' ideal. Lucilla's words, encouraging the senators and Praetorians to carry the hero's body from the arena, sum up the film's theme:

> Is Rome worth one good man's life? We believed it once. Make us believe it again. He was a soldier of Rome. Honor him.

This dream of a Rome that was noble in origin but now has decayed is almost as old as Roman historiography itself. In the preface to his monumental work on the history of Rome from its foundation down to his own time, Livy describes the state as being undermined by disorder, first slowly, then in a downhill rush, before descending to an age when its citizens could neither stand their faults nor their cure.[1] But since continual deterioration without reaching a nadir over a period of almost a thousand years was difficult to envision, Romans often believed that the process could be halted and the direction reversed by the intervention of great men. Such was the imperial propaganda of emperors Augustus and Trajan, for example. In *Gladiator*, Maximus' sacrifice is supposed to effect a similar escape. His virtues are authentic, his spiritual and family values undeniable, and the ethics of the productive farmer contrast with the corruption of the metropolis.

So Scott's depiction of Antonine Rome is initially plausible, but the means by which he persuades the viewer of the corruption of Rome are worth examining more closely. The depiction of Commodus' entry into Rome is clearly derived from one particular visual source, Leni Riefenstahl's *Triumph of the Will* (1935), her controversial film of the 1934 Nazi party rally at Nuremberg. In its opening sequence, Riefenstahl gave the Germans aerial views of Hitler arriving by plane, the masses eagerly awaiting him. The aerial view of Rome with which Scott gives his audience its first glimpse of the imperial city is a clear homage to his predecessor.[2] Hitler's descent through the clouds in *Triumph of the Will* is mirrored in *Gladiator*. Both filmmakers employ an Olympian viewpoint to impress the importance of the moment on us. This kind of shot had for years been a feature of German alpine adventure films (*Bergfilme*, i.e.,

---

1   Livy, Preface 9.
2   So Ridley Scott in his commentary on the DVD release and in *Gladiator: The Making of the Ridley Scott Epic*, ed. Diana Landau (New York: Newmarket Press, 2000), 120. One of the first to point to *Triumph of the Will* as a model for *Gladiator* was Anthony Lane, "The Empire Strikes Back," *The New Yorker* (May 8, 2000), 125–6; rpt. as "*Gladiator*" in Lane, *Nobody's Perfect: Writings From the New Yorker* (New York: Knopf, 2002), 309–12.

"mountain films"), a virtual subgenre of German cinema. Riefenstahl herself had learned her craft from these films. She had acted in some that were directed by her mentor, Dr. Arnold Fanck. The title of one of the best-known mountain films and the one to give Riefenstahl her first acting part, Fanck's *The Holy Mountain* (1926), reveals the highly mystical celebration of nature and the naïvely romantic reaction against modern times that these films evinced and that appealed to Riefenstahl. She acted in two more in 1929–30 and then directed and starred in one herself: *The Blue Light* (1932).[3] The mountain films were spiritual precursors of Riefenstahl's own films and of most Nazi cinema in general, as historians and film scholars have long recognized.[4] To powerful effect, Riefenstahl adapted the mountain-film style to lend emotional resonance to the landing of Hitler's plane in *Triumph of the Will*. Moreover, the Roman eagle as a symbol of power in *Gladiator*, the first thing we see after the aerial "fly-over," recalls the Nazi eagle which is the first thing to be seen in *Triumph of the Will*. Even the imperial procession past cheering crowds in *Gladiator* appears in some shots from the viewpoint of Commodus in his chariot, just as Riefenstahl had repeatedly shown the Führer from a camera angle close above and behind him, in this way giving him a larger-than-life appearance and making him dominate his adoring followers. Scott even quotes a brief but famous moment from the opening sequence of *Triumph of the Will*, in which a little girl in the arms of her mother offers flowers to Hitler in his car as he is passing them. At the conclusion of his triumphal procession through Rome, Commodus is greeted on the steps of the senate house, and a little girl steps forward to present him with flowers.

3   Riefenstahl later directed and starred in *Tiefland* ("Lowlands"), on which she had begun work in 1934. Filmed between 1940 and 1945 but not released until 1954, this film opposes the purity and simplicity of life in the mountains to the corruption found in the valleys.

4   On Riefenstahl and the mountain film see now David B. Hinton, *The Films of Leni Riefenstahl*, 3rd edn. (Lanham and London: Scarecrow Press, 2000), 1–18. For her own comments on her films see Leni Riefenstahl, *A Memoir* (1993; rpt. New York: Picador, 1995). Cf. in general Siegfried Kracauer, *From Caligari to Hitler: A Psychological History of the German Film* (Princeton: Princeton University Press, 1947; several rpts.), and Erwin Leiser, *Nazi Cinema*, tr. Gertrud Mander and David Wilson (1974; rpt. New York: Macmillan, 1975). – The best version of *Triumph of the Will* currently available is a "special edition" DVD, published in 2001 with a historical audio commentary. A 1993 German-French documentary on Riefenstahl, directed by Ray Müller, is available in English as *The Wonderful Horrible Life of Leni Riefenstahl*, both on videotape and DVD. In general, see Richard Meran Barsam, *Filmguide to* Triumph of the Will (Bloomington: Indiana University Press, 1975; rpt. 1980); Glenn B. Infield, *Leni Riefenstahl: The Fallen Film Goddess* (New York: Crowell, 1976), 3–11 and 73–112; and Hinton, 19–46.

Cinematic technology increases the Fascist overtones in this sequence of *Gladiator*. Computer-generated images impart a cold blue light and a forbidding atmosphere to the city and deny it the warm colors we might expect to find in the Mediterranean. Instead of the light that Maximus had associated with Rome, he and the audience get a city full of alienating and eerie darkness, although not one as bleak as the dystopian Los Angeles of Scott's *Blade Runner* (1982). Soldiers in precise military formations fill the sides of the enormous square outside the senate house and contrast with the relatively small train accompanying Commodus. Similarly, the most arresting sequence of *Triumph of the Will* had contrasted the massed ranks of thousands with the individual figures of Hitler and the leaders of the SA and SS as they were walking down the length of the enormous space at Nuremberg in a ceremony commemorating the party dead. In *Triumph of the Will* and *Gladiator* alike, massive architecture dominates the surroundings and makes the humans minuscule. In Scott's Rome, the senate is at one end of the square, the Colosseum at the other. This vision of Rome is closer to what Hitler and his architects had envisioned for "Germania," their new and hubristically gigantic Berlin, than it is to the historical Rome, even the idealized Rome of its Mussolini-era model.[5] In classicizing Fascist architecture, wide-open spaces suitable for rallies and surrounded by huge buildings dwarf the individual and emphasize the power of the regime able to erect them.[6] The Rome that possesses such buildings can easily bring forth a

5   Many of the models for grandiose buildings intended to celebrate the Nazi regime are shown in the documentary film *Architektur des Untergangs* (1989), directed by Peter Cohen. An English-language version is available on DVD as *Architecture of Doom* (1999). For recent work on Nazism and antiquity see Alex Scobie, *Hitler's State Architecture: The Impact of Classical Antiquity* (University Park and London: College Art Association/Pennsylvania State University Press, 1990), especially 9–36 (chapter on "Mussolini, Hitler, and Classical Antiquity"); and Volker Losemann, "The Nazi Concept of Rome," in *Roman Presences: Receptions of Rome in European Culture, 1789–1945*, ed. Catharine Edwards (Cambridge: Cambridge University Press, 1999), 221–35. Detailed overviews with references mainly to Italian and German scholarship, respectively, are Salvatore Pisani, "Faschismus: I. Kunst und Architektur," and Mariella Cagnetti and Claudio Schiano, "Faschismus: II. Politik und Gesellschaft," both in *Der Neue Pauly: Enzyklopädie der Antike*, 13 (1999), cols. 1084–96 and 1096–105; Volker Losemann, "Nationalsozialismus: I. NS-Ideologie und die Altertumswissenschaften, " and Hans-Ernst Mittig, "Nationalsozialismus: II. Kunst und Architektur," both in *Der Neue Pauly*, 15.1 (2001), cols. 723–54 and 754–67. Klaus Kreimeier, *The Ufa Story: A History of Germany's Greatest Film Company 1918–1945*, tr. Robert and Rita Kimber (1996; rpt. Berkeley: University of California Press, 1999), 247–54, examines the connections between Nazi architecture and cinema, with discussion of *Triumph of the Will*; additional references at 410–11.
6   An example is the first Nazi forum, a redesign of the Königsplatz in Munich, described in Scobie, *Hitler's State Architecture*, 56–68.

tyrant like Commodus. Small wonder that in *Gladiator* the Praetorian Guards, dressed in black, look like forerunners of Hitler's SS. They even have square standards that are shaped like those of the SA. These appear in large numbers toward the conclusion of *Triumph of the Will*, displaying the ominous inscription *Deutschland Erwache* ("Germany, Awake").[7] The Praetorians act not only as the emperor's bodyguard, as the SS did with its elite *Leibstandarte Adolf Hitler*, but they also function as his spies and assassins, another historical analogy between this Roman Empire and the Third Reich. (*Reich* is German for "empire.") As a force separate from the regular army, the Praetorians are the backbone of Commodus' tyranny, just as the SS were for Hitler's.[8] In a scene deleted from the final release version of *Gladiator* but available on its DVD edition, the Praetorians provide Commodus with an anachronistic firing squad when they execute those who had failed to alert him to Maximus' escape. The excision of this scene simplifies the narrative but leaves unexplained Lucilla's earlier remark to her brother that he "must let the legions know that treachery will not go unpunished." This diverts possible criticism from the regular troops who are shown as willing to join Maximus and the other conspirators in staging a coup d'état. The Praetorians prevent the overthrow of Commodus by military means, but they finally side against him when, in the film's climactic duel, his cowardice in fighting an already maimed adversary appalls them.

Scott's depiction of a Fascist Rome is visually impressive and in keeping with Hollywood's presentation of imperial Rome in the 1950s, but it is not mandatory. An alternative is to be found in the most obvious model of *Gladiator*, Anthony Mann's epic *The Fall of the Roman Empire* (1964), which gives its audiences a positive view of Rome as a Great Power.[9] Mann, too, responds to Riefenstahl, but how he differs from that model and its later imitators, especially Mervyn LeRoy's *Quo Vadis* (1951), is instructive. For instance, there is no descent through the clouds when Mann first takes us to Rome from the German frontier. Instead, he dissolves from the smoke rising from Marcus Aurelius' pyre, the camera following it up into a dark and cloudy sky. The smoke ascending suggests the deification of the wise old emperor, not the descent of a new god. Rome then appears out of a cloudless blue sky with a shot of a

7   Leiser, *Nazi Cinema*, was originally published in German in 1968 as *Deutschland, erwache*. The book accompanied his documentary film by the same title. Cf. Leiser, *Nazi Cinema*, 7–9 (on the phrase) and 134–42 (documents on Riefenstahl's films).

8   The SS had been established as an autonomous organization as early as 1934; cf. Leiser, *Nazi Cinema*, 25.

9   So Martin M. Winkler, "Cinema and the Fall of Rome," *Transactions of the American Philological Association*, 125 (1995), 135–54.

statue of Victory in her chariot, set on top of an arch. The visual signal telling us that we are now in Rome is not an emblem of political power – the eagle of Riefenstahl and Scott – but one that indicates to the viewer the beauty and high culture of an advanced civilization. Mann does not show Commodus during his triumphal procession from higher up but from the viewpoint of the cheering crowd, as the new ruler winds his way in his chariot along the Roman Forum. His destination is not a place of power or government but the temple of Jupiter Optimus Maximus, patron god of the Romans. In the final shot of this sequence inside the temple, Commodus deposits his triumphal wreath on Jupiter's altar. Only then does a wry smile cross his face. He is aware, as we are now, too, that he has indeed succeeded to absolute power and has deceived everyone about his real character into the bargain.

Unlike Mann's film, *Gladiator* reflects a modern filmmaker's difficulties of working with epic or historical themes that have a long cinematic tradition. In order to make his hero, the most important individual in the whole Roman military, a sympathetic character, Scott had to counter the popular impression that the Romans were aggressive warriors or, in modern terminology, imperialists.[10] This Scott did by showing Maximus' desire to return to the peaceful haven of his farm in Spain after the conclusion of warfare.[11] Similarly, Maximus shows little enthusiasm for the phony and pointless warfare of the arena until he realizes that gladiatorial success will allow him the access to the emperor that he requires in his quest for revenge. Yet the depiction of imperial Rome as Fascist serves

10   Martin M. Winkler, "*Star Wars* and the Roman Empire," in *Classical Myth and Culture in the Cinema* ed. Martin M. Winkler (New York: Oxford University Press, 2001), 272–90, at 276, has shown how the depiction of the imperial army units in *Star Wars* as storm troopers and legionaries refers to both the Roman Empire and Hitler's Germany. For Riefenstahl's influence on and Nazi overtones in *Star Wars* (1977; later *Star Wars: Episode IV – A New Hope*) see Dan Rubey, "*Star Wars*: Not So Far Away," *Jump Cut*, 18 (1978), 9–14. For the Fascist appearance of the Roman Empire in Hollywood films see in general Martin M. Winkler, "The Roman Empire in American Cinema After 1945," *The Classical Journal*, 93 (1998), 167–96; rpt. in a slightly different version in *Imperial Projections: Ancient Rome in Modern Popular Culture*, ed. Sandra R. Joshel, Margaret Malamud, and Donald T. McGuire, Jr. (Baltimore and London: Johns Hopkins University Press, 2001), 50–76.

11   This might give the impression that the Roman army was a volunteer force recruited for specific campaigns. While this was so in the republic, the imperial army was comprised of professional soldiers who served for a fixed term, not simply until the end of a particular war. Elsewhere *Gladiator* suggests that a standing army not engaged in military activities will deteriorate quickly: Maximus' soldiers wintering at Ostia are said to have become "fat and bored." Classical historians were usually suspicious of the corrupting power of inactivity and urban leisure.

to reinforce the impression that this was indeed a highly militaristic society. So the display of violence in the cinematic arena continues to possess a comparable fascination for viewers of *Gladiator* as its historical counterpart had done for the Romans in the real Colosseum. It may be repulsive, but the thrill of combat is exciting as well, particularly since we often see events from the viewpoint of the combatants. When traditional Roman film epics were produced in the first half of the twentieth century, audiences came to see sex and violence as perpetrated by the Roman conquerors, not the goodness of their victims, usually Christians.[12] Likewise, modern audiences may well be attracted primarily to blood and guts and to what has been described as "war porn" in reference to Scott's *Black Hawk Down* (2001).[13] A commercial film director thus runs the risk of being an amoral showman, a modern kind of Proximo. Proximo, a champion of the arena during his time of enslavement, is now himself the owner of gladiators. As such, he best understands the extraordinary power of the successful gladiator in the Colosseum: "Win the crowd, win your freedom."

The danger of propagandizing a view one may despise is a common problem for a film director. Paul Verhoeven's *Starship Troopers* (1997) is a recent example. The film was intended to be a critical depiction of the neo-Fascist views of Robert Heinlein, author of the book on which it was based. Heinlein's views indirectly derived from Plato's suggestion that only those who will fight for their country deserve to gain citizenship.[14] Unfortunately, audiences failed to perceive the irony in this because the all-out glorification of violence against aliens was far too attractive. (The studio even produced a series of animated sequels.) Such public response reflects the contradictions inherent in these cinematic enterprises and recalls the similar incoherence of those political movements between the two World Wars that are now labeled Fascist. In Mussolini's Italy, colonial imperialism, which led to the portrayal of his Ethiopian campaign as a Fourth Punic War, was combined with the more recent theme of Italian nationalism. Furthermore, the idealization of the Roman past, particularly that of the age of Augustus, the first Roman emperor, on whom Mussolini came to model himself, could be associated with a pride

12 Cf. Maria Wyke, *Projecting the Past: Ancient Rome, Cinema and History* (New York and London: Routledge, 1997), 31.

13 Brian D. Johnson, "Oh! What a Lovely War" (review), *Maclean's* (January 21, 2002), 45.

14 Fascism had long been of interest to Verhoeven, from *Portrait of Anton Adriaan Mussert* (1968), his early documentary on the Dutch Fascist Party, to *Soldier of Orange* (1977), a film set in the Holland of World War II.

in modern technological advances.[15] For the Fascists, the ideal Rome was not the city that had grown haphazardly throughout the Middle Ages and later but a re-creation of classical themes in a modern context. The Palazzo della Civiltà Italiana in Rome's EUR district, generally called after its arches the *Colosseo quadrato* ("square Colosseum"), was regarded to be the essence of Italian architectural style, a re-creation, if a rectangular one, of the ancient Colosseum intended to serve a new government and society.[16] In a comparable manner, Hitler's Germany was meant to represent the culmination of a great and glorified past. Modern political ideologies looked for legitimacy to classical antiquity, the foremost cultural model in the entire history of Western civilization.

Still, despite its totalitarian imagery, it would be too easy to describe *Gladiator* as a Fascist film in the style of *Starship Troopers*. The praise of Roman imperialism is muted, not least because the new head of state is shown to be an irremediable villain. And in keeping with modern multiculturalism and the ethnic mixture of the American population, racism is largely absent from *Gladiator*. Indeed, the friendship between Maximus and the Nubian Juba is portrayed as entirely unproblematic, in marked contrast to the tension between the Thracian hero and the African Draba in Stanley Kubrick's *Spartacus* (1960). Nevertheless, even now the black among the gladiators unhesitatingly accepts and appreciates the white hero's leadership qualities without question. The theme of racism does, however, briefly appear in *Gladiator* when Commodus announces to his sister in a display of Hitlerian megalomania that he intends to marry her and "produce an heir of pure blood so that Commodus and his progeny will rule for a thousand years." This reflects Nazi fantasies of eugenics but is clearly regarded as an isolated case and a moral aberration.

While denial of social conflict might in itself be a political theme, it is perhaps best to regard the portrayal of politics in *Gladiator* as being no more than deeply conservative.[17] The desire to return Rome to the control

---

15   The juxtaposition of the classical and the modern is instructively described by Tim Benton, "Epigraphy and Fascism," in *The Afterlife of Inscriptions: Reusing, Rediscovering, Reinventing and Revitalizing Ancient Inscriptions*, ed. Alison Cooley (London: Bulletin of the Institute of Classical Studies, supplement 75; 2000), 163–92. Perhaps this blend is most obvious in the inscription *SPQR* (*Senatus populusque Romanus*, "the Roman senate and people") on manhole covers in modern Rome.

16   Cf. Scobie, *Hitler's State Architecture*, 82.

17   In the first version of the script, Maximus defines a republican as "a man who strives to create equality among all classes," a definition which in its rejection of class struggle is closer to European Fascism than to the Roman idea of republicanism. Contrast Cicero's declaration that there can be no equity when all are equal (*Republic* 1.43).

of the senate rather than to allow it to continue to be governed by a single leader dependent on an unstable mob is hardly new. It reflects republican longings among the Roman upper classes of the early empire, as both Suetonius and Tacitus have recorded.[18] In addition, this republicanism is one of the main themes of Robert Graves' novel *I Claudius*, which was the basis of a popular BBC television series in 1976.[19] Graves' portrayal of Emperor Claudius at least in part reflects upper-middle-class British attitudes in the first half of the twentieth century, especially their distrust of the rising power of the proletariat and of their own leaders. It is probably no coincidence that Gracchus, the noblest of the senators in *Gladiator* and one with a highly charged republican name, should be played by Derek Jacobi, the actor who had portrayed Claudius a quarter century before. This republican vision can also be seen in the hero of *Gladiator*: Maximus is a leader, but he is not *the* leader, neither *il Duce* nor *der Führer*. Hans Zimmer provided the film with a stirring neo-Wagnerian score, as is most obvious during the initial fighting in Germany. This changes to a parodic waltz in the Battle of Carthage sequence. Yet the music associated with Maximus when he appears alone on screen separates him from the rest of the characters. He is given an exotic, vaguely Arab-Celtic motif by Lisa Gerrard, as befits the erstwhile Spanish landowner and head of a family, not the general and leader of the gladiators.

So we are probably justified to regard *Gladiator* as commending not an outright Fascist ideology but a neo-conservative rural utopianism, one that follows classical models more or less accurately. Such a perspective on antiquity may be found today, for instance, in the works of American classical scholar Victor Davis Hanson. His writings on Greek hoplite warfare, the American family farm, and the greatness of a number of military leaders stress the importance of the agrarian heartland for the defense of the state, a kind of ancient Greek "homeland security" before the term became topical in America.[20] Scott's vision for *Gladiator* seems

18   Suetonius mentions a suggestion by Drusus, brother of Tiberius, that the republic should be restored (*Tiberius* 50.1), a debate about restoring senatorial rule after the death of Caligula (*Caligula* 60), and the claim that Otho had overthrown Galba in order to restore the republic and its liberty (*Otho* 12.2). In Tacitus, *libertas* ("freedom"), especially in the sense of non-tyrannical, senatorial government, is a common motif. For instance, at *Agricola* 3.1, Tacitus observes that Nerva and Trajan have achieved the blending of polar opposites, rule by one man (*principatus*) and freedom (*libertas*).

19   On this see now Sandra R. Joshel, "*I, Claudius*: Projection and Imperial Soap Opera," in *Imperial Projections*, 119–61.

20   Cf. Victor Davis Hanson, *Fields Without Dreams: Defending the Agrarian Idea* (New York: Free Press, 1996; rpt. 1997); *The Other Greeks: The Family Farm and the Agrarian Roots of Western Civilization*, 2nd edn (Berkeley: University of California Press, 1999); *The Soul of*

to parallel this, as is most obvious at the film's conclusion. As dawn rises above the Colosseum, we are presented with a panoramic vista across the city, with buildings and temples on the hills, the Tiber, and the country-side beyond. The new dawn is meant to signal a bright, hopeful, and better tomorrow, now that the traditional values that Maximus embod-ies have triumphed over evil and Fascist Rome. So the future looks prom-ising. We might almost expect a voice-over to tell us: "It's morning again in the Roman Empire." This is the sort of thing that Ronald Reagan's television ads had told the American people about their country during his re-election campaign in 1984. Some of these showed vistas of peace-ful scenery. Scott, who directed the famous Orwellian "1984" television advertisement for the new Apple Macintosh computer that same year, would have been aware of the power of such images.[21] Hence, the ending of *Gladiator* is politically as reactionary as Marcus Aurelius' and the sen-ators' anachronistic and fictitious zeal for the restoration of the repub-lic. Stylistically, the film's last shot, with its sun rays breaking through the morning clouds, resembles the kind of pictorial Kitsch that was beloved of German reactionaries in the nineteenth and twentieth centuries. It is but a small step from there to the standards of the SA proclaiming "Germany, Awake."

   Gladiator is by no means an attempt to portray Roman history authen-tically. Although its depiction of the Colosseum is based on sound archi-tectural knowledge and looks convincing even in its details, the other elements in its presentation of Rome are strictly imaginary, created from a combination of partially built sets, computer graphics, a pair of hills in Provence, a painted backdrop, and a French sky.[22] Scott is reverting to romantic portrayals of the city and its empire, such as appear in Thomas Cole's famous series of allegorical paintings, *The Course of Empire* (1836). Cole's depiction of the rise and fall of Rome was intended as a warning to the newly formed United States. Scott has also referred to the inspira-tion he derived from Jean-Léon Gérôme's well-known gladiatorial paint-ing *Pollice Verso* ("Thumbs Down"; 1872).[23] This image has come back

Battle: From Ancient Times to the Present Day: How Three Great Liberators Vanquished Tyranny (1999; rpt. New York: Anchor Books, 2001); and *The Western Way of War: Infantry Battle in Classical Greece*, 2nd edn (Berkeley: University of California Press, 2000). Page duBois, *Trojan Horses: Saving the Classics from Conservatives* (New York: New York University Press, 2001), 34–8, provides a brief critique of Hanson's views.

21   On this cf. Paul M. Sammon, *Ridley Scott* (New York: Thunder's Mouth Press, 1999), 74–6.

22   Scott's interest in exactitude in the depiction of the Flavian Amphitheater and the technology of the underground elevators is detailed in the book *Gladiator*, 80–9.

23   So Scott at the beginning of his "Introduction" to *Gladiator*, 7–9; the book reproduces Gérôme's painting at 23–4.

into vogue in recent years, adorning the covers of several books on gladiators and arena games. To no small degree, its force derives from the power of the masses that, on occasions such as the scene depicts, erupt into violence. The Fascist and Nazi movements exploited this fear of the uncontrolled masses to impose their own leaders.

By such references to classical themes in the art of the nineteenth century, by his recourse to the visual style of *Triumph of the Will*, and by a plot line that is as hoary in its politics as it is unhistorical to begin with, Scott is offering the world his own conservative vision of the past. Maximus' heroic sacrifice provides an escape from tyranny and mob rule and allows a return to aristocratic rule balanced by popular acceptance. This is modeled on Greek historian Polybius' analysis of the rise of Rome. Polybius sees the main cause for Rome's political ascendance in its mixed constitution, one that allows an escape from the cycle of monarchy/autocracy, aristocracy/oligarchy, and democracy/ochlocracy (mob rule) in a process of constant political decay from one stage to the next. This system strongly influenced the Founding Fathers when they devised the mixed constitution of the United States, in which the popular representatives, the senate, and the president correspond to the positive side of each of the three Roman pairs.[24] Paternalistic government is, of course, a reassuring ideal, both in the Roman past and in our present. But the final scene of *Gladiator* implies more than that the cycle of political conflict and decline has been broken or at least halted, if only temporarily. The final panorama suggests that it is possible to combine an original Arcadian state with technological urbanism. This utopianism is visually dazzling and emotionally satisfying after two and a half hours of spectacle, but in its inherent political contradictions it comes dangerously close to being irrational. Historically, the death of Commodus did not usher in a new age. There was no new morning for Rome. And in the twenty-first century, individual heroic martyrdom, even in the name of liberty, should not be such a political panacea.

---

24   Polybius 6.11–18. For the English text see Polybius, *The Rise of the Roman Empire*, tr. Ian Scott-Kilvert (Harmondsworth: Penguin, 1979; several rpts.), 311–18.

CHAPTER NINE

Gladiator and Contemporary American Society

Monica S. Cyrino

Gladiator opened on Friday, May 5, 2000, which was also my birthday. So it was something of a celebration when several of my students and I arrived at the brand-new local movie theater for the film's first showing. The impact of *Gladiator* in that huge, glossy, luxurious Colosseum of a theater is unforgettable: plush love-seat-style rows stacked vertically in a sheer rise of tiers; the pounding state-of-the-art sound system that rendered every shout and whisper, every slash and stab, into an extra-sensory auditory experience, as if we were witnessing real combat: "Brothers, what we do in life echoes in eternity" – and in THX. And not to forget the upscale fare of cappuccino and cheesecake, the modern spectators' equivalents of rich and decadent "Roman imperial tidbits," and, of course, the steep metropolitan ticket prices.[1] But as Maximus might have shouted to our eager provincial crowd: "Are you not enter-tained?" Of course we were! "Is that not why you are here?" Yes, it was! So began an intense love-affair between me and *Gladiator* or, to be more precise, a *ménage à multiplex*. We in the audience were magically trans-formed into the Roman mob, breathless with excitement and roaring for more thrilling diversions. We had become Romans, those ancient people both alluring and alarming to Americans.

1   The quotation is from *Monty Python's Life of Brian* (1979), directed by Terry Jones. Brian works a snack concession at a provincial Roman arena and sells excessively exotic foods.

The opening of *Gladiator* initiated a sudden resurrection of toga films after thirty-six years in disgrace and exile. But exciting as it is for fans of epic movies, the film prompts the question about its significance today. In his discussion of how history is employed in films as a subtle device to express the present, film historian Pierre Sorlin puts the question this way: "What did the film-makers or their audiences expect from a return to the past?"[2] *Gladiator* is a product of its makers' personal vision and an act of their creative will; yet the film's achievement in speaking to contemporary society reflects something that society desires or needs to hear. The epic genre is exceptionally well suited for this: "The film epic has taken up one of the most ancient art-forms and propelled it into the present day covered in twentieth-century ambitions, anxieties, hopes and fantasies."[3] *Gladiator* has become part of our cultural consciousness, and its financial and artistic success continues to inspire popular entertainment, including a throng of upcoming epics. So it is important to explore its contemporary relevance and the way modern American audiences identify themselves with the Romans in their respective arenas. As screenwriter David Franzoni has said: "The movie is about us. It's not just about ancient Rome, it's about America."[4] Like General Maximus' soldiers, "lean and hungry" and ready to do battle at his command, the American audience of the early twenty-first century is listening and responding to the issues *Gladiator* raises. If we are the Romans, then the film is a sign of our own time. *Gladiator* tells our story.

1. A New Epic

Any interpretation of *Gladiator* must take into account its relationship to the Roman epics made in Hollywood in the 1950s and early 1960s. It is fair to inquire why the long-defunct genre was revived at all. Like the earlier films, *Gladiator* reinvents ancient Rome, the city of power, intrigue, cruelty, and lust, and the ultimate symbol of both the sublime and the corrupt, and exhibits our own desires and doubts. In the spirit of those mid-century epics, *Gladiator* re-creates and adapts what Peter

2   Pierre Sorlin, *The Film in History: Restaging the Past* (New York: Barnes and Noble, 1980), 208.
3   Derek Elley, *The Epic Film: Myth and History* (London: Routledge, 1984), 1.
4   This and my later quotations from Franzoni are taken from an interview with John Soriano for the Writers Guild of America, published electronically at *http://www.wga.org/craft/interviews/franzoni2001.html*.

Bondanella has called "the myth of Rome" in order to express and examine contemporary social and political concerns:

> The myth is not so much a relic to be venerated as it is a flexible and limitless source of self-expression, a common heritage which has met the needs of successive generations . . . Something in the myth of Rome has helped us to understand our human condition, our world, and ourselves.[5]

Yet three and a half decades after the last chariot wheel came to a stand-still in Anthony Mann's *The Fall of the Roman Empire* (1964), *Gladiator*, with its unexpected popularity and profits, offers the public a different kind of film. *Gladiator* is more overtly aware of its own involvement in manipulating and retelling the myth of Rome. The announcement of Cassius, the emcee in the Colosseum ("On this day we reach back to hallowed antiquity to bring you a re-creation of the second fall of mighty Carthage"), highlights what epic film itself is engaged in doing. Moreover, state-of-the-art computer technology allowed the creators of *Gladiator* to display the previously buried images of Roman spectacle on an unprecedented scale. In this way, "Rome can be built in a day" after all.[6] But special effects and brazen self-consciousness alone cannot explain the astonishing success of *Gladiator*.

At a time when critics of the American film industry claimed that there was a dearth of new ideas, when remakes of old war horses and frequent replications of the tried and true ruled the box office, *Gladiator* dared to go beyond an opportunistic reproduction of a seemingly obsolete genre. Instead, it wove together some of the most intelligent, provocative, and entertaining aspects of those earlier epics. Mervyn LeRoy's *Quo Vadis* (1951) had been a campy riot of color and sound, with delightfully debauched characters scheming and seducing their way through fabulous orgies on the Palatine and dramatically staged martyrdoms in the arena. On the other hand, *The Fall of the Roman Empire*, a dignified epic set in the same period as *Gladiator*, attempted to achieve solemnity and to portray the greatness of Roman culture, but it may have gone too far in neglecting the flashy, crowd-pleasing features that audiences had come to anticipate from Roman extravaganzas. The film was instead judged to be somber, even tedious, and was often blamed for the collapse of the entire epic genre, together with Joseph L.

5   Peter Bondanella, *The Eternal City: Roman Images in the Modern World* (Chapel Hill and London: University of North Carolina Press, 1987), 1.
6   Herbert Muschamp, "Throwing Our Anxieties to the Lions," *The New York Times* (April 30, 2000), section 2A, pages 1 and 33; quotation at 1.

Mankiewicz's *Cleopatra* of the year before. But *Gladiator* managed to unite these two cinematic approaches. Director Ridley Scott grew up watching these and other legendary epic films and so was well aware of the need to update this classic genre to win contemporary audiences: "I loved the costume drama of it all and remembered that world vividly. But I also knew you can't bring that to bear today. You've got to reinvent it."[7] So he and his writers and crew combined the spectacular decadence and imperial intrigue from earlier films with the sober narrative of an appealing hero's tragic journey along the lines of Stanley Kubrick's *Spartacus* (1960), all of it enhanced by computer technology. As a result, *Gladiator* delivers a compelling new kind of film: enjoyable, impressive-looking, and moving. As Scott said before filming started: "I hope to design the film in such a way that when people see it, they'll think, 'Gee, Rome's never been done like *this* before.' . . ."[8]

Just as those earlier epics used ancient Rome to address issues relevant to mid-twentieth-century America, *Gladiator*, too, functions as an allegory of its time and evokes themes and concerns unique to contemporary American society. It provides a new critical tool for the exploration of recent debates in American politics and culture. Scholars of classical antiquity and cinema have elucidated how the earlier films ambiguously invited American audiences both to distance themselves from and to identify themselves with the spectacle of Roman power, luxury, and superiority. The process of projection offered in those mid-century films was complex in that Rome, presented as a corrupt oppressor, troubled and repelled post-war viewers, while Rome in its self-confident and materially comfortable aspects attracted favor in the consumer-oriented economy of the time.[9] But as the first Roman epic made after the end of the Cold War, *Gladiator* arrived in an altogether different social and political world. As such, the film introduces a new and extraordinary problem of interpretation. Its prologue, set against a sepia-toned background and with haunting female vocals as its only accompaniment, informs us rather

7 Quoted from Richard Corliss, "*Gladiator*: The Empire Strikes Back," *Time* (May 8, 2000), 83–4, at 83.
8 Quoted from Paul M. Sammon, *Ridley Scott* (New York: Thunder's Mouth Press, 1999), 130.
9 Cf. Sandra R. Joshel, Margaret Malamud, and Maria Wyke, "Introduction," in *Imperial Projections: Ancient Rome in Modern Popular Culture*, ed. Sandra R. Joshel, Margaret Malamud, and Donald T. McGuire, Jr. (Baltimore and London: Johns Hopkins University Press, 2001), 1–22, at 6–13; further Maria Wyke, *Projecting the Past: Ancient Rome, Cinema and History* (New York and London: Routledge, 1997), 23–32. On tensions in the modern identification with Rome see in particular William Fitzgerald, "Oppositions, Anxieties, and Ambiguities in the Toga Movie," in *Imperial Projections*, 23–49, especially 24–8.

portentously that Rome is "at the height of its power." The American spectators in the year 2000, supremely confident and unencumbered by doubts about their country's geo-political dominance, experience not an indecisive tug or a double-sided connection with ancient Rome but rather a shock of recognition. The Romans depicted in *Gladiator* undeniably stand in for us; the film is "a meditation on the perplexity of the world's sole surviving superpower."[10] Such bewilderment is represented by two very distinct depictions of Rome, as *Gladiator* poses the very question of the direction and purpose of American cultural and political hegemony.

The main theme of the film is the conflict between two competing visions of what kind of superpower Rome – or, by analogy, America – should be. *Gladiator* takes us to a world completely conquered by Roman military might. "There is no one left to fight, sire," General Maximus tells Emperor Marcus Aurelius. But the worldwide spread of the *pax Romana*, the Roman peace, does not extend to Rome itself. Rather, Rome is on the verge of a breakdown under increasing pressure from within, as two opposing sides clash in an ideological battle between totalitarian oppression, epitomized by the wicked new emperor Commodus, and a just and noble republicanism, embodied by Maximus and a senatorial conspiracy against Commodus.[11] In an ingenious plot turn, *Gladiator* introduces the improbable objective of restoring the Roman republic in A.D. 180 and allows this fantasy to represent Good in its everlasting conflict against Evil.[12] Earlier films traditionally made Rome the imperialistic oppressor of implausibly virtuous and racially harmonious groups, the most common narrative formula being the subjugation of Christians, Hebrews, or slaves. *Spartacus* and *The Fall of the Roman Empire* focused on Roman political factions in their examination of the corrupting influence of power. But *Gladiator* presents an imaginative new development by casting the Roman Empire as the oppressor of its true self, the republic.

Thus the conflict between Maximus and Commodus is a battle for Rome's very soul, as each tries to define his idea of Rome on his own

10   Muschamp, "Throwing Our Anxieties to the Lions," 1.

11   For echoes of republican Roman values in the film see Jon Solomon, *The Ancient World in the Cinema*, 2nd edn (New Haven and London: Yale University Press, 2001), 94–5. Cf. also below.

12   On the Roman republic as a good Rome and the empire as an evil one see Martin M. Winkler, "*Star Wars* and the Roman Empire," in *Classical Myth and Culture in the Cinema*, ed. Martin M. Winkler (New York: Oxford University Press, 2001), 272–90, at 273–80. Cf. Bondanella, *The Eternal City*, 4–5.

terms. Maximus' dream of a republican Rome, in which family farmers become soldiers only when necessary to fight genuine external enemies, is set against Commodus' spectacle of a Rome whose staged battles mask the internal erosion of an empire. In a demonstration of the Roman Empire's military strength and limitless power, professional gladiators engage in mock warfare with women and animals in the arena, diverting the mindless mob into a blithe state of numbness and oblivion to the struggles for control that are going on upstairs in the marble "corporate" boxes.[13] "I will give the people a vision of Rome," promises Commodus, "and they'll love me for it." Soon the bloodthirsty crowd demands ever more stunning and bizarre entertainment. "He will bring them death," observes Senator Gracchus, "and they will love him for it." The key question – whether or not we should identify with the Romans – *Gladiator* answers with a resounding affirmative. But the film adds a subtle new twist when it speculates on which vision of Rome, or America, will ultimately prevail.

2. The Rebirth of Rome

Gladiator offers overwhelming evidence of its successful response to the American cultural consciousness. The film has generated a revival of the epic genre and a resurgence of interest in classical studies in popular literature, art, and classrooms across America. But in June of 1998, the creative forces behind *Gladiator* knew they were taking a great risk. Then DreamWorks' production head Walter Parkes noted a trend in the box-office success of recent "classic" films like James Cameron's *Titanic* (1997) and thought it was time for a rebirth of the toga film: "The Roman epic occupies a strange, special place in the heart of moviegoers. We love the good ones like *Ben-Hur* and *Spartacus*, but even the bad ones are guilty pleasures."[14] Scott, however, had to be persuaded into taking the helm of the film. He was presented with a reproduction of the painting *Pollice Verso* (1872) by Jean-Léon Gérôme, in which a victorious gladiator stands over fallen foes in an arena crowded with rabid spectators, and he was inspired by the dramatic and visual possibilities of a gladiator epic that would tap into contemporary

13   Alison Futrell, *Blood in the Arena: The Spectacle of Roman Power* (Austin: University of Texas Press, 1997; rpt. 2000), 44–51, examines the political importance of the imperial games.
14   Quoted from Corliss, "*Gladiator*," 83.

social issues.[15] As Sorlin observed: "The main advantage of history is that it allows people to describe the present time in a free, imaginary way."[16] *Gladiator* had all the promise to be a major summer blockbuster for a public eager to see a recognizable yet original image of ancient Rome. On its opening weekend (May 5–7, 2000), it grossed more than the next seven films combined. In spring of 2001, *Gladiator* earned five Academy Awards, including Best Picture and Best Actor for Russell Crowe.

Modern cinematic techniques and special effects update the epic narrative of *Gladiator* and present a fresh reconstruction of Roman antiquity. The initial battle sequence in Germania recalls the turmoil of the Normandy invasion in Steven Spielberg's World War II drama *Saving Private Ryan* (1998): "It's a bravura sequence . . . that doesn't copy *Private Ryan*'s famous opening tour de force of carnage so much as raise a banner in admiration."[17] All the fight sequences in *Gladiator* represent a breathtaking technical advance upon the combat scenes of earlier epics, which used to be filmed mainly in a single wide-angle shot "like a ballet," in Scott's words.[18] The main setting in the city of Rome was an impressive replica of the Colosseum that cost over $1 million and took months to build. In an appropriate metaphor for the way the film combines and reprocesses earlier images of Rome with contemporary technology, the lower two tiers of the model were constructed at full scale – about forty percent of the original four tiers that were 157 feet high – and the rest was added by computer. There is a striking moment when the provincial gladiators enter the Colosseum for their first fight and are staggered by its sheer immensity as the roar of 50,000 spectators envelops them. The film audience follows their stunned eyes as they sweep upward to the last tier of that marvelous feat of human imagination and engineering, both ancient and modern. "I didn't know men could build such things," declares the Nubian Juba, as awe-struck as we are.

15   Cf. Chris Nashawaty, "Chairman of the Sword," *Entertainment Weekly* (May 12, 2000), 26–31, at 26–7. *Gladiator: The Making of the Ridley Scott Epic*, ed. Diana Landau (New York: Newmarket, 2000), 24–5, reproduces the painting, about which Scott has said: "That image spoke to me of the Roman Empire in all its glory and wickedness" (*Gladiator*, 26).

16   Sorlin, *The Film in History*, 209.

17   Lisa Schwarzbaum, "Fight Club," *Entertainment Weekly* (May 12, 2000), 47–8, at 47.

18   Quoted from Nashawaty, "Chairman of the Sword," 30.

3. The New Romans

The figure of Maximus, the fictional protagonist of *Gladiator*, prompts the question about what kind of heroism the film wants its audiences to accept. Its tag-line is "A Hero Will Rise," but what kind of hero is Maximus? Some critics suggested that the character of Maximus reaches back to an idea of masculine bravery and goodness that is old-fashioned by both modern and ancient standards. One reviewer described him as "a brother-in-attitude" of the quietly dignified Captain Miller in *Saving Private Ryan*: "They're decent men forced by circumstance to perform extraordinary feats."[19] Jon Solomon has suggested a comparison with the farmer-turned-general Cincinnatus, "an early Roman exemplar of nobility."[20] Like him, Maximus wants to return to his farm after the fighting. It is not surprising that Maximus displays old-fashioned virtues. In this film, the historical Roman republic serves to represent the same powerful retro glamour and gilded integrity that "the greatest generation" of World War II fighters now does for Americans. *Gladiator* invites us, as do the democratic-minded Romans in the film, to view Maximus in the soft, admiring light of nostalgia. Franzoni has remarked on the appeal of his Roman hero to contemporary Americans: "We're stewing in self-indulgent mediocrity, and here's a noble figure who's almost swallowed up by the Roman equivalent, and he endures." Others have asserted that the depiction of Maximus improves upon the conventional Hollywood action hero by offering a more psychologically substantive character; they imply that modern sensibilities require a hero of greater sensitivity and emotional depth: "I think our idea of what an action hero is has changed," said Joaquin Phoenix, who plays Commodus. "Now we care about heroes with flaws and humanity."[21] Maximus' character responds to our tendency to romanticize the rugged heroes of the past, infusing them with personality traits that expose and emphasize their sentiments and imperfections.

Certain unusual aspects of Maximus' humanity might appear rather disturbing to modern viewers, principally his tragic self-consciousness, his single-minded focus on bloody revenge, and his gloomy preoccupation with his mortality. Maximus demonstrates all the furious rage, brooding menace, and pitiless aggression of a whole history of insulted heroes from Achilles in Homer's *Iliad* to Mad Max in George Miller's

19 Schwarzbaum, "Fight Club," 47.
20 Solomon, *The Ancient World in the Cinema*, 94.
21 Quoted from Nashawaty, "Chairman of the Sword," 30.

apocalyptic film trilogy. On the surface, Maximus seems to owe much to Kubrick's Spartacus. Both are gladiators turned into heroic leaders who fight for their own freedom and that of their enslaved brothers-at-arms against an autocratic and corrupt Roman government. Like Spartacus, proud Maximus is subjected to humiliation and brutality in the arena. Both die virtually sacrificial deaths in a daring effort to achieve their goals, a fate rarely visited upon Hollywood action heroes. Yet the freedom-fighter Spartacus believes unconditionally in the justice of his struggle to liberate his people. Maximus, however, is an unwilling savior, one who initially refuses to take on the role Marcus Aurelius intends to bestow on him, that of a protector who will return Rome to senate rule. When the old and weary emperor asks him: "Won't you accept this great honor that I have offered you?" Maximus answers: "With all my heart, no." "Maximus," the emperor sighs, "that is why it must be you." At the beginning, Maximus confidently articulates his faith in the ideal of Rome despite Marcus Aurelius' frustration over his succession, but soon Maximus is forced to realize that this ideal does not exist.

Although he embodies the values and virtues of republican Rome, Maximus is a reluctant instrument in all the political maneuvering and only decides to assist the revolt against Commodus out of a sense of personal outrage. In this, he resembles Judah Ben-Hur in William Wyler's *Ben-Hur* (1959), who is driven by his bitter quarrel with the Roman tribune Messala, once his intimate boyhood friend. Like Maximus, Judah is brutalized and enslaved by the Roman system, loses his family, and seeks vengeance against the man who had injured him and them. Both heroes play out their personal revenge in the arena in scenes of extreme violence that show not a shred of forgiveness. Judah beats Messala in the famous chariot race, and Maximus slays Commodus in a bloody duel. Judah is ultimately redeemed and his family is restored to him by the grace of Jesus, but, before, his destiny had been shaped by his adoptive Roman father, the consul Quintus Arrius. In a similar way, Marcus Aurelius is Maximus' surrogate father. "You are the son that I should have had," the emperor tells his favorite general, and Maximus, about whose parents the film says nothing, calls him "father" in several scenes. Yet it is only in the arena, when he realizes that he is about to die, that Maximus accepts his political duty out of love and respect for the memory of his imperial father figure. "There was a dream that was Rome. It shall be realized," he commands. "These are the wishes of Marcus Aurelius." For Maximus, the ideal of the Good Rome is inextricably bound to his filial relationship with Marcus and underscored by his old-fashioned idea that Roman power can be a just and positive force in the world. For the heroes of earlier epic films, the concept of Rome itself was linked to the role of paternal figures: "Rome is the name for the unrequited desire for an authority that would restore the public world to these anachronistic men."[22] In keeping with this perspective, actor Russell Crowe had to be talked into donning breastplate and sword. After reading an early version of the script, he was not happy with its "semi-cynical take on life in ancient times."[23]

The interactions of various others with Maximus reveal a range of problematic, broken, and often reconfigured familial bonds that suggests a parallel to contemporary American concerns and criticisms about the collapse of the nuclear family. Domestic affairs take on a conspicuously modern tenor. At the beginning, Marcus Aurelius presides over the simmering tensions that finally break out between his son Commodus and his chosen heir Maximus. He justifies his choice thus: "Commodus is not a moral man." *Gladiator* follows the convention of earlier epic films in complicating the father figure, for whose affection and attention his "sons" must compete in a dangerous, often deadly, struggle. Unstable Commodus is desperate for the love and approval of Marcus, who withholds it from him but acknowledges: "Your fault as a son is my failure as a father." Commodus only receives the paternal embrace he has longed for when he strangles Marcus to death. When Maximus accuses him of the murder in a scene that sets up their final fight, Commodus transfers his lethal embrace to Maximus and stabs him with a poisoned knife in the back, whispering in his ear: "You loved my father, I know. But so did I. That makes us brothers, doesn't it?" This moment builds on an earlier awkward embrace after the battle in Germania, when Commodus first calls Maximus "brother" and incurs an agonizing pang of jealousy over his father's display of favoritism toward Maximus.

As evil young Commodus, Joaquin Phoenix avoids the archetype of the effeminate Roman tyrant. He plays the autocrat coming unhinged with petulant perversity. When confronted with Maximus' enduring popularity, he whines elegantly, in one of the film's most often-repeated lines: "It vexes me . . . I'm terribly vexed." Commodus' insecurity and cruelty betray a very modern psychological motivation as the result of his having been "an unloved child with vivid plans for vengeance."[24] As an adult, Commodus harbors vicious fantasies of hurting others to assuage his own emotional pain. His depravity arises from his twisted

22   Fitzgerald, "Oppositions, Anxieties, and Ambiguities in the Toga Movie," 45.
23   Quoted from Nashawaty, "Chairman of the Sword," 29.
24   Corliss, "*Gladiator*," 84.

and unsuccessful need to form family bonds with others. When Senator Gracchus questions his limited experience of the Roman people, Commodus airily, and eerily, counters: "I call it love, Gracchus. The people are my children, I am their father. I shall hold them to my bosom and embrace them tightly." Commodus' incestuous cravings for his elder and politically more mature sister Lucilla also indicate his search for maternal affection. He curls up next to her in the fetal position and longs for the peaceful security enjoyed by her son Lucius: "He sleeps so well because he is loved." But Commodus has no true understanding of love. When Lucilla does not respond to his creepy overtures, and when he discovers that she is at the heart of the plot to depose him, he attributes the loss of her devotion, like his father's, to the interference of Maximus. As Lucilla explains to Maximus: "My brother hates all the world and you most of all." Maximus assents: "Because your father chose me." But Lucilla corrects him: "No. Because my father loved you. And because I loved you." The more love Maximus finds, the less Commodus gets. In one of the film's most astonishing updates of epic genre conventions, even the wicked tyrant is not totally unsympathetic. His main defect is that he lacks his family's love.

So far there has been little comment on Lucilla, perhaps not surprisingly, since hers is the only female speaking part in the entire film: "As happens in such muscle-bound extravaganzas, Lucilla appears to be the only woman residing in all of the Eternal City."[25] But the portrayal of Lucilla resists the traditional good woman–bad woman polarity of earlier epics. She is neither a feline seductress, like Empress Poppaea in *Quo Vadis*, nor the pure Christian (or proto-Christian) maiden who becomes the male protagonist's redeemer, like Lygia in *Quo Vadis*, Diana in Henry Koster's *The Robe* (1953), or Esther in *Ben-Hur*. Instead, *Gladiator* suggests a more nuanced portrayal of sexuality, power, femininity, and domesticity. Her on-screen precursor might be Elizabeth Taylor's incarnation of a sexually liberated and politically visionary Cleopatra. As was Cleopatra, so Lucilla is the one with natural talent and disposition for just rule, although their younger brothers are the ones in line for the throne. "If only you'd been born a man," her father tells Lucilla, "what a Caesar you would have made!" Both Cleopatra and Lucilla are mothers, fiercely protective and concerned for the political futures of their sons. Commodus explicitly compares Lucilla to Cleopatra in his "busy little bee" speech to Lucius: "Royal ladies behave very strangely and do very odd

25   Schwarzbaum, "Fight Club," 48.

things in the name of love." Lucilla's ability to instigate and guide the republican coup attempt reflects our contemporary attitudes about female political skills and our familiarity with women in positions of power, but the film also presents a modern view of the importance of family by highlighting Lucilla's maternal instincts.[26] The ruptures and dysfunctions in Lucilla's relationships create an emotional space for a temporary bond between her and Maximus, one that is imbued with both politics and eroticism. In this, too, *Gladiator* goes against earlier epics, in which the most powerful scenes tended to take place between male characters. Because Lucilla is different from the one-dimensional women of previous films, the scenes between her and Maximus are just as important to the narrative as any of his scenes with other males, if not more so in that Lucilla succeeds in convincing him of his responsibility to Rome. Moreover, because their lingering sexual desire for each other is expressed but not consummated, the scenes between Lucilla and Maximus maintain a palpable tension. Combining sensuality and domesticity with political intelligence, Lucilla responds to issues relevant to women in today's society who attempt to manage competing personal and professional roles and who, like her, accomplish this with varying degrees of success. Graceful Lucilla in her sleek costumes evokes the languid luxury and urban affluence of ancient Rome in a way that modern followers of fashion can appreciate.

Proximo, the owner and trainer of the gladiators who was freed by Marcus Aurelius, takes over the parental function left vacant by the old emperor's death. Maximus is surprised to find himself emotionally drawn to Proximo, who presides over his rebirth into his new public role. Proximo's rhetoric is permeated with the language of transitions and parenthood. "I shall be closer to you for the next few days, which will be the last of your miserable lives, than that bitch of a mother who first brought you screaming into this world!" he barks at his new purchases. "And just as your mother was there at your beginning, I shall be there at your end." Proximo is the unwitting midwife present at the birth of the hero Maximus. *Gladiator* permits an unconventional attachment to form between two initially opposed male characters and allows that bond to develop the theme of the protagonist's destiny.

The ways in which these reinvigorated ancient characters engage with one another respond to contemporary concerns about domestic and romantic relationships. As Russell Crowe has commented: "I'd be

26   Cf. Solomon, *The Ancient World in the Cinema*, 94.

surprised if I have a second movie that becomes as much a part of the zeitgeist."[27]

4. Alienation

Gladiator is a story of alienation. Maximus' disaffection with the idea of Rome offers a compelling analogy to the modern sense of estrangement from politics in all its corrupt irrelevance. Contemporary culture critics speak of "the crisis of confidence in American institutions" and point to several examples of popular media that exhibit "few convictions beyond pandering to viewers' feelings of superiority to all those bad people in Washington."[28] Maximus' journey of transition from general to slave to gladiator exemplifies such isolation from national or group identity, followed by a decisive turn toward pure self-interest. At the beginning, Maximus the general can fight for an ideal Rome because, never having been to the city, he has remained undefiled by its reality. Maximus demonstrates his patriotism and personal valor on the battlefield, and when he utters the army's motto "Strength and Honor," it is clear that he embodies these virtues. The opening scene illustrates the organization and corporate integrity of the Roman army. Maximus can conceive of no other idea of Rome than as rightful conqueror and civilizing force over the world. This idea is manifest to him in the cooperative spirit of his legions. The courage, commitment, and unity of the Roman soldiers make the idea of Rome a reality.

But soon Maximus is harshly awakened from his dream of Rome by Commodus' distorted imperial vision and loses all faith in the idea he had defended with his life. The scene in which he finds his wife and son murdered marks the moment of his alienation from everything he once valued. Maximus later scrapes off his flesh the insignia of the legions – SPQR: "The senate and people of Rome" – with a knife. Shortly after, the film cuts to the massive SPQR engraved on marble in Rome as Commodus holds his hollow victory parade. This is a visual equation indicating that Maximus now spills his own blood to reject what Rome has become under the new tyrant; he excises the Roman part of himself. Now a nameless slave, Maximus is loyal solely to his desire for revenge, and his

---

27   Quoted from Benjamin Svetkey, "Counting Crowes," *Entertainment Weekly* (January 4, 2002), 20–6, at 24.
28   James Poniewozik, "The Big Fat Year in Culture," *Time* (December 30, 2002–January 6, 2003), 141–53, at 145, and "No Coattails," *Time* (January 13, 2003), 58.

only community with the other gladiators is for the sake of survival in the arena. Like a modern urban gang, the gladiators form a brotherhood that develops a code of honor and organizes a system of allegiances but exists outside the law, alienated from any civil or social conventions.

Maximus' fighting skill and courage, once employed in the service of Rome's greatness, are now trivialized into bloody entertainment for the masses. As a visual symbol of this sudden degradation, the brave wolf-dog, who had accompanied Maximus into the opening battle as emblem of Rome's legendary and noble fighting spirit, has disappeared from the film and is briefly replaced by the leashed hyena in Proximo's tent. In the arena Maximus fights to stay alive, but he displays his contempt for the crowd by scowling and spitting on the sand. After one particularly gory show he even hurls his sword into the official viewing box of the local VIPs. Such moments emphasize Maximus' utter disillusion with the concept of Roman authority.

Maximus' alienation from a degenerate Rome and his deep-seated ambivalence about his role in restoring Roman government to the people suggests a parallel to post-Cold War America. Despite the temporary boost in the rhetoric of national unity and superficial displays of patriotism after September 11, 2001, current political and social commentators remark on the apathy of the American electorate, citing low voter turnout and a persistent lack of interest in political debate as evidence of the general disenfranchisement of individual Americans and the pervasive attitude that politics is a dirty game. Because of their profound hostility to and suspicion of the government in Washington, more and more Americans assume postures of self-interest. Maximus first lays eyes on Rome as a slave and feels nothing but revulsion at the corruption he sees. He eventually realizes what he has already begun to understand: "The mob is Rome." The disillusioned general, now turned free-agent hero, is driven by his anger and isolation to re-enact his ideal of Rome from within the arena.

5. *Athletics as Spectacle*

The transformation, even trivialization, of Maximus' military skill into gladiatorial entertainment also suggests a present analogy through the prominence of professional athletics in American popular culture and the cult of the celebrity athlete. Most superstar athletes are free agents, idolized by their admirers and celebrated by the media as individual icons separate from any team, further evidence of the trend toward alienation from group or even corporate identities. These highly paid athletes are among the most influential figures in modern society, with the capacity to affect people in what they buy, eat, and wear on the strength of their commercial endorsements. Famous Roman gladiators, who also attained celebrity status through specialized types of fighting, were known to endorse products, too; some of these endorsements survive in ancient frescoes and wall graffiti. Ironically, the makers of *Gladiator* downplayed this historical angle on the assumption that modern audiences would not believe it.[29] Yet *Gladiator* evokes the influence of the superstar athlete in a child's wide-eyed worship of celebrity when young Lucius approaches Maximus, his new idol, as he waits in his cell to enter the arena. Lucius is about the same age as Maximus' dead son. In this poignant scene, a father without a son comes face to face with a son without a father. The moment even reminds us of current debates about professional athletes' responsibility to provide effective role models for America's youngsters.

The gladiatorial fights are reminiscent of the way in which contemporary sports competitions, especially professional football and wrestling, are filmed for television. *Gladiator* makes the combat scenes in the ancient arena visibly accessible to its viewers and connects the gladiatorial bouts explicitly with athletic events in modern ballparks and stadiums. Franzoni was conscious of the film's visual and thematic resonance with contemporary big-ticket professional sports: "This movie is about modern athletic contests, the power entertainment holds over the people and then in turn [is] exploited for the sake of power." Screenwriter John Logan contributed an emphasis on Maximus and his fellow gladiators as the objects of the Roman mob's ardent gaze. The camera watches from a series of vantage points that are easily recognizable to any viewers of Monday Night Football. Logan had written *Any Given Sunday* (1999) for director Oliver Stone, a story of corruption in the National Football League with a reference to an earlier epic film: The voluble head coach barks out his philosophy to his quarterback while the chariot race from *Ben-Hur* plays on his big-screen television in the background.[30] In *Gladiator*, the contests in the provincial arena in Zucchabar exhibit a number of sports camera angles, including a dramatic circular pan sweeping around Maximus and Juba, who are chained together for their first fight. But the Battle of Carthage evinces the most striking use of filming techniques honed at modern sports events. Several spectacular

29   Tricia Johnson, "Far From Rome," *Entertainment Weekly* (May 19, 2000), 8–9, at 9.
30   As noted by Solomon, *The Ancient World in the Cinema*, 25.

elements in this battle are intended to recall the opening sequence in Germania, and the reversal underscores the degradation of Maximus' military skills. The performance staged in the arena replaces the true glory of Rome. "The beating heart of Rome is not the marble of the senate," observes Senator Gracchus grimly, "it is the sand of the Colosseum."

For the Battle of Carthage, the gladiators enter the arena in a narrow shot from inside the athletes' tunnel or "chute," emerging in a camera view typical of televised sporting events. Like a modern general manager, Proximo watches through a broad horizontal slit in his box. The battle itself is shot from diverse angles familiar from television sports: from above the stadium, from end zones and sidelines, and from gladiatorial-helmet angles. The bird's-eye shots of the Colosseum in particular are an astounding sight, as if originating from a blimp hovering high above a modern sports arena. Later, a triumphant Maximus does a victory lap around the arena on a white horse, and the crowd goes wild with applause for the newcomers' unexpected win. The reversal in the Battle of Carthage – the Roman legions lose – parallels underdog sports films like David Anspaugh's *Hoosiers* (1986) and John Lee Hancock's *The Rookie* (2002), in which a downtrodden or disadvantaged team or individual is shown to succeed against all odds. Amid the sound of ecstatic fans chanting "Maximus!" the gladiators exit the arena in a wide-angle shot as if they were a victorious football team leaving the field. A close-up of Maximus' face reveals that look of pure satisfaction before an athlete is named his team's Most Valuable Player.

The connection between gladiatorial spectacle and sports events extends to the language appropriate to sports journalism in reviews of *Gladiator*. One critic described Maximus as if he were an underdog athlete: "He battles back through the gladiatorial bush leagues to become a blood sport superstar."[31] Another commented that the historical Commodus himself loved "to climb into the ring" as a gladiator: "His fights, however, were as fixed as an episode of *WWF Smackdown!*"[32] Some reviewers addressed contemporary anxieties about the amount of violence in popular entertainment and sports. One noted: "It has lots of fighting, but with a posh accent; this may be the first culturally acceptable version of WrestleMania."[33] The commercial success of *Gladiator*

31   Joe Morgenstern, "Crowe Sizzles As Rome Burns in Epic 'Gladiator'; An Empire Strikes Back," *The Wall Street Journal* (May 5, 2000), section W, pages 1 and 9; quotation at 1.
32   Johnson, "Far From Rome," 9.
33   Corliss, "*Gladiator*," 83.

can in part be attributed to its realistic and exciting depiction of physical action and violence in "the contemporary style of hyperrealism."[34] The film's glamorization of brutal force and conquest and their association with spectacle and scoreboard are directly evoked in the recent naming of a new team in the American Arena Football League: "The Gladiators." *Gladiator* is also inspiring Reality TV, which has lately taken on a distinctly Roman guise. On December 1, 2002, The Learning Channel presented "Chariot Race 2002" with an advertisement featuring a Russell Crowe look-alike standing arms akimbo in a chariot under the headline "The Original Action Hero" and with the tag: "Join four modern day competitors as TLC recreates the mother of all drag races." Long before "Survivor" and "Fear Factor," the ancient Romans were producing their own "reality entertainment" in packed arenas throughout the empire.

In a virtuoso twist of reciprocity, *Gladiator* is also influencing the way contemporary sports are shown on television. During the playoff games of the National Football League for the 2002 season, televised on network stations in January, 2003, the musical theme from *Gladiator* was used before commercial breaks and before and after half-time. A comparison of any football audience with the spectators in the ancient arena suggests that our sporting events are so enormous and extravagant that they equal or exceed the grandeur of the Romans. Thus the depiction of the Roman mob in *Gladiator* offers the American audience an unnerving mirror-image of themselves, eager to be entertained at all costs and demanding ever more intricate, dangerous, and realistic spectacles, as when the Colosseum emcee cries with familiar gusto: "Caesar is pleased to bring you the only undefeated champion in Roman history: Tigris of Gaul!"

6. Back to Simple Values

Another strong link between *Gladiator* and contemporary society is the current movement toward simplicity and the longing to return to the plain ideals of the mid-twentieth century and to a down-to-earth hearth and family. While American society may be eager to celebrate the simple values of past decades, the mocking and often exaggerated way this retro trend appears in popular culture shows that we are also reluctant to give up the irony and self-consciousness that has become "cool." Yet

34   Solomon, *The Ancient World in the Cinema*, 93.

Americans are wistful about the times when it was generally believed that an individual could achieve the American Dream through hard work and commitment to family, God, and country. Maximus, too, looks back to a time when the idea of Rome meant something decent, true, and easily comprehensible, not least in regard to the validity of empire. Loyal service to Rome had raised him from the fields of his farm to chief general of the legions, to victories for Rome on the field of honor, and to closest confidant of the emperor.

As Jon Solomon has observed: "*Gladiator* reveals another twenty-first-century bias. Contemporary Hollywood family values interject themselves into the ancient Roman zeitgeist."[35] The film principally explores the theme of a return to traditional ideals of home and family through Maximus, originally a farmer and so "a working-class hero."[36] "Dirt cleans off a lot easier than blood," he tells the senators. The ideal has special relevance for the American viewer familiar with Thomas Jefferson's veneration of his farm at Monticello and with his concept of the gentleman farmer as the archetype of American nobility and virtuous citizenship. When Marcus Aurelius asks Maximus after the battle in Germania: "Tell me about your home," Maximus delivers a sentimental speech about the simple beauty and tranquillity of his farm, with its fecund soil "black like my wife's hair." His wistful reverie evokes the modern individual's yearning for the simplicity of the land. Russell Crowe wrote this speech himself, drawing on his feelings of homesickness for his own ranch: "That's the way I feel about missing my home too."[37] Marcus Aurelius tells Maximus that his home is "worth fighting for" and thereby suggests that the protection of the small family farm is one of the purposes of Roman military conquest. The old emperor, beset by doubts about the legacy of his rule, has come to realize that the countryside, not the city, is the true Rome. Maximus' speech anticipates and fortifies his depiction as an old-fashioned man of the land in the rest of the film, one who has been brutally displaced. Maximus "has a farmer's vanity-free self-confidence."[38] He picks up a handful of dirt and smells it before each fight, drawing strength from his connection to the soil. Franzoni explained why: "We wanted a character trait that humanized the hero before battle . . . Some thought he did it when his life was in danger. But really, the impulse was, he does it when he's about

35   Solomon, *The Ancient World in the Cinema*, 93.
36   Corliss, "*Gladiator*," 84. This is a common feature in Scott's films, on which cf. Richard A. Schwartz, *The Films of Ridley Scott* (Westport and London: Praeger, 2001), 144–5.
37   Quoted from Nashawaty, "Chairman of the Sword," 31.
38   Schwarzbaum, "Fight Club," 48.

to kick ass." Maximus cannot lose as long as he keeps in contact with the earth.

This portrayal of Maximus as a simple man of the soil responds to modern society's idealization of the countryside and its supposed virtue and purity, in stark contrast to the crime-ridden metropolis. *Gladiator* recalls the spectacle of Roman corruption and debauchery lavishly presented in earlier toga epics that equated oppressive political power with social and sexual deviance. *Gladiator* also employs the image of transgressive sexuality to suggest moral depravity and the abuse of tyrannical power. Commodus reveals incestuous yearnings for Lucilla, connecting his aberrant desires with his despotic plans for Rome. His perverse sexuality parallels the bisexuality of Crassus in *Spartacus*, which indicated "aristocratic promiscuity and political rapacity."[39]

By contrast, Maximus honors his wife and remains celibate – to the considerable exasperation of Crowe's female fans. *Gladiator* shows Maximus and Lucilla negotiating the tricky boundaries of their past relationship. Only when Maximus lies dying in her arms are the former lovers almost restored to being a couple, since, like a good husband, he has provided her with security for herself and her son ("Lucius is safe"). So, through Maximus the old-fashioned soldier, gentleman farmer, and faithful Roman husband and father, *Gladiator* reaffirms the ideals of family and simplicity.

Maximus is also a man of personal spirituality. By representing Maximus, devoted father and husband, as someone who honors his household gods in the manner of a traditional Roman *paterfamilias*, the head of the family, the film combines "modern familial sensitivity and ancient Roman Republican virtues."[40] This spirituality seems to acknowledge the present movement toward alternative and individualized religious expression and a concurrent disaffection with the structures and strictures of institutional religions. *Gladiator* effectively contrasts the arrogance and hedonism of imperial Rome with the genuine religiosity of the individual. Franzoni wanted a hero who "transcends traditional religious morality"; as he put it: "I believe there is room in our mythology for a character who is deeply moral, but who's not traditionally religious." Maximus encourages his troops to fight bravely until the final moment with the promise of a peaceful and painless transition to the world beyond: "And if you find yourself alone, riding

---

39   Alison Futrell, "Seeing Red: Spartacus as Domestic Economist," in *Imperial Projections*, 77–118; quotation at 105.

40   Solomon, *The Ancient World in the Cinema*, 95.

through green fields with the sun on your face, do not be troubled, for you are in Elysium, and you are already dead!"

Popular interest in the afterlife, in particular the possibility of contact with the spirits of one's family or friends, is prevalent in American popular culture. This is readily apparent in films with a protagonist who grapples with his indissoluble connection to his dead wife, as in Tom Shadyac's *Dragonfly* (2002) or Steven Soderbergh's *Solaris* (2002). These two films, and comparable examples on television, highlight the unbreakable spiritual bonds among family and friends. What they have in common is the theme of reunion and the belief that our loved ones are accessible to us after death. Maximus' conversation with Juba about his dead family evokes the Roman concept of the afterlife but also resonates with the modern idea or hope that the souls of our loved ones exist where they can still communicate with us. The loss of his family is the single most powerful force that motivates Maximus, and the viewers' feeling of assurance that he will be reunited with them after his death gives the film a kind of positive resolution. Lucilla closes Maximus' eyes and tells him: "Go to them . . . you're home." Yes, you *can* go home again.

Maximus' loneliness and sense of impending catastrophe mirror the condition of Rome itself, as the viewers are shown an empire poised on the brink of crisis and collapse. This is consistent with the growing appeal of apocalyptic theology in mainstream American churches and even among secular Americans, in particular after the terrorist attacks of September 11, 2001. As a critic has observed about the anxious mood in contemporary America:

> There are times in human history when instinct, faith, myth and current events work together to create a perfect storm of preoccupation. Visions of an end point lodge in people's minds in many forms, ranging from entertainment to superstitious fascination to earnest belief. Now seems to be one of those times.[41]

There is now a widespread demand for "apocalyterature" that provides evidence that the current fascination with the concept of "the End Times" is not a fringe phenomenon. The extraordinary success of the *Left Behind* series of books and films based on the mysterious prophecies in the biblical Book of Revelation points to the need of many to be reassured by divine providence that they will not be lost amid moral decay and cul-

---

41   Nancy Gibbs, "Apocalypse Now," *Time* (July 1, 2002), 40–8, at 45.

tural breakdown. Even beyond the realm of such believers, apocalyptic fervor has been infusing the American public. "What we do in life echoes in eternity," Maximus proclaims to his men. Three years after becoming a popular quotation, these words are beginning to take on added meaning.

7. The Exhaustion of Empire

Marcus Aurelius looks wearily around the frozen battlefield, notes the calculated late arrival of Commodus, and sighs: "So much for the glory of Rome." On his face we can see what an absolute empire has come to: from an opportunity for positive change in the world to the responsibility for that world and, in turn, the recognition of the burdens imposed by imperial obligation, all resulting in inescapable exhaustion. Social and political events since the release of *Gladiator*, accompanied by a rising sense of imminent calamity, permit us to measure the film's achievement in expressing today's fraying consciousness. Following on general relief after dire warnings about the Y2K virus and terrorism, the film emerged during a brief moment of calm before a series of unsettling and demoralizing incidents. First a disputed presidential election, then a severe economic recession caused in large part by the criminal negligence of several overcompensated CEOs of large corporations. Then, and worst, terrorist attacks. With confidence in the safety of its borders shattered, the United States was plunged into a deep depression. It was attended by a rise in patriotism among the people and a noisy bout of saber-rattling from a government of questionable legitimacy. The loss of the space shuttle in February, 2003, struck a blow to America's assertion of global pre-eminence in scientific technology. Meanwhile, the military campaign in Afghanistan had failed to show any major results. Subsequently, things came to a head with the almost global isolation of the world's only superpower over war in Iraq and the start of this war in March, 2003. All this allows us to evoke comparisons between the unilateralist goals of the United States and those of imperial Rome. In such an environment, *Gladiator* offers a vision – some might say, a prescient vision – of the perils that an internally challenged empire faces. It is the more significant now that Americans contemplate the outcome of a highly technological war, a rising sense of discomfort with the volatile situation in the Middle East, and the uncertain position of their country in the world.

Recent discussions among diplomats and journalists about the current state of American global supremacy and the unrestrained growth of a new American empire reinforce the analogy between Rome and the United States. Like the Romans, and despite their unrivaled martial, economic, and cultural power, Americans today are confronted by tensions arising from imperial ambitions, isolationism, and a lack of understanding of, respect for, and attention to their geo-political alliances. One analyst has referred to this ingrained national attitude as "the narcissistic confidence of Americans in the superiority of American values and practices, and their rootless inattentiveness to history and tradition – their own and other people's."[42] Some commentators have called on the United States to embrace its hegemonic role in response to terrorism, with one right-wing observer calling American dominance "a liberal and humanitarian imperialism, to be sure, but imperialism all the same."[43] Others here and abroad are openly critical of an incautious American leadership that refuses to acknowledge international concerns.

Washington's policy of brash unilateralism has heightened the general perception that America ignores or disdains international opinion and foreign allegiances. This leaves the United States in the precarious position of a lonely, self-righteous, and determinedly bellicose superpower. The 2003 State of the Union address was delivered on January 28 by a president indifferent to foreign opinion: "The course of this nation does not depend on the decisions of others." Like Commodus in *Gladiator*, who plans to dissolve the Roman senate so that the emperor can from now on act with sole power, President Bush has devalued the United Nations' role in maintaining global accord and pledged that America will act alone, if necessary. It has begun to do so.

Gladiator offers us an opportunity to draw some uncanny analogies between the unskilled young Roman emperor and the American president. Both attempt to govern in the shadow of a father who had previously ruled, and both use and distort their fathers' memory to further their political ambitions. Jealous Commodus is keen to acquire the love and respect of the Roman people that his father had enjoyed but criticizes Marcus Aurelius for his intellectualism: "My father spent all his time at study . . . books, learning, and philosophy. He spent his twilight hours reading scrolls from the senate." A number of Americans view President Bush's demeanor of anti-intellectual swagger and macho posturing as an anxious attempt to do better than Bush Sr., who failed to

42   Tony Judt, "Its Own Worst Enemy," *The New York Review of Books* (August 15, 2002), 12–17; quotation at 12.
43   Max Boot, "The Case for American Empire," *The Weekly Standard* (October 15, 2001), 27–30; quotation at 28.

capitalize on his popularity after the Gulf War or to be re-elected. The film also suggests some eerie verbal analogies, as both Commodus and Bush Jr. employ rhetoric imbued with overly emotional and sometimes childish tones. When Commodus faces Maximus' defiance in the arena, he reacts petulantly: "You simply won't die!" Similarly, Bush has reacted with sullen irritability to Iraqi president Saddam Hussein's lack of compliance with his wishes: "He must disarm. I'm sick and tired of games and deception!"[44] Commodus and Bush publicly decry the insubordination of their opponents in language showing that they take things altogether too personally for men in their exalted positions of world power. The film characterizes Commodus as immature, unreasonable, and ill-prepared for the demands of governing – utterly unlike his father; some critics have described Bush as initially unprepared for the global arena: "Bush junior, who came to the presidency without any knowledge of foreign affairs, could not make decisions or manage dissent as his more knowledgeable and experienced father had."[45] Both men describe the resultant political problems that plague them in terms of a world difficult to comprehend. Commodus exclaims: "The whole thing is like some crazy nightmare!" Bush grumbles: "This looks like a rerun of a bad movie, and I'm not interested in watching it."[46] Both are fully aware of their absolute power. But their behavior and attitudes are more palatable when they come from a cinematic Roman emperor than from a real American president. Commodus attempts to win Lucilla for his idea of disbanding the senate and rendering sole authority unto himself and tells her: "Rome has changed. It takes an emperor to rule an empire." Bush is likewise enamored of imperial power: "I'm the commander. See, I don't have to explain why I say things . . . maybe somebody needs to explain to me why they say something, but I don't feel like I owe anyone an explanation" and: "If this were a dictatorship, it'd be a heck of a lot

44   Quoted from Richard Reeves, "Bush Is Taking Saddam and Kim Too Personally," Universal Press Syndicate (January 17, 2003).
45   Frances FitzGerald, "George Bush and the World," *The New York Review of Books* (September 26, 2002), 80–1 and 84–6; quotation at 81 (on a statement made to her by Brent Scowcroft). Cf. the more recent assessment of Bush and his cabinet by Tony Judt, "America and the World," *The New York Review of Books* (April 10, 2003), 28–31, at 30: "when American leaders throw fits of pique at European dissent, and provoke and encourage internal European divisions, these are signs of incipient weakness, not strength. Real power is influence and example, backed up by understated reminders of military force. When a great power has to buy its allies, bribe its friends, and blackmail its critics, something is amiss."
46   Quoted by Ron Fournier, "Bush Scolds U.N. Members On Iraq: 'How Much Time Do We Need?'" Associated Press (January 21, 2003).

easier. Just as long as I'm the dictator."[47] Commodus and Bush are con-
temptuous of guidance from advisory councils and express their scorn
by means of anti-intellectual bluster. Commodus is fed up with the senate
("Who are they to lecture me?") and says threateningly that the world
will "soon forget the tedious sermonizing of a few dry old men." Bush
disdains the United Nations, which will "fade into history as an ineffective, irrelevant debating society."[48] As a result, America has come to be
regarded abroad as a new empire.[49]

The general analogies drawn frequently between imperial
Roman history and imperious American politics have in at least one
current case found a specific expression, linking the present US
government and its inner circle of leaders who have been pushing for
war in the Middle East – a modern Praetorian Guard? – to a Roman
emperor, although not to Commodus. In a widely publicized letter of resignation after twenty years in the Foreign Service, addressed to Secretary
of State Colin Powell, a high-ranking career diplomat asks, rhetorically
but seriously:

> Why does our president condone the swaggering and contemptuous
> approach to our friends and allies this administration is fostering, includ-
> ing among its most senior officials? Has *oderint dum metuant* really become
> our motto?[50]

The appearance of the Latin phrase in this letter is revealing: "Let them
hate as long as they fear" – an expression originally from the mouth of
a mythical tyrant in a Roman tragedy but made famous, or rather, infamous, as a saying of Emperor Caligula. In the popular imagination of the

47 Quoted from Reeves, "Bush Is Taking Saddam and Kim Too Personally."
48 Bush was speaking at Mayport Naval Station in Mayport, Florida, on February 13,
2003; quoted from CNN.
49 Cf. Andres Oppenheimer, "Information Divide Explains Split with U.S. Over Iraq," *The
Miami Herald* (March 23, 2003), 5A: "Even the words both sides use to characterize what
is going on are different. While U.S. media talk about the 'coalition forces' or the 'U.S.-led
war' on Iraq, the overwhelming majority of foreign press is talking about 'the U.S. war' or
– I'm not making this up – 'the empire's war.' . . . Such is the conviction abroad that Bush
is embarked on a neo-imperialist campaign to Middle Eastern oil and dominate the world
that many normally restrained foreign newspapers have stopped worrying about subtleties.
Brazil's influential *Folha de Sao Paulo* is carrying the daily news of the war under the
thematic heading 'Ataque do Imperio' ('Attack of the Empire')."
50 John Brady Kiesling, "Iraq: A Letter of Resignation," *The New York Review of Books*
(April 10, 2003), 91–2; quotation at 92. Prior to this publication, Kiesling's letter had
circulated on the Internet for several weeks.

West, Caligula has come to be regarded as the second-worst quintessential Roman tyrant after Nero.[51]

Gladiator could not have predicted the type of president Americans would have, but the film strongly suggests that there are serious risks inherent in unchecked executive leadership. It argues in favor of a government marked by respect for republican principles and tempered by constitutional representation.

Rome survived Commodus. America, like Rome, persists. Empire is carried forward by its own institutional momentum even as its internal structure begins to unravel. At the time of the Iraqi war, Commodus' words about the Roman border campaigns took on new meaning, both for international and domestic affairs: "My father's war against the barbarians – he said it himself: it achieved nothing. But the people loved him." *Gladiator* asks Americans to contemplate whether purely national interests will be enough to discharge their imperial obligations. Unless it accepts the responsibilities that are part of the opportunities of empire, in particular the need to maintain rather than squander the high esteem it has earned from people and nations all over the world, America may be compelled to admit with Marcus Aurelius: "I brought the sword, nothing more." *Gladiator* also invites us to ponder the brittleness of the idea that an empire has the right to export its definition of what is just and good for the world and how vulnerable that idea can be to the indifference of its own leaders. "There was a dream that was Rome," says Marcus Aurelius. "You could only whisper it. Anything more than a whisper and it would vanish, it was so fragile." The frequently invoked American Dream occupies a similarly precarious place: "American power and influence are actually very fragile, because they rest upon an idea, a unique and irreplaceable myth: that the United States really does stand for a better world and is still the best hope of all who seek it."[52] Maximus is unwilling to identify himself with the debased concept of Rome as an empire. The ending of the film suggests that the noble and honorable idea of empire represented by Marcus Aurelius and Maximus continues to be in a state of risk. Maximus himself becomes a symbol of Rome's fragility.

In the end, viewers must themselves decide if *Gladiator* sends a positive message about heroism and empire or presents rather a bleak

51   Suetonius, *Caligula* 30.1. The phrase, preserved by Cicero and so becoming proverbial, is a fragment from the lost tragedy *Atreus* by Accius. Nero's tutor Seneca cites it in his philosophical essays *On Anger* (1.20.4) and *On Clemency* (1.12.4 and 2.2.2); the latter work is addressed to Nero.
52   Judt, "Its Own Worst Enemy," 16.

outlook on the subordination of individual heroes to the dictates of a callous ruler and the fading ideals of an unraveling empire. The film leaves us uncertain. Does it matter that Maximus never goes home until he is dead? Is fighting the good fight enough? Can the great dream of Rome ever be realized? *Gladiator* might not echo in eternity, but it has acquired an unexpected topicality. Lucilla asks: "Is Rome worth one good man's life?" The answer ought to be: "We believed it once. Make us believe it again."

CHAPTER TEN

The Politics of *Gladiator*

Peter W. Rose

The fundamental appeal of antiquity today lies in what cultural historian Peter Bondanella has termed the "myth of Rome." He defines that myth as part of a "secular political mythology":

> At the core of the myth of Rome are two diametrically opposed models of political and ethical behavior: a virtuous Roman republic defended by stalwart citizen-soldiers and ever vigilant guardians of public liberty, on the one hand; and a corrupted empire, on the other, whose citizens are occupied by an overriding lust for power, lust for wealth, or lust pure and simple.[1]

This formulation of a secular political myth does not, however, adequately cover the major function of Rome in the cinema, especially during the 1950s, when pagan Rome was the decadent and oppressive antithesis of emergent Christianity. The power of films set in ancient Rome lies only partly in their success in offering credible images of an actual period of history, imaginatively portraying the mentality of the past, or enlightening us about our own historical consciousness.

---

1 Peter Bondanella, *The Eternal City: Roman Images in the Modern World* (Chapel Hill and London: University of North Carolina Press, 1987), 4.

1. The Politics of History and Pedagogy

Educators in particular should turn their students' attention to stereo-types and anachronisms as important indicators of our society's ideol-ogy. Highly important for modern students' critical interactions with films about antiquity are the films' silences, their conscious or uncon-scious repressions of important aspects of the past that may be relevant to a particular film's image of that past.[2] In the case of Ridley Scott's *Gladiator*, a true appreciation of its politics is only possible through an exploration of the political meanings omitted from it despite their rele-vance to the political climate at the time of its production. Moreover, a true sense of the historical differences of the past on the one hand and of its most significant continuities on the other can best emerge from an examination of what a contemporary filmmaker projects onto antiquity or excises from it by either design or ignorance. One advantage of this approach, too rarely acknowledged, is that it offers the prospect of getting students, the majority of whom rarely read newspapers or watch news on television, to think about the times they are living in. Even historically attested accurate elements of the past in a well-made film cannot simply be assumed to appear on the screen because of the filmmakers' dutiful commitment to history. Rather, these reflect the filmmakers' selection of details that fit their specific ideological and com-mercial intentions. Furthermore, a key element of teachers' pedagogical responsibility is to bring students to a clearer awareness of the resources, possibilities, and limitations of specific forms of storytelling, here that of film, which in our society is the prime means to perpetuate dominant ide-ologies. As Bertold Brecht argued: "For as long as one does not criticize the social function of cinema, all film criticism is only a criticism of symp-toms and has itself a merely symptomatic character."[3]

One aspect of film deserves particular emphasis in connection with any analysis of its ideological role. The more expensive a medium, the greater the likelihood that its ideological messages will be mixed. To recover their enormous costs of production and to garner profits, most films aim at appealing to the broadest spectrum of opinions and values through avoidance of any message that might directly offend a

2   My focus on silences and repressions within a text is indebted to Pierre Macherey, *A Theory of Literary Production*, tr. Geoffrey Wall (1978; rpt. London: Routledge, 1989). This work has long influenced my approach to cultural criticism.
3   Quoted from Stephen Heath, *Questions of Cinema* (Bloomington: Indiana University Press, 1981), 16 (in a chapter on film and ideology).

significant portion of the target audience. Setting a narrative in the distant past offers a kind of ideological deniability. At the same time, a film has to address the actual concerns, anxieties, and ideologies of its audience in order to be successful. Films often do not merely reflect but respond to reality and at times even anticipate social or political developments, as became obvious with Barry Levinson's *Wag the Dog* (1997).

A full appreciation of the differences of a particular period of the past from all others, when it is represented as accurately as possible, is undeniably valuable. But I believe Walter Benjamin came closer to the truth:

> To articulate the past historically does not mean to recognize it "the way it really was" (Ranke). It means to seize hold of a memory as it flashes up at a moment of danger . . . The danger affects both the content of the tradition and its receivers. The same threat hangs over both: that of becoming a tool of the ruling classes. In every era the attempt must be made anew to wrest tradition away from a conformism that is about to overpower it . . . Only that historian will have the gift of fanning the spark of hope in the past who is firmly convinced that *even the dead* will not be safe from the enemy if he wins. And this enemy has not ceased to be victorious.[4]

Our students deserve our strenuous efforts to struggle against all appropriations of the past in the service of a complacent status quo.

2. The Politics of Empire

The specific appeal of ancient Rome is the widespread perception that it offers a well-documented model of the rise and fall of the most successful empire in history and therefore carries the potential for useful lessons about contemporary empires. Anthony Mann's 1964 film *The Fall of the Roman Empire*, whose plot *Gladiator* lifts almost in its entirety, presents itself by its very title as a cautionary tale to a country that, at least in the twentieth century, has rarely acknowledged itself to be an empire but is widely perceived as one by most of the world.[5] The film begins with an omniscient narrator confronting us with historiographic questions:

4   Walter Benjamin, "Theses on the Philosophy of History," in *Illuminations*, ed. Hannah Arendt, tr. Harry Zohn (1968; slightly different new edn New York: Schocken, 1969; rpt. 1986), 253–64; quotation at 255.
5   William Appleman Williams, *Empire As Way of Life: An Essay on the Causes and Character of America's Present Predicament, Along with a Few Thoughts About an Alternative* (Oxford and New York: Oxford University Press, 1980; rpt. 1982), 35–54 (chapter entitled "A

Two of the greatest problems in history are how to account for the rise of Rome and how to account for her fall. We may come nearer to understanding the truth if we remember that the fall of Rome, like her rise, had not one cause but many. It was not an event but a process, spread over three hundred years. Some nations have not lasted as long as Rome fell.

This last comment sounds rather ominous. The slowly unfolding drama soon hints at the anxieties of empire that inspired the title. Emperor Marcus Aurelius, campaigning on the Danube frontier against German tribes, explains to his general, the fictitious Livius: "Rome has existed for a thousand years. It is time we found peaceful ways to live with those you call barbarians." Soon after, a massive procession of representatives of the whole empire assembles in the emperor's military base. This is one of the most daring violations of historical plausibility in the whole film and attests to the importance Mann attaches to the theme of empire.[6] The sequence culminates in a key speech by Marcus Aurelius, in which he lays out his utopian vision of a peaceful world of equals:

You have come from the deserts of Egypt, from the mountains of Armenia, from the forests of Gaul, and the prairies of Spain. You do not resemble each other, nor do you wear the same clothes, nor sing the same songs, nor worship the same gods. Yet like a mighty tree with green leaves and black roots, you are the unity which is Rome. Look about you and look at yourselves, and see the greatness of Rome . . . Rome wants and needs human frontiers. We've had to fight long wars. Your burdens have been great. But we come now to the end of the road. Here, within our reach, golden centuries of peace, a true *pax Romana*. Wherever you live, whatever the color of your skin, when peace is achieved, it will bring to all, *all*, the supreme right of Roman citizenship. [*Huge cheering.*] . . . No longer provinces or colonies, but Rome, Rome everywhere. A family of equal nations, that is what lies ahead.

The injection of a Latin phrase into a film requiring our suspension of disbelief as we listen to Romans speaking English highlights the film-makers' eagerness to drive home an ideological message. The *pax Romana*

Revolution for Self-Government and Empire"), and R. W. Van Alstyne, *The Rising American Empire* (1960; rpt. Chicago: Quadrangle Books, 1965), trace the use of the term by the Founding Fathers. On its re-emergence in the second Bush era see John Bellamy Foster, "The Rediscovery of Imperialism," *Monthly Review*, 54 no. 6 (2002), 1–16.

6   So Martin M. Winkler, "Cinema and the Fall of Rome," *Transactions of the American Philological Association*, 125 (1995), 135–54, at 144.

is presented to us as a historical ideal, a model option to the audience, who may have heard the phrase *pax Americana*.

Once Marcus Aurelius has been murdered by Commodus' friends conspiring to prevent Livius from becoming his heir, we learn that the new emperor is committed to a policy of maximum extortion from the provinces, backed by brutal military repression of all rebellions. The ideological conflict between Marcus Aurelius' utopian vision and this policy of Commodus is the subject of a historically implausible debate in the Roman senate much later in the film, when the case is made again for the utopian vision of Marcus Aurelius in language calculated to recall his speech.

At one point in this debate, Commodus' spokesman exclaims, in language calculated to mark him as the voice of America's own paranoid, militaristic, xenophobic, and anti-Semitic conservatives:

> Equality. Freedom. Peace. Who is it that uses these words but Greeks and Jews and slaves? Behind him and his people are the Vandals – untold millions of them, waiting for a moment of weakness, ready to destroy us. If we take these barbarians in amongst us, our enemies will say it is because we are weak, and they will pour in on us from everywhere. It will be the end of the Roman Empire. [*Dramatic pause.*] It will be the end – of Rome.

Here the title of the film takes on importance. But an aged senator now intervenes. He is played by an actor whose earlier roles as patriarchal Christian authority figures give his voice additional weight.[7] The old senator takes up the last speaker's final words:

> The end of Rome? How does an empire die? Does it collapse in one terrible moment? No! No! But there comes a time when its people no longer believe in it. Then, then does an empire begin to die. Fathers of Rome, I have lived under four great emperors: Trajan, Hadrian, Antoninus, Marcus Aurelius. And during all those years our empire grew, changed. The law of life is: grow or die. But you, the senators, are the heart of Rome, it is through you that the people speak. Speak up! Let the world hear you. Let the world know that Rome will not die. There are millions like *them* waiting at our gates. If we do not open these gates, they will break them down and destroy us. But, instead, let us grow ever bigger, ever greater; let us take them among us, let the heart of the empire grow with us. Honorable Fathers, we have changed the world. Can we not change ourselves?

7   Winkler, "Cinema and the Fall of Rome," 149.

We hear shouts of "Yes! It is time to change! An end to war! *Pax Romana!*" The debate is now over, apparently a triumph for Marcus Aurelius' vision.

The speech assumes an obvious connection between an imperial people believing in their empire and the decision to welcome an enormous influx of new citizens into the existing body politic. The final rhetorical question acknowledges that such a decision entails a fundamental change. Most striking about the invocation of belief is its apparent gratuitousness. Certainly Commodus' mouthpiece and those who had shouted their approval gave no hint of a lack of faith in the traditional Roman way of doing things. Instead, Marcus Aurelius and Livius have articulated their own lack of faith in the Roman way of treating allies and enemies and have called for a radical change from methods no longer commanding *their* belief. Classical scholars will recognize a defense of empire previously articulated by Herodotus' Xerxes and Thucydides' Alcibiades.[8] But a contemporary audience is more likely to have internalized this as an eternal law constantly reiterated in their own socio-economic system. Invocation of the logic of "grow or die" in connection with the fate of empires may even point toward the necessity of new wars of conquest, thus supporting the previous speaker's argument. "Grow or die" is also the most concise statement of the inner logic of capitalism. Economists regard the rate of growth as the most important indicator of economic health.

How are we to envision the American people processing these arguments? On the one hand, they are invited to see the Roman senate as an analogy of their own senate and, by extension, of the whole system of representative government, a vehicle capable of effecting meaningful transformations of fundamental social relations. They are offered a vague but ominous warning that they need to believe in the American empire if it is to survive. At the same time they are exhorted to change radically the character of their empire away from paranoia.

The end of the film returns to preaching about empire. As cynical plutocrats haggle openly to buy the throne from a thoroughly corrupted military, the narrator tells us:

> This was the beginning of the fall of the Roman Empire. A great civilization is not destroyed from without until it has destroyed itself from within.

This warning recalls the senator's invocation of the role of belief – the inner character of a civilization – and, in its immediate context, points

---

8 Herodotus, *Histories* 7.8; Thucydides, *The Peloponnesian War* 6.18.

to the combination of greed with brutality as the chief causes for the fall of Rome.

The Fall of the Roman Empire does not simply reflect political and economic developments; rather, it offers a creative response and seeks, unfortunately futilely, to shape future realities. The break-up of the British Empire after World War II evidently provided the filmmakers with raw material for their utopian vision of the peaceful transformation of a vast empire built mostly on conquest into a more or less friendly family of nations with formally equal sovereignty.

In view of its heavy dependence on the plot of this film, one of the most striking aspects of *Gladiator* is the virtual absence of any anxiety over empire. In this connection it is revealing to compare the explicitly cautionary opening voice-over of *The Fall of the Roman Empire* with the message, entirely in capital letters, with which *Gladiator* begins:

> At the height of its power, the Roman Empire was vast, stretching from the deserts of Africa to the borders of northern England. Over one quarter of the world's population lived and died under the rule of the Caesars. In the winter of 180 A.D. Emperor Marcus Aurelius' twelve-year campaign against the barbarian tribes in Germania was drawing to an end. Just one final stronghold stands in the way of Roman victory and the promise of peace throughout the empire.

The specific nature of Rome emerges immediately in this reference to its unique success as an empire. The passage is the very opposite of the anxiety-haunted opening of the earlier film. Now we find simple admiration for the sheer extent of Roman power and for the confident triumphalism of an empire that perceives no more problems on the horizon. After his victory over the Germans, General Maximus confidently declares to Marcus Aurelius: "There's no one left to fight, sire." Despite a dour reply by the emperor – "There is always someone left to fight" – the rest of the film shows no concern at all for the future of the empire. When Commodus triumphantly enters Rome, dissident senator Gracchus observes skeptically: "He enters Rome like a conquering hero. But what has he conquered?" The name Gracchus echoes the dissident senator in Stanley Kubrick's *Spartacus* (1960), whose name in turn echoes the radical Roman brothers Tiberius and Gaius Gracchus of the second century B.C. The implication of Gracchus' comment in *Gladiator* is that the chief criterion for an emperor is conquest. In its confidence and militarism, the Rome of this film perfectly echoes the arrogance and naiveté of the world's only current superpower after the collapse of the

Soviet Union, a superpower for whose Republican government "nation-building" is not a priority. Political developments since the release and success of *Gladiator* have only reinforced this perspective, most clearly in the sometimes scornful American interactions with the United Nations and with some European governments.

At the same time that *Gladiator* eschews any explicit engagement with issues of empire, the ferocious efficiency of the Roman army in the film's opening battle sequence leaves an indelible impression of the invincibility of Roman might, based on superior discipline and a high level of military technology. This is a clear analogy to the military arrogance of today's United States. Even the protagonist's name – Maximus means "The Greatest" – attests to this general aura of supreme confidence.

A brief exchange between Maximus and his second in command, Quintus, strongly anticipates the indifference of our present government to the costs of militarism:

> Quintus: Soldier, I ordered you to move those catapults forward; they're
> out of range.
> Maximus: Range is good.
> Quintus: The danger to the cavalry –
> Maximus [*interrupting*]: – is acceptable. Agreed?

Maximus is a commander not likely to be troubled by "collateral damage," even as his performances in the arena will later suggest that no amount of bloodshed is too much.

3. Totalitarianism vs. Democracy, or The Politics of Class

In the 1950s, Roman films carried two heavy, often overlapping, ideological messages, the conflict of Christianity and paganism and the conflict of totalitarianism and freedom.[9] In *Spartacus*, this opposition took on a more complex character.[10] Both novelist Howard Fast, on whose novel the film was based, and screenwriter Dalton Trumbo had been targets of

9   Cf. William Fitzgerald, "Oppositions, Anxieties, and Ambiguities in the Toga Movie," in *Imperial Projections: Ancient Rome in Modern Popular Culture*, ed. Sandra R. Joshel, Margaret Malamud, and Donald T. McGuire, Jr. (Baltimore and London: Johns Hopkins University Press, 2001), 23–49.

10   On this film see Maria Wyke, *Projecting the Past: Ancient Rome, Cinema and History* (New York and London: Routledge, 1997), 60–72, and Alison Futrell, "Seeing Red: Spartacus as Domestic Economist," in *Imperial Projections*, 77–118.

anti-Communist crusades, but something of their vision of the struggle of labor-versus-capital and of capitalism's recourse to totalitarian repression remains in the film. At the same time, producer and star Kirk Douglas overlaid this message with his own Zionist vision of the protagonist as a second Moses attempting to lead his people back to their traditional homeland. In *The Fall of the Roman Empire*, the senate debate, in spite of the menacing presence of the emperor, offers some semblance of a deliberative process that an American audience might consider democratic. Certainly it is a more positive image of the Roman senate than the vision of oligarchy represented in the senate scenes of *Spartacus*.[11] In *The Fall of the Roman Empire*, the climactic ending with the empire for sale to the highest bidder suggests the underlying reality of a government by plutocracy. The utopian hope for a peaceful and just world order is subverted not only by the utterly irresponsible self-indulgence and brutality of a monomaniacal monarch, but also by a greed that conquers all – the people, dancing mindlessly in the streets, and the leaders. The response of the protagonists, Livius and Lucilla, his beloved, reflects the privatism of those who see themselves as too decent for politics. They just walk away.[12]

The opposite dynamic is at work in *Gladiator*: a lack of interest in the workings of empire, concern about the internal politics of monarchy, and a vague, ultimately cynical, populism. The future of Rome lies in Marcus Aurelius' dream of giving power back to the people through a revived senate. Early on, Marcus asks Maximus: "Tell me again, Maximus, why are we here?" Maximus dutifully replies: "For the glory of the empire, sire." Marcus now expresses such scorn and indifference for his own conquests that Maximus is provoked to protest in the name of his soldiers: "I will *not* believe that they fought and died for nothing." The emperor then voices his dying wish that he be remembered as "the emperor who gave Rome back her true self." He soon asks Maximus "to become the protector of Rome after I die. I will empower you to one end alone, to give power back to the people of Rome and end the corruption that has crippled it." The equivocations in these words are the most revealing anachronism in the film. Not only had the people of Rome never really held power, but the need to end corruption first opens a wide temporal and political gap between the people's empowerment and the process by which this unspecified corruption must be removed. An absurd claim of Senator Gracchus to Commodus later compounds this

11   Cf. Wyke, *Projecting the Past*, 67.
12   Cf. Fitzgerald, "Oppositions, Anxieties, and Ambiguities in the Toga Movie," 33.

disingenuous populism: "But the senate is the people, sire, chosen from among the people, to speak for the people." The Roman senate, originally an advisory group consisting of the heads of the richest land-owning families, was at its most powerful a strictly oligarchic group. During the civil wars of the late republic it was repeatedly purged, then packed with the supporters of whichever war lord was in control. During the empire the senate degenerated into an increasingly irrelevant body. It is true that the five good emperors Nerva, Trajan, Hadrian, Antoninus Pius, and Marcus Aurelius carefully cultivated good relations with the senate, but modern historians have long been aware of the reality of imperial Roman power:

> if the emperors of the second century were at pains to restore to the Senate a sense of partnership with themselves, they were equally careful to retain in their hands all the powers exercised by the [preceding] Flavian dynasty ... By the end of the second century the Senate had become fairly representative of the empire as a whole; but it was now of small practical importance, except as a panel for the future recruitment of high imperial officials.[13]

The film's utopian pseudo-populism soon turns out to be an enlightened paternalism at best. Gracchus, with whom Maximus eventually negotiates, says about himself to another senator: "I don't pretend to be a man of the people, senator, but I do try to be a man *for* the people." This is a cynical appropriation of Abraham Lincoln's famous utopian vision, expressed in his Gettysburg Address, of government "of the people, by the people, for the people." Soon after, Commodus proposes to abolish the senate altogether, thus provoking an exchange with his sister Lucilla that articulates a vision of imperial and domestic politics as pure illusion. Lucilla replies sternly:

> Lucilla: Don't even think it! There has always *been* a senate.
> Commodus: Rome has changed. It takes an emperor to rule an empire.
> Lucilla: Of course, but leave the people their –
> Commodus: Illusions?

13   M. Cary, *A History of Rome Down to the Reign of Constantine*, 2nd edn (London: Macmillan; New York: St. Martin's Press, 1954; several rpts.), 632–3. With the term "representative" Cary refers to the addition of provincial members to the senate, which still remained a strictly elite group. As he points out at 475, Octavian had even specified substantial property requirements as one of the preconditions for membership.

Lucilla: – traditions.

Commodus: My father's war against the barbarians – he said it himself: it achieved nothing. But the people loved him.

Lucilla: People always love victories.

Commodus: Why? They didn't see the battles. What do they care about Germania?

Lucilla: They care about the greatness of Rome.

Commodus: The greatness of Rome? But what is that?

Lucilla: It's an idea, greatness. Greatness is a vision.

Commodus: Exactly. A vision. Do you not see, Lucilla? I will give the people a vision of Rome and they'll love me for it. They will soon forget the tedious sermonizing of a few dry old men. I will give the people the greatest vision of their lives.

The most striking feature of this exchange is the hollowness of Lucilla's replies. She is presented as a very strong character, fully capable of governing, and at this point she is not so thoroughly terrorized by Commodus that we cannot expect her to speak her mind. In an age of *Wag the Dog* media politics, there is no challenge to Commodus' childish phrase about an emperor ruling an empire to justify hereditary autocracy or to his conception of politics as the manipulation of images. Here, popular art does not simply reflect but anticipate reality. So a newspaper article presented the case for a Bush dynasty, expecting Jeb Bush to assume the throne when his brother vacates it.[14] The term "empire" for the United States, largely taboo in mainstream media in 2000, has now made a remarkable comeback, and the current president's advisors speak openly of imposing a *pax Americana* on the world.

After Commodus expresses his vision, Scott cuts to the Colosseum, where games are in progress. Outside, Gracchus is discussing with a fellow senator the political effectiveness of Commodus' approach to domestic politics:

Gaius: Games! 150 days of games!

Gracchus: He's cleverer than I thought.

Gaius: Clever? The whole of Rome would be laughing at him, if they weren't so afraid of his Praetorians.

Gracchus: Fear and wonder. A powerful combination.

Gaius: You really think the people are going to be seduced by that?

---

14   Adam Clymer, "Defying Expectations, A Bush Dynasty Begins to Look Real," *The New York Times* (November 10, 2002), section 4, pp. 1 and 3. Cf. the unsigned "Florida's Governorship: How Dynasties Happen, Maybe," *The Economist* (November 9–15, 2002), 33.

Gracchus: I think he knows what Rome is. Rome is the mob. He will conjure magic for them and they will be distracted. He'll take away their freedom, and still they'll roar. The beating heart of Rome is not the marble of the senate; it's the sand of the Colosseum. He'll bring them death, and they will love him for it.

The general cynicism of this perspective is reinforced visually by a reminder of the famous Roman saying "Bread and Circuses." Loaves of bread are indeed being thrown to the crowd before the performances in the Colosseum begin.

Gracchus' view of the Roman people comes from the leftmost pole of the political spectrum in *Gladiator*. The combination of utter scorn for the people and profound cynicism in regard to any alternative confirms Commodus' vision of reality and completely undercuts the pseudo-populism of Marcus Aurelius' vision. This political configuration reflects a specifically Republican response – in the modern American sense – to others' anxieties over the displacement of democracy by plutocracy. Scott's film is far less self-conscious in its ideological messages than Mann's, except for its awareness of the power of film itself.

Even if we are invited to be shocked by Commodus' plan to abolish the senate, his repeated denunciations of it as a hotbed of corrupt and conniving politicians are borne out by the betrayal of the republican ideal on the part of Senator Falco, who becomes Commodus' advisor and confidant, and by Maximus' skepticism about the senate. Before Marcus has asked Maximus to take power after his death, the issue of the republic and of the nature of the senate occurs in a brief exchange when Commodus, still confident that his father will designate him as heir to the throne, introduces two senators to Maximus:

Commodus: Senator Gaius, Senator Falco. Beware of Gaius. He'll pour honeyed potion in your ear and you'll wake up one day and all you'll say is "Republic! Republic! Republic!"

Gaius: Well, why not? Rome *was* founded as a republic.

Commodus: Yes and in a republic, the senate has the power. But Senator Gaius isn't influenced by that, of course.

Falco: Where do you stand, General? Emperor or senate?

Maximus: A soldier has the advantage of being able to look his enemy in the eye, Senator.

Maximus' jibe implies that he shares Commodus' and Marcus' view that the senate is a place of backroom scheming. *Gladiator* is quintessentially the film of an anti-politics politician. Marcus Aurelius prefers Maximus because Maximus does not even want power and because he has never been to Rome. He is therefore presumed free of and proof against all its corruption, a corruption symbolized by the senate itself. The film's presentation of Maximus as a farmer who is always picking up a handful of dirt, communing with spring birds, and fondling ripe fields of grain fits the campaign rhetoric of Jimmy Carter, Ronald Reagan, Bill Clinton, and George W. Bush, who all represented themselves as outsiders and therefore the right men to clean up Washington. Reagan and Bush especially favored kitschy shots of themselves in the country.

Maximus' heroism in the arena is consistently associated with his military status. The chief means by which the film censors any hint that the gladiators, who are slaves, constitute a potentially rebellious class is the consistent focus on Maximus' success in re-enacting his role as general that had been impressed on us in the opening battle. He succeeds in his first fight in the Colosseum by recruiting the black gladiator Juba as his assistant, and he achieves his most dazzling reversal of crowd expectations during the Battle of Carthage when he organizes the other gladiators into a disciplined military machine, for which cooperation equals strict adherence to the general's orders. Maximus' creation of a gladiatorial army is emphasized when the gladiators adopt for themselves the slogan of the Roman army heard in the opening: "Strength and Honor!" In this respect *Gladiator* anticipates a slightly later prison film, Rod Lurie's *The Last Castle* (2001), in which an imprisoned general manages to organize a rebellion against the evil warden. This film, too, is a paean to militarism and patriotism. Its use of a Roman-style catapult to hurl fire at the guard posts may be a borrowing from *Gladiator*.

4. The Politics of Race, Gender, Family, and Spirituality

A further side of the domestic politics of *Gladiator* is its presentation of race. *Spartacus* had shown contemporary racial tensions in the bonding of Spartacus with the African slave and gladiator Draba, played by Woody Strode, whose starring role in John Ford's *Sergeant Rutledge* earlier in 1960 had established him as a figure of integrity in the face of pervasive prejudice.[15]

Maximus' rise to power from wounded slave to gladiator to threat to the empire has close similarities to the development of the hero of

15   So Wyke, *Projecting the Past*, 68.

Spartacus. But the radical potential of *Spartacus* is expunged from *Gladiator*, despite a visual allusion to the earlier film. Draba, instead of killing his friend Spartacus, defiantly hurls his weapon at the group of decadent Roman aristocrats who have come to watch slaves kill each other. For his attack on them he is killed, and his naked corpse is hung head down in the gladiators' quarters as a warning. Draba's refusal to kill Spartacus leads to his martyrdom and to the gladiators' rebellion. Maximus, in his second performance in the provincial arena, also hurls a weapon at some of his audience, screaming bitterly: "Are you not entertained? Are you not entertained? Is this not why you are here?" But instead of being punished, he is cheered wildly. This confirms Proximo's subsequent analysis of the power of winning the crowd: "Win the crowd, and you'll win your freedom."

The relationship in *Gladiator* between Maximus and the Nubian Juba is clearly inspired by *Spartacus.* But the differences are a good indication of the later film's ideology. Djimon Hounsou, who plays Juba, had been the rebellious slave leader in Steven Spielberg's *Amistad* (1997) and had achieved a public image as a representative of black liberation struggles. In *Gladiator,* however, he plays a diametrically opposite role. Juba is at first a kind of loving nurse to wounded and enslaved Maximus, then a naïvely obedient gladiator who cannot comprehend Maximus' defiance of his master. In the arena, Juba becomes Maximus' subordinate and obedient partner. Finally, he is the pious friend who buries Maximus' family idols after his death. Here again we have a specifically Republican image of nostalgia for a lost golden age of race relations, in which blacks do not question whites and obey their white superiors.

Scott's Commodus is a far starker villain than Mann's, who seemed to have a thing not for his sister but for Livius. He and Commodus are represented from the outset as warm friends of long standing. Their initial reunion culminates in a suggestive bout of arm-in-arm drinking from leather wine-bags, liquid squirting over their happy faces. But politics shatters their intimate bond. Such hints at homoerotic bonding do not entail any negative judgment; they simply add to the drama of enmity between former friends. Moreover, the far more obvious romance between Livius and Lucilla counterbalances this lightly homosexual subtext. When Commodus offers him the opportunity to spend the rest of his life happily with Lucilla, Livius refuses in order to pursue his radical initiative in the senate. At the end, the lovers walk away from Rome and its corruptions, thereby confirming that perennial favorite of American cinema, romantic love.

The film also hints at a harmony between this romantic avoidance of politics and a particular spiritual reason for turning away from it. Early in the film, after a fervent prayer, Lucilla speaks to Livius of a time when she had turned away from the world in hopes of finding peace but had found only loneliness. A stronger hint at a new alternative to the Roman way of life comes toward the end of the film. On the corpse of Timonides, who had been living peacefully with his free agricultural community of Germans, we see a pendant cross with the Greek letters *chi* and *rho*, the first letters of the word "Christos" and the only clear hint at Christianity in the film.

In *Spartacus*, the romance of love and marriage mutes and even supersedes a potentially Communist vision of a slave rebellion against a corrupt and exploitative empire. In lieu of a verbally explicit presentation of a communal alternative to Roman hierarchy and discipline, we are shown utopian images of the slave army as an extended family under the benign patriarchal leadership of Spartacus, who actually becomes a father in the course of the film. Moreover, the final vision of the leader hanging on a cross offers an unmistakable image of Rome's eventual redemption by Christianity. And homoerotic relations are given a specifically political spin as a sign of Roman decadence.[16]

In *Gladiator*, Maximus carries even further the displacement of any hint of class rebellion by a relentless devotion to family values in combination with fervent religiosity.[17] Except for one kiss with his former girl-friend Lucilla, Maximus is firmly committed to his farm and the memory of his family. The opening image of Maximus the farmer fondling ripe grain in a field and wistfully smiling at a robin is echoed by his repeated reaching down to feel the quality of the soil (and to give his hands extra traction before fighting). This longing for home and family becomes explicit in his interview with Marcus Aurelius. Immediately after, Maximus is accosted by Lucilla, who hints at a former relationship between them about which he is cold and distant. When they speak of their sons, who are about the same age, the screenplay tells us: "Again a moment of peace overcomes him as he speaks of his family." The camera cuts immediately to Maximus kneeling in his tent before a shrine devoted to his ancestors and family, holding some clay figurines. We hear him praying:

16 Wyke, *Projecting the Past*, 70.
17 Cf. Jon Solomon, *The Ancient World in the Cinema*, 2nd edn (New Haven: Yale University Press, 2001), 93–4.

Ancestors, I ask for your guidance. Blessed Mother, come to me with the gods' desire for my future. Blessed Father, watch over my wife and son with a ready sword. Whisper to them I live only to hold them again.

When Maximus learns after the murder of Marcus Aurelius that he will be executed, he reacts stoically but pleads with his former subordinate Quintus to look after his family. He is told: "Your family will meet you in the afterlife." Only now does Maximus resist his fate for the first time. His escape is immediately followed by his frantic ride all the way from Germany to Spain, and we hear again bits of his conversation about his family with Marcus and of his prayer. Maximus displays the greatest emotion when he is in agony at the sight of his murdered wife and son. His only motive for staying alive and pursuing success in the arena is to kill Commodus: "I will have my vengeance, in this life or the next." Even his bonding with Juba contains speculation about reunion with their families in the afterlife, and the film ends with Juba dutifully burying Maximus' figurines.

Roman aristocrats indeed practiced ancestor worship, but they did so in a form heavily entwined with political ambitions. Images of ancestors were carried in funeral processions, and public funerals were a favorite means to boast of all the glorious accomplishments of earlier family members. Romans also engaged in a great deal of public religious activity focused on their anthropomorphic divinities. One of the major attractions of Christianity to Romans was the general absence from Roman religion of any compelling vision of an afterlife. A striking distortion of this in the case of Maximus is that his ancestors are meaningful only in relation to his immediate family, that the whole of his religious experience is fused with his devotion to them, and that his references to an afterlife are confined to hopes of reunion with them. There is only one exception. Just before the battle with the Germans Maximus jokingly alludes to the Elysian Fields and declares bombastically: "What we do in life echoes in eternity." Subsequently he shows no interest in the idea of immortality through military achievement.

Maximus is also proof against all sexual temptations offered him by Proximo, by the women of the street who hang on his neck, and by Lucilla, who emerges as a sympathetic figure largely because of her intense devotion to her son, with whom Maximus forges a close bond. When Lucilla first visits him in his gladiatorial prison, she comments playfully: "Rich matrons pay well to be pleasured by the bravest champions." This hint at her continuing sexual attraction to Maximus inspires his responding – "viciously," as the script indicates – with the accusation that she is an assassin. His kiss seems at least as much inspired by his belated recognition of her maternal devotion to her threatened son as by desire.

The only explicit references in *Gladiator* to homosexuality, which was an openly acknowledged if not universally approved aspect of Roman life, are confined to Proximo, a down-to-earth and cynical realist from near the bottom of the social hierarchy. We first see him complaining to a Bedouin slave trader, whose testicles he grasps in a painful gesture of intimidation: "Those giraffes you sold me, they won't mate. They just walk around eating and not mating. You sold me queer giraffes." Subsequently, after Maximus has distinguished himself in the arena, Proximo asks him about a reward: "What do you want? Hmmmm? Girl? Boy?" Audiences know that Maximus is faithful to his wife even beyond death and that he is as unwaveringly straight as they expect their epic heroes (and the actors who play them) to be.[18]

As regards Lucilla, her interactions with her father and brother go as far as *Gladiator* can go to present some less appealing truths about the institution of the nuclear family as a counter to this film's general celebration of family values. In *The Fall of the Roman Empire*, Lucilla was a dutiful daughter, agreeing without protest but not without pain to marry the king of Armenia, a perfect stranger, for the good of the empire as soon as her father requested it, and this despite her love for Livius. Even Commodus seemed to take Marcus' rejection of him as future emperor with a curious blend of anger and frantic humor, referring repeatedly to the gods' laughter. The plot also absolved him from guilt for the murder of Marcus.

Gladiator dramatizes the pain inherent in a dysfunctional family far more strongly. Lucilla is told by her dying father: "I need your help, with your brother . . . He loves you, he always has and . . . he will need you now, more than ever." But Marcus does not confide to her his plans to name Maximus his heir. Instead he breaks off: "Enough of politics. Let us pretend that you are a loving daughter and I am a good father." She replies with a bitter look: "This is a pleasant fiction, isn't it?" Years of pain and guilt are distilled into this brief exchange. Marcus' failure as a father is even more prominent in his encounter with Commodus that will culminate in the father's murder by his son. Commodus shows intense pain

---

18   *Gladiator* no more than hints at the possibility that Senator Gracchus may also be homosexual. In the scene of his arrest, an effeminate-looking young man warns Gracchus about the approach of the Praetorians. Shortly after, Commodus asks Lucilla: "Does Gracchus have a new lover?"

at his father's rejection. His pathetic acknowledgment that he has none of the qualities his father most admires leads to his agonized declaration:

> it was as if you didn't want me for your son . . . I searched the faces of the gods for ways to please you, to make you proud . . . One kind word, one full hug while you pressed me to your chest and held me tight would have been like the sun on my heart for a thousand years . . . What is it in me you hate so much? All I ever wanted was to live up to you, Caesar, Father.

In the image of the hug there is an ironic anticipation of the murder by suffocation that will soon follow, but Commodus' expression of pain at paternal love withheld is compelling. He murders Marcus with a passionate and weirdly touching embrace, one that suffocates him with twisted love. So Commodus' incestuous longings for his sister in the absence of his father's love gain a kind of logic. Although the audience may be titillated by the prospect of brother–sister incest when Commodus, using his threat upon the life of her son, informs Lucilla that she will provide him "an heir of pure blood so that Commodus and his progeny will rule for a thousand years," we see nothing but Commodus' kisses and Lucilla's refusal. The only bedroom scene in the entire film turns out to be another defeat for love-starved Commodus. Willy-nilly, audiences may even feel sorry for this Commodus, but when he later threatens sexual violence to his pre-teenage nephew, he again turns into a standard villain whose socially unsanctioned sexual desires mark him as irredeemable, the kind of character audiences love to hate. That this dysfunctional family is part of a patriarchal system is confirmed by Marcus' first words to Lucilla: "If only you had been born a man. What a Caesar you would have made. You would have been strong." This is no idle compliment, for when in the senate Commodus displays his complete indifference to pressing public concerns, Lucilla takes over the responsibility for necessary actions from the senators. But the workings of the plot confirm that for her biology is destiny. Her maternal love compels her to betray the conspiracy she herself has plotted.

5. *From Gender to Genre: The Politics of Filmic Form*

In a review essay published just before *Gladiator* was released, Herbert Muschamp poses the question: "Why revive this genre of movie now?" His conclusion is compelling:

The postwar Roman epics were sprawling adventures in hypocrisy: moral tales that allowed audiences to indulge vicariously in pull-out-the-stops orgies . . . Still, despite the Roman settings and violent plots, the epics actually depict the moral climate in the Age of Eisenhower, when the tyranny of normalcy ruled the cultural landscape . . . The DreamWorks revival of this campy entertainment genre reflects, in part, the New Normalcy of our time.

Muschamp describes *Gladiator* as a throwback "to a time when the American moral fiber was held together by the strict segregation of men and women into acting subjects and passive objects."[19]

In this, he echoes an influential article by radical feminist Laura Mulvey, who had used Freudian theory to unmask the mechanisms of manipulation inherent in the classic Hollywood film. Mulvey argued that "the pleasure of the look" specific to film consists of two different kinds. One, fostered by the darkened theater, is the Peeping-Tom pleasure that Freud called scopophilia ("love of looking"), a reflection of the child's excited, but essentially passive, curiosity about sex, especially that of its parents. Mulvey sees this pleasure manifested most obviously in the display of women's bodies on the screen as "passive objects." The second form of pleasure is vicariously active. The male viewer identifies with the active hero as a projection of his ideal image of himself.[20] In *Gladiator*, Maximus is nothing if not active. But the most striking difference between this film and its progenitors is the almost complete absence of female objects of male visual pleasure. Lucilla is certainly an object of desire for Commodus and for male audiences, and we are invited to be titillated by Commodus' exercise of totalitarian power when he manipulates her maternal instincts into sexual submission. But she remains fully clothed throughout the film, even during the bed scene mentioned before. There are no scantily clad women's bodies, no lewd dances, no orgiastic parties. All the visual pleasure of the film is directed toward male bodies engaged in violent conflict in the arena. The utter repression of heterosexual desire in the eternally grieving protagonist finds its only outlet in his efficient beheadings and mutilations of male rivals. (A student pointed out to me that all the opponents of Maximus in the Colosseum are masked and thus dehumanized.) William Fitzgerald's

19 Herbert Muschamp, "Throwing Our Anxieties to the Lions," *The New York Times* (April 30, 2000), section 2A, pp. 1 and 33.
20 Laura Mulvey, "Visual Pleasure and Narrative Cinema," in *Visual and Other Pleasures* (Bloomington and Indianapolis: Indiana University Press, 1989), 14–26. Mulvey's article first appeared in *Screen* (Autumn, 1975).

comment on the 1950s films is apposite here: "The male look at the male body must be motivated in such a way that its erotic component is repressed, hence the sadism and violence connected with many of the scenes in which the male body is displayed."[21] But in *Gladiator* the erotic element of violence can be more explicit. The murderous thrust with which Commodus mortally wounds Maximus is self-consciously staged as an act of love, recalling Commodus' loving murder of his father. Commodus says:

> You loved my father, I know. But so did I. That makes us brothers, doesn't it? Smile for me now, brother. *Commodus embraces Maximus and with one cowardice* [sic], *fierce thrust, stabs him with his dagger that has been hidden in his sleeve, and then kisses him on the neck.*

Besides the pervasive repression of heterosexual desire and this murderous homoeroticism, *Gladiator* contains one scene of explicit misogyny. The Battle of Carthage is set in a Colosseum bristling with large gray phallic objects for which there is no historical justification. (They are *metae*, turning points for chariots, that belong in the Circus Maximus.) The scythed chariots of the Romans carry female archers, all covered with golden masks and sporting golden breastplates with prominent breasts. All these women are gleefully slaughtered; one of them is beheaded and another cut in two by a scythe. The presence of women in the arena is a case of historically accurate detail, but its implications exceed any historical justification for its inclusion. With some exceptions, this genre of film does not show women becoming victims in the arena except when they are Christian martyrs. The inclusion of female archers in *Gladiator* and their defeat fit the film's ideological pattern of sexual repression and fear of assertive women.

Even in the most historically accurate films, narrative necessarily comes first: "narrative is there immediately in film . . . to lay out the images . . . to suggest laws to hold the movement, to ensure continuity, to *be* 'cinematic form'."[22] The presence of an individual protagonist with whom we are meant to identify is fundamentally at odds with the depiction of a complex historical process.[23] One reason why *Gladiator* has been far more successful at the box-office than *The Fall of the Roman Empire* is

21 Fitzgerald, "Oppositions, Anxieties, and Ambiguities in the Toga Movie," 37.
22 Heath, *Questions of Cinema*, 12–13.
23 On this and on historical cinema in general see especially Robert Rosenstone, *Visions of the Past: The Challenge of Film to Our Idea of History* (Cambridge and London: Harvard University Press, 1995).

its relentless focus on Maximus, who is on screen most of the time and the main topic of discussion when he is not. Russell Crowe's Maximus is more appealing to audiences than Stephen Boyd's Livius because Crowe shows us the type of the primary narcissist: completely self-absorbed and seemingly utterly autonomous, a type of personality to which, Freud observed, we are drawn as we are to cats.[24] Boyd, on the other hand, projected an image of the perpetually needy type who tends to induce anxiety. It is fitting, then, that the rapid editing in the arena scenes of *Gladiator*, especially of the Battle of Carthage, reinforces the film's overall presentation of male psychology. In this way *Gladiator* becomes a commodity ready for an audience used to constant interruptions by advertising. Its only long sequences are the opening battle and the blood sports. But even these have fast action and "were shot to mimic the way modern-day sporting events are shown on television."[25] Instead of the long panoramic shots that gave *The Fall of the Roman Empire* its striking visual beauty, we get a plethora of very short scenes in *Gladiator*.

Narrative envisions the possibility of change. Classic narrative at its simplest entails three phases: an initial static state, then a period of change and potential chaos that leads to the third stage, in which a static state is re-established.[26] Initially in *Gladiator*, the Roman imperial order is firmly established and the protagonist is firmly a part of it, placed to assume its highest position. Commodus' murder of his father plunges Maximus into a fundamental disorientation, a precipitous descent to the bottom of the political and social hierarchy. We follow his upward movement in terms that none other than Commodus articulates for us just before the duel in the arena that will end both their stories:

> Maximus. Maximus. Maximus. They call for you. The general who became a slave. The slave who became a gladiator. The gladiator who defied an emperor. A striking story. Now the people want to know how the story ends. Only a famous death will do.

This summary of Maximus' story makes meaningful change in the Roman order possible, but despite the death of the evil emperor the death

24   Sigmund Freud, "On Narcissism: An Introduction" (1914), in *The Standard Edition of the Complete Psychological Works of Sigmund Freud*, ed. James Strachey, vol. 14 (London: Hogarth Press, 1957), 73–102.
25   Rick Lyman, "Building Rome By Computer," *The New York Times* (April 28, 2000), section E, p. 26.
26   Cf. Mulvey, "Changes: Thoughts on Myth, Narrative and Historical Experience," in *Visual and Other Pleasures*, 159–76. This essay previously appeared in the journal *Discourse* (1985) and in the *History Workshop Journal* (1987).

of Maximus denies that possibility. His mystical return to the ghosts of his wife and child are this film's equivalent of the retreat to privacy at the end of *The Fall of the Roman Empire*. While the earlier film at least confronted the audience with the problem of fundamental historical change, the ending of *Gladiator* confirms the unshakable power of the status quo. The rebels have all been rounded up or killed off. In spite of Maximus' final words – "There was a dream that was Rome. It shall be realized. These are the wishes of Marcus Aurelius" – and in spite of the final words of the film spoken by Juba – "Now we are free . . ." – we have no faith that the liberated senator Gracchus can transform a system in which he himself has no faith.

The tension between history and the demands of narrative is the subject of Fredric Jameson's analysis of the role of cinema in the era of globalization and postmodernism, a period in which we are compelled "to think a system so vast that it cannot be encompassed by the natural and historically developed categories of perception." Jameson focuses on the "conspiratorial text" of films which represent "an unconscious, collective effort at trying to figure out where we are and what landscapes and forces confront us in a late twentieth century whose abominations are heightened by their concealment and their bureaucratic impersonality."[27] For this it is necessary "to test the incommensurability between an individual witness – the individual character of a still anthropomorphic narrative – and the collective conspiracy which must somehow be exposed or revealed through these individual efforts."[28] Although neither *The Fall of the Roman Empire* nor *Gladiator* is primarily such a conspiratorial text, both tackle the problem of representing a global political system to global audiences in order to offer a meaningful commentary on the contemporary world. In this regard, *The Fall of the Roman Empire* is the more explicit and ambitious work. From the leaders' gathering at the edge of the empire to the extensive panoramic views of the heart of the empire in Rome, including the highly symbolic moment of Emperor Commodus stepping on the map of the empire, to the battle scenes in the Middle East and the frequent switches from the border to Rome in the film's second half, we are confronted with a global system that is fundamentally dysfunctional. *Gladiator* is far more reluctant to raise explicit questions about such a global system, just as it visually withholds from us the panoramic views of the Roman Empire and even

27   Fredric Jameson, *The Geopolitical Aesthetic: Cinema and Space in the World System* (Bloomington and Indianapolis: Indiana University Press; London: BFI [British Film Institute], 1992; rpt. 1995), 2–3.
28   Jameson, *The Geopolitical Aesthetic*, 10.

of the city of Rome. We see instead the frozen forests of Germany, a Spain not at all sunny, a North African desert village, and, most tellingly, a dark and claustrophobic Rome. Only the very last image in the film briefly grants us a full panorama of the city.

Still, the sense of conspiracy is strong in *Gladiator*. *The Fall of the Roman Empire* showed us the successful conspiracy to kill Marcus Aurelius, and Livius is finally drawn into another conspiracy to overthrow Commodus and to bring about Marcus' plan to transform an exploitative and violent domination over the world into a multicultural and peaceful global system. In *Gladiator*, the family-revenge plot is connected to the conspiracy of Lucilla, Gracchus, and his fellow-senator Gaius to murder Commodus and fulfill Marcus Aurelius' vision of a restored republic run by the senate. It is only Maximus' obsession with farming and revenge that lends credibility to his pledge that once he has killed Commodus he will withdraw from politics altogether. The conspiratorial atmosphere of the film is reinforced by the counterplotting of Commodus and Senator Falco and by Commodus' menacing narrative to Lucius and Lucilla of a conspiracy against Emperor Claudius long ago. Taken together, the spatial panoramas of the empire and the conspiracy plots or subplots of both films convey a message of the overwhelming complexity of a worldwide system that escapes the control of individual protagonists. With their endings, both films despair of meaningful change.

To Scott, the fundamental flaw in the system is the mob, the people of Rome seen as the audience in the arena, who in turn stand in for the cinema audience. This self-reflexive aspect, absent from *The Fall of the Roman Empire*, is central to *Gladiator*. Lucilla and Maximus, the conspirators, confirm Commodus' observation that the people will love him for the "vision" he will give them with the games in the arena:

> Lucilla: The gods have spared you. Don't you understand? Today I saw a slave become more powerful than the emperor of Rome.
> Maximus: The gods have spared me? I am at their mercy with the power only to amuse a mob.
> Lucilla: That is power. The mob is Rome.

The director's cynical self-congratulation about the power of the medium he controls and manipulates is built into the politics of his film as a whole. Glorying in the fictive universe which the bottomless pockets and complex technology of Hollywood can create and at the same time despairing of any truly meaningful deployment of that power, he might say with Proximo: "I am an entertainer."

The Major Ancient Sources

Cassius Dio on Commodus

EDITOR'S NOTE: Greek historian Cassius Dio (ca. A.D. 163–ca. 235) came to Rome as a young man. He was senator under Commodus and went on to a distinguished political career, twice holding the consulship. He wrote his *Roman History* in eighty books from the arrival of Aeneas down to his own time.

The following excerpts are from the epitome by Xiphilinus of Dio's Book 73. Translator's annotations have been omitted. Editor's additions appear in ⟨ ⟩; textual omissions are indicated by [. . .].

Reprinted by permission of the publishers and trustees of the Loeb Classical Library from *Dio's Roman History in Nine Volumes*, tr. Earnest Cary, vol. 9 (LCL 177; Cambridge: Harvard University Press; London: Heinemann, 1927; rpt. 1969). The Loeb Classical Library is a registered trademark of the President and Fellows of Harvard College.

1. This man [Commodus] was not naturally wicked, but, on the contrary, as guileless as any man that ever lived. His great simplicity, however, together with his cowardice, made him the slave of his companions, and it was through them that he at first, out of ignorance, missed the better life and then was led on into lustful and cruel habits, which soon became second nature. And this, I think, Marcus ⟨Aurelius⟩ clearly perceived beforehand. Commodus was nineteen years old when his father died, leaving him many guardians, among whom were numbered the best men of the senate. But their suggestions and counsels Commodus rejected, and after making a truce with the barbarians he

hastened to Rome; for he hated all exertion and craved the comfortable life of the city.

2. The Marcomani by reason of the multitude of their people that were perishing and the constant ravaging of their lands no longer had an abundance of either food or men. At any rate they sent only two of their chief men and two others of inferior rank as envoys to sue for peace. And, although Commodus might easily have destroyed them, yet he made terms with them; for he hated all exertion and was eager for the comforts of the city. In addition to the conditions that his father had imposed upon them he also demanded that they restore to him the deserters and the captives that they had taken in the meantime, and that they furnish annually a stipulated amount of grain – a demand from which he subsequently released them. Moreover, he obtained some arms from them and soldiers as well, thirteen thousand from the Quadi and a smaller number from the Marcomani; and in return for these he relieved them of the requirement of an annual levy. However, he further commanded that they should not assemble often nor in many parts of the country, but only once each month and in one place, and in the presence of a Roman centurion; and, furthermore, that they should not make war upon the Iazyges, the Buri, or the Vandili. On these terms, then, he made peace and abandoned all the outposts in their country beyond the strip along the frontier that had been neutralized.

3. Commodus granted peace to the Buri when they sent envoys. Previously he had declined to do so, in spite of their frequent requests, because they were strong, and because it was not peace that they wanted, but the securing of a respite to enable them to make further preparations; but now that they were exhausted he made peace with them, receiving hostages and getting back many captives from the Buri themselves as well as fifteen thousand from the others, and he compelled the others to take an oath that they would never dwell in nor use for pasturage a five-mile strip of their territory next to Dacia. [. . .] Sabinianus also, when twelve thousand of the neighbouring Dacians had been driven out of their own country and were on the point of aiding the others, dissuaded them from their purpose, promising them that some land in our Dacia should be given them.

4. Commodus was guilty of many unseemly deeds, and killed a great many people.

Many plots were formed by various people against Commodus, and he killed a great many, both men and women, some openly and some by means of poison, secretly, making away, in fact, with practically all those who had attained eminence during his father's reign and his own, with the exception of Pompeianus, Pertinax and Victorinus; these men for some reason or other he did not kill. I state these and subsequent facts, not, as hitherto, on the authority of others' reports, but from my own observation. On coming to Rome he addressed the senate, uttering a lot of trivialities; and among the various stories that he told in his own praise was one to this effect, that once while out riding he had saved the life of his father, who had fallen into a deep quagmire. Such were his lofty pratings. But as he was entering the hunting-theatre, Claudius Pompeianus formed a plot against him: thrusting out a sword in the narrow entrance, he said: "See! This is what the senate has sent you." This man had been betrothed to the daughter of Lucilla, but had intimate relations both with the girl herself and with her mother; in this way he had become friendly with Commodus, so that he was his companion both at banquets and in youthful escapades. Lucilla, who was no more modest or chaste than her brother Commodus, detested her husband, Pompeianus. It was for this reason that she persuaded him to make the attack upon Commodus; and she not only caused his destruction but was herself detected and put out of the way. Commodus also put Crispina to death, having become angry with her for some act of adultery. But before their execution both women were banished to the island of Capreae ⟨Capri⟩.

There was a certain Marcia, the mistress of Quadratus (one of the men slain at this time), and Eclectus, his cubicularius ⟨domestic steward⟩; the latter became the cubicularius of Commodus also, and the former, first the emperor's mistress and later the wife of Eclectus, and she saw them also perish by violence. The tradition is that she greatly favoured the Christians and rendered them many kindnesses, inasmuch as she could do anything with Commodus.

5. Commodus also killed Salvius Julianus and Tarrutenius Paternus, who was enrolled among the ex-consuls, and others with them, including even a woman of the nobility. And yet Julianus, after the death of Marcus, could have done at once anything whatever that he wished against Commodus, since he was a man of great renown, was in command of a large army, and enjoyed the devotion of his soldiers; but he had refused to make any rebellious move, both because of his own probity and because of the good will that he bore to Marcus even after that emperor's death. And Paternus, if he had plotted against Commodus, as he was accused of doing, could easily have killed him while he himself was still in command of the Pretorians; but he had not done so.

Commodus likewise killed the two Quintilii, Condianus and Maximus; for they had a great reputation for learning, military skill, brotherly accord, and wealth, and their notable talents led to the suspicion that, even if they were not planning any rebellion, they were nevertheless displeased with existing conditions. And thus, even as they had lived together, so they died together, along with the son of one of them. They had offered the most striking example ever seen of mutual affection; and at no time had they ever been separated, even in the offices they held. They had grown prosperous and exceedingly wealthy, and were wont to hold office together and to act as assistants to each other.

6. Sextus Condianus, the son of Maximus, who surpassed all others by reason both of his native ability and his training, when he heard that sentence of death had been pronounced against him, too, drank the blood of a hare (he was living in Syria at the time), after which he mounted a horse and purposely fell from it; then, as he vomited the blood, which was supposed to be his own, he was taken up, apparently on the point of death, and was carried to his room. He himself now disappeared, while a ram's body was placed in a coffin in his stead and burned. After this, constantly changing his appearance and clothing, he wandered about here and there. And when this story got out (for it is impossible that such matters should remain hidden very long), diligent search was made for him high and low. Many were punished in his stead on account of their resemblance to him, and many, too, who were alleged to have shared his confidence or to have sheltered him somewhere; and still more persons who had perhaps never even seen him were deprived of their property. But no one knows whether he was really slain, – though a great number of heads purporting to be his were brought to Rome, – or whether he made good his escape. Some other man, however, after the death of Commodus boldly claimed to be Sextus and undertook to recover his wealth and rank. And he played the part bravely, though questioned much by many persons; yet when Pertinax asked him something about Grecian affairs, with which the real Sextus had been well acquainted, he showed the greatest embarrassment, being unable even to understand the question. Thus, though nature had made him like Condianus in appearance and practice had made him similar in other respects, yet he did not share in his learning.

7. As for this matter, now, that I have just related, I myself was present and heard it; and I will mention another thing, that I saw. There is in the city of Mallus, in Cilicia, an oracle of Amphilochus that gives responses by means of dreams. Now it had given a response also to Sextus, that he had indicated by means of a drawing; the picture which he had put on the tablet represented a boy strangling two serpents and a lion pursuing a fawn. I was with my father, who was governor of Cilicia

at the time, and could not comprehend what the figures meant, until I learned that the brothers had been strangled, so to speak, by Commodus (who later emulated Hercules), just as Hercules, when an infant, is related to have strangled the serpents sent against him by Juno (for the Quintilii, too, had been strangled), and until I learned also that Sextus was a fugitive and was being pursued by a more powerful adversary.

I should render my narrative very tedious were I to give a detailed report of all the persons put to death by Commodus, of all those whom he made away with as the result of false accusations or unjustified suspicions or because of their conspicuous wealth, distinguished family, unusual learning, or some other point of excellence.

Commodus displayed in Rome itself many indications of wealth and very many more, even, of a love of the beautiful. In fact, he occasionally performed an act of public service. Thus, when Manilius, who had been associated with Cassius, had been secretary of his Latin correspondence, and had possessed the greatest influence with him, was captured after taking to flight, the emperor would not listen to a word from him, though he offered to give a great deal of information, and he burned all the conspirator's papers without reading them.

8. He also had some wars with the barbarians beyond Dacia, in which Albinus and Niger, who later fought against the emperor Severus, won fame; but the greatest struggle was the one with the Britons. When the tribes in that island, crossing the wall that separated them from the Roman legions, proceeded to do much mischief and cut down a general together with his troops, Commodus became alarmed and sent Ulpius Marcellus against them. This man [. . .] ruthlessly put down the barbarians of Britain, and later, when, thanks to his peculiar excellence, he was all but on the point of being put to death by Commodus, he was nevertheless pardoned.

9. Perennis, who commanded the Pretorians after Paternus, met his death as the result of a mutiny of the soldiers. For, inasmuch as Commodus had given himself up to chariot-racing and licentiousness and performed scarcely any of the duties pertaining to his office, Perennis was compelled to manage not only the military affairs, but everything else as well, and to stand at the head of the State. The soldiers, accordingly, whenever any matter did not turn out to their satisfaction, laid the blame upon Perennis and were angry with him.

The soldiers in Britain chose Priscus, a lieutenant, emperor; but he declined, saying: "I am no more an emperor than you are soldiers."

The lieutenants in Britain, accordingly, having been rebuked for their insubordination, – they did not become quiet, in fact, until

Pertinax quelled them, – now chose out of their number fifteen hundred javelin men and sent them into Italy. These men had already drawn near to Rome without encountering any resistance, when Commodus met them and asked: "What is the meaning of this, soldiers? What is your purpose in coming?" And when they answered, "We are here because Perennis is plotting against you and plans to make his son emperor," Commodus believed them, especially as Cleander insisted; for this man had often been prevented by Perennis from doing all that he desired, and consequently he hated him bitterly. He accordingly delivered up the prefect to the very soldiers whose commander he was, and had not the courage to scorn fifteen hundred men, though he had many times that number of Pretorians. So Perennis was maltreated and struck down by those men, and his wife, his sister, and two sons were also killed.

10. Thus Perennis was slain, though he deserved a far different fate, both on his own account and in the interest of the entire Roman empire, – except in so far as his ambition for office had made him chiefly responsible for the ruin of his colleague Paternus. For privately he never strove in the least for either fame or wealth, but lived a most incorruptible and temperate life; and as for Commodus and his imperial office, he guarded them in complete security.

Commodus was wholly devoted to pleasure and gave himself up to chariot-racing, caring nothing for anything of that nature ⟨his duties as emperor⟩; and, indeed, even if he had been deeply concerned, he would not have been able to administer them by reason of his indolence and his inexperience.

And the imperial freedmen, with Cleander at their head, after getting rid of this man [Perennis], refrained from no form of mischief, selling all privileges, and indulging in wantonness and debauchery.

Commodus devoted most of his life to ease and to horses and to combats of wild beasts and of men. In fact, besides all that he did in private, he often slew in public large numbers of men and of beasts as well. For example, all alone with his own hands, he dispatched five hippopotami together with two elephants on two successive days; and he also killed rhinoceroses and a camelopard ⟨giraffe⟩. This is what I have to say with reference to his career as a whole.

11. A statue was set up to Victorinus, who had been prefect of the city. He had not died as the victim of any plot; in fact, at one time, when a persistent rumour and many reports, one may almost say, were being circulated about his death, he became emboldened, and approaching Perennis, said: "I hear that you men wish to kill me. Why, then, do you delay? Why do you put it off, when you might do it this very day?" Yet

not even after that was he molested by any outside person, but he took his own life; and yet he had been honoured among the foremost men by Marcus, and in point of moral excellence and forensic eloquence stood second to none of his contemporaries. [. . .]

12. As for Cleander, who possessed the greatest influence after Perennis, he had formerly been sold as one of a group of slaves and had been brought to Rome with the others to be a pack-carrier; but in the course of time he advanced to such a point that he actually became Commodus' cubicularius, married the emperor's concubine Damostratia, and put to death Saoterus of Nicomedeia, his predecessor in this office, together with many others. Yet Saoterus, too, had possessed very great influence, so great, in fact, that thanks to it the Nicomedeians had obtained from the senate the privilege of celebrating some games and of erecting a temple to Commodus. So Cleander, raised to greatness by the favour of Fortune, bestowed and sold senatorships, military commands, procuratorships, governorships, and, in a word, everything. In fact, some men became senators only after spending all they possessed, so that it was said of Julius Solon, a very obscure man, that he had been stripped of all his property and banished to – the senate. Besides all this, Cleander appointed twenty-five consuls for one year, a thing that never happened before or since; one of these consuls was Severus, who later became emperor. Cleander, accordingly, was obtaining money from every source, and he amassed more wealth than any who had ever been named cubicularii. A great deal of it he gave to Commodus and his concubines, and he spent a great deal on houses, baths, and other works of benefit either to individuals or to cities.

13. So this Cleander, too, who had been raised to so exalted a station, fell suddenly and perished in dishonour. It was not the soldiers, however, that killed him, as in the case of Perennis, but the populace. A famine occurred, sufficiently grievous in itself; but its severity was vastly increased by Papirius Dionysius, the grain commissioner, in order that Cleander, whose thefts would seem chiefly responsible for it, might incur the hatred of the Romans and be destroyed by them. And so it came to pass. There was a horse-race on, and as the horses were about to contend for the seventh time, a crowd of children ran into the Circus, led by a tall maiden of grim aspect, who, because of what afterwards happened, was thought to have been a divinity. The children shouted in concert many bitter words, which the people took up and then began to bawl out every conceivable insult; and finally the throng leaped down and set out to find Commodus (who was then in the Quintilian suburb), invoking many blessings on him and many curses upon Cleander. The latter sent some

soldiers against them, who wounded and killed a few; but, instead of being deterred by this, the crowd, encouraged by its own numbers and by the strength of the Pretorians, pressed on with all the greater determination. They were already drawing near to Commodus, whom no one had kept informed of what was going on, when Marcia, the notorious wife of Quadratus, reported the matter to him. And Commodus was so terrified (he was ever the greatest coward) that he at once ordered Cleander to be slain, and likewise his son, who was being reared in the emperor's charge. The boy was dashed to the earth and so perished; and the Romans, taking the body of Cleander, dragged it away and abused it and carried his head all about the city on a pole. They also slew some other men who had enjoyed great power under him.

14. Commodus, taking a respite from his amusements and sports, turned to murder and was killing off the prominent men. Among these was Julianus, the prefect, whom he had been wont even in public to embrace and kiss and address as "father." Another was Julius Alexander, who was executed for having brought down a lion with his javelin while on horseback. This man, when he learned of the arrival of the assassins, murdered them at night, and also destroyed all his enemies at Emesa, his native city; then he mounted a horse and set out to go to the barbarians. And he would have escaped, had he not taken along a boy-favourite with him, since he himself was an excellent horseman; but he could not bring himself to desert the lad, who had become wearied, and so, when he was being overtaken, he killed both the boy and himself. Dionysius, the grain commissioner, also met his death by the orders of Commodus.

Moreover, a pestilence occurred, the greatest of any of which I have knowledge; for two thousand persons often died in Rome in a single day. Then, too, many others, not alone in the City, but throughout almost the entire empire, perished at the hands of criminals who smeared some deadly drugs on tiny needles and for pay infected people with the poison by means of these instruments. The same thing had happened before in the reign of Domitian.

15. Now the death of these victims passed unheeded; for Commodus was a greater curse to the Romans than any pestilence or any crime. Among other reasons was this, that whatever honours they had been wont to vote to his father out of affection they were now compelled out of fear and by direct command to assign also to the son. He actually ordered that Rome itself should be called Commodiana, the legions Commodian, and the day on which these measures were voted Commodiana. Upon himself he bestowed, in addition to a great many other names, that of Hercules. Rome he styled the "Immortal, Fortunate Colony of the

Whole Earth"; for he wished it to be regarded as a settlement of his own. In his honour a gold statue was erected of a thousand pounds' weight, representing him together with a bull and a cow. Finally, all the months were named after him, so that they were enumerated as follows: Amazonius ⟨Amazonian⟩, Invictus ⟨Invincible⟩, Felix ⟨Fortunate⟩, Pius ⟨Dutiful⟩, Lucius, Aelius, Aurelius, Commodus, Augustus, Herculeus ⟨Herculean⟩, Romanus ⟨Roman⟩, Exsuperatorius ⟨Conquering⟩. For he himself assumed these several titles at different times, but "Amazonius" and "Exsuperatorius" he applied constantly to himself, to indicate that in every respect he surpassed absolutely all mankind superlatively; so superlatively mad had the abandoned wretch become. And to the senate he would send messages couched in these terms: "The Emperor Caesar Lucius Aelius Aurelius Commodus Augustus Pius Felix Sarmaticus Germanicus Maximus Britannicus, Pacifier of the Whole Earth, Invincible, the Roman Hercules, Pontifex Maximus, Holder of the Tribunician Authority for the eighteenth time, Imperator ⟨Supreme Commander⟩ for the eighth time, Consul for the seventh time, Father of his Country, to consuls, praetors, tribunes, and the fortunate Commodian senate, Greeting." Vast numbers of statues were erected representing him in the garb of Hercules. And it was voted that his age should be named the "Golden Age," and that this should be recorded in all the records without exception.

16. Now this "Golden One," this "Hercules," this "god" (for he was even given this name, too) suddenly drove into Rome one afternoon from his suburb and conducted thirty horse-races in the space of two hours. These proceedings had much to do with his running short of funds. He was also fond, it is true, of bestowing gifts, and frequently gave largesses to the populace at the rate of one hundred and forty denarii per man; but most of his expenditures were for the objects I have mentioned. Hence he brought accusations against both men and women, slaying some and to others selling their lives for their property. And finally he ordered us, our wives, and our children each to contribute two gold pieces every year on his birthday as a kind of first-fruits, and commanded the senators in all the other cities to give five denarii apiece. Of this, too, he saved nothing, but spent it all disgracefully on his wild beasts and his gladiators.

17. In public he nowhere drove chariots except sometimes on a moonless night, for, though he was eager to play the charioteer in public, too, he was ashamed to be seen doing so; but in private he was constantly doing it, adopting the Green uniform. As for wild beasts, however, he slew many both in private and in public. Moreover, he used to contend as a

gladiator; in doing this at home he managed to kill a man now and then, and in making close passes with others, as if trying to clip off a bit of their hair, he sliced off the noses of some, the ears of others, and sundry features of still others; but in public he refrained from using steel and shedding human blood. Before entering the amphitheatre he would put on a long-sleeved tunic of silk, white interwoven with gold, and thus arrayed he would receive our greetings; but when he was about to go inside, he put on a robe of pure purple with gold spangles, donning also after the Greek fashion a chlamys ⟨cloak⟩ of the same colour, and a crown made of gems from India and of gold, and he carried a herald's staff like that of Mercury. As for the lion-skin and club, in the street they were carried before him, and in the amphitheatres they were placed on a gilded chair, whether he was present or not. He himself would enter the arena in the garb of Mercury, and casting aside all his other garments, would begin his exhibition wearing only a tunic and unshod.

18. On the first day he killed a hundred bears all by himself, shooting down at them from the railing of the balustrade; for the whole amphitheatre had been divided up by means of two intersecting cross-walls which supported the gallery that ran its entire length, the purpose being that the beasts, divided into four herds, might more easily be speared at short range from any point. In the midst of the struggle he became weary, and taking from a woman some chilled sweet wine in a cup shaped like a club, he drank it at one gulp. At this both the populace and we [senators] all immediately shouted out the words so familiar at drinking-bouts, "Long life to you!"

And let no one feel that I am sullying the dignity of history by recording such occurrences. On most accounts, to be sure, I should not have mentioned this exhibition; but since it was given by the emperor himself, and since I was present myself and took part in everything seen, heard and spoken, I have thought proper to suppress none of the details, but to hand them down, trivial as they are, to the memory of those who shall live hereafter, just like any events of the greatest weight and importance. [. . .]

19. On the first day, then, the events that I have described took place. On the other days he descended to the arena from his place above and cut down all the domestic animals that approached him and some also that were led up to him or were brought before him in nets. He also killed a tiger, a hippopotamus, and an elephant. Having performed these exploits, he would retire, but later, after luncheon, would fight as a gladiator. The form of contest that he practised and the armour that he used were those of the *secutores* ⟨pursuers⟩, as they were called: he held the

shield in his right hand and the wooden sword in his left, and indeed took great pride in the fact that he was left-handed. His antagonist would be some athlete or perchance a gladiator armed with a wand; sometimes it was a man that he himself had challenged, sometimes one chosen by the people, for in this as well as other matters he put himself on an equal footing with the other gladiators, except for the fact that they enter the lists for a very small sum, whereas Commodus received a million sesterces from the gladiatorial fund each day. Standing beside him as he fought were Aemilius Laetus, the prefect, and Eclectus, his cubicularius; and when he had finished his sparring match, and of course won it, he would then, just as he was, kiss these companions through his helmet. After this the regular contestants would fight. The first day he personally paired all the combatants down in the arena, where he appeared with all the trappings of Mercury, including a gilded wand, and took his place on a gilded platform; and we regarded his doing this as an omen. Later he would ascend to his customary place and from there view the remainder of the spectacle with us. After that the contests no longer resembled child's play, but were so serious that great numbers of men were killed. Indeed, on one occasion, when some of the victors hesitated to slay the vanquished, he fastened the various contestants together and ordered them all to fight at once. Thereupon the men so bound fought man against man, and some killed even those who did not belong to their group at all, since the numbers and the limited space had brought them together.

20. That spectacle, of the general character I have described, lasted fourteen days. When the emperor was fighting, we senators together with the knights always attended. Only Claudius Pompeianus the elder never appeared, but sent his sons, while remaining away himself; for he preferred even to be killed for this rather than to behold the emperor, the son of Marcus, conducting himself in such a fashion. For among other things that we did, we would shout out whatever we were commanded, and especially these words continually: "Thou art lord and thou art first, of all men most fortunate. Victor thou art, and victor thou shalt be; from everlasting, Amazonian, thou art victor." But of the populace in general, many did not enter the amphitheatre at all, and others departed after merely glancing inside, partly from shame at what was going on, partly also from fear, inasmuch as a report spread abroad that he would want to shoot a few of the spectators in imitation of Hercules and the Stymphalian birds. And this story was believed, too, because he had once got together all the men in the city who had lost their feet as the result of disease or some accident, and then, after fastening about their knees

some likenesses of serpents' bodies, and giving them sponges to throw instead of stones, had killed them with blows of a club, pretending that they were giants.

21. This fear was shared by all, by us [senators] as well as by the rest. And here is another thing that he did to us senators which gave us every reason to look for our death. Having killed an ostrich and cut off its head, he came up to where we were sitting, holding the head in his left hand and in his right hand raising aloft his bloody sword; and though he spoke not a word, yet he wagged his head with a grin, indicating that he would treat us in the same way. And many would indeed have perished by the sword on the spot, for laughing at him (for it was laughter rather than indignation that overcame us), if I had not chewed some laurel leaves, which I got from my garland, myself, and persuaded the others who were sitting near me to do the same, so that in the steady movement of our jaws we might conceal the fact that we were laughing.

After the events described he raised our spirits. For when he was intending to fight once more as a gladiator, he bade us enter the amphitheatre in the equestrian garb and in our woollen cloaks, a thing that we never do when going to the amphitheatre except when one of the emperors has passed away; and on the last day his helmet was carried out by the gates through which the dead are taken out. These events caused absolutely every one of us to believe that we were surely about to be rid of him.

22. And he actually did die, or rather was slain, before long. For Laetus and Eclectus, displeased at the things he was doing, and also inspired by fear, in view of the threats he made against them because they tried to prevent him from acting in this way, formed a plot against him. It seems that Commodus wished to slay both the consuls, Erucius Clarus and Sosius Falco, and on New Year's Day to issue forth both as consul and *secutor* from the quarters of the gladiators; in fact, he had the first cell there, as if he were one of them. Let no one doubt this statement. Indeed, he actually cut off the head of the Colossus ⟨the huge statue of Nero next to the amphitheater⟩, and substituted for it a likeness of his own head; then, having given it a club and placed a bronze lion at its feet, so as to cause it to look like Hercules, he inscribed on it, in addition to the list of his titles which I have already indicated, these words: "Champion of *secutores*; only left-handed fighter to conquer twelve times (as I recall the number) one thousand men."

For these reasons Laetus and Eclectus attacked him, after making Marcia their confidant. At any rate, on the last day of the year, at night, when people were busy with the holiday, they caused Marcia to administer poison to him in some beef. But the immoderate use of wine and baths, which was habitual with him, kept him from succumbing at once, and instead he vomited up some of it; and thus suspecting the truth, he indulged in some threats. Then they sent Narcissus, an athlete, against him, and caused this man to strangle him while he was taking a bath. Such was the end of Commodus, after he had ruled twelve years, nine months, and fourteen days. He had lived thirty-one years and four months; and with him the line of the genuine Aurelii ceased to rule.

23. After this there occurred most violent wars and civil strife. [. . .]

24. Before the death of Commodus there were the following portents: many eagles of ill omen soared about the Capitol and moreover uttered screams that boded nothing peaceful, and an owl hooted there; and a fire that began at night in some dwelling leaped to the temple of Pax ⟨Peace⟩ and spread to the storehouses of Egyptian and Arabian wares, whence the flames, borne aloft, entered the palace and consumed very extensive portions of it, so that nearly all the State records were destroyed. This, in particular, made it clear that the evil would not be confined to the City, but would extend over the entire civilized world under its sway. For the conflagration could not be extinguished by human power, though vast numbers both of civilians and soldiers carried water, and Commodus himself came in from the suburb and encouraged them. Only when it had destroyed everything on which it had laid hold did it spend its force and die out.

The *Augustan History*: *Commodus*

EDITOR'S NOTE: The *Augustan History* (*Historia Augusta*, also referred to as *Scriptores Historiae Augustae*) is a collection of biographies of emperors and usurpers ostensibly written by six authors in the late third to early fourth centuries A.D. Scholars now believe that it is the work of a single author writing in the late fourth century.

The following biography of Commodus in the *Historia Augusta* is taken from *Lives of the Later Caesars*, tr. Anthony Birley (Harmondsworth: Penguin, 1976; several rpts.). Reprinted by permission of Penguin Books. Translator's annotations have been omitted. Editor's additions appear in ⟨ ⟩; textual omissions are indicated by [. . .].

Concerning Commodus Antoninus' parents there has been sufficient discussion in the *Life* of Marcus Antoninus. Now he himself was born at Lanuvium with his twin brother Antoninus on the day before the Kalends of September, his father and uncle being the consuls [31 August A.D. 161], in the place where his maternal grandfather is also said to have been born. Faustina, when pregnant with Commodus and his brother, dreamed that she was giving birth to snakes, one of which however was fiercer than the other. But when she had given birth to Commodus and to Antoninus, the latter, for whom the astrologers promised a horoscope equal to Commodus, was carried off at the age of four. So when his brother was dead, Marcus tried to educate Commodus both by his own precepts and by those of great and excellent men. [. . .] But teachers in so many disciplines profited him nothing. So great is the power either of innate qualities or of those kept as tutors at court. For straight from his earliest boyhood he was base, shameless, cruel, lecherous, defiled of mouth too and debauched, already adept at those arts which do not accord with the position of emperor, in that he could mould cups, dance, sing, whistle, even play the buffoon and the gladiator to perfection. He gave advance warning of his future cruelty in his twelfth year, at Centumcellae. For when he happened to have taken a bath in rather tepid water, he ordered the bath-keeper to be cast into the furnace. Whereupon a sheepskin was burned in the furnace by the slave-tutor to whom this order had been given, to make him believe from the smell of the fumes that the penalty had been paid.

He was called Caesar as a boy with his brother Verus, and in the fourteenth year of his age he was enrolled in the college of priests. He was [. . .] Leader of the Youth [. . .] when he assumed the toga. While still wearing the bordered tunic of a boy he gave largess and presided in Trajan's basilica. He was in fact robed in the toga on the Nones of July [7 July A.D. 175], the day on which Romulus disappeared from the earth, and at the time when Cassius ⟨Avita⟩ revolted from Marcus. Having been commended to the soldiers he set out with his father for Syria and Egypt, and returned with him to Rome. After this, when exemption from the law of the appointed year had been granted, he was made consul, and with his father he was hailed *imperator* ⟨"supreme commander"⟩ on the fifth day before the Kalends of December, when Pollio and Aper were the consuls [27 November A.D. 176], and he celebrated a triumph with his father. Then he accompanied his father to the German war.

Of those appointed to supervise his life he could not endure the more honourable, but retained all the most evil men and those that were dismissed he yearned for to the point of falling ill. When they were reinstated through his father's soft-heartedness, he always kept cookshops and low dives for them in the palace, and never spared either decency or expense. He played at dice in his house. Women of particular beauty of appearance he gathered together like bought harlots, creating a brothel to make sport of their chastity. He purchased chariot-horses for himself and drove chariots in the dress of a charioteer. He conducted himself like a procurer's attendant, so that you would have believed him born rather for shameful things than for that station to which fortune had advanced him. His father's older ministers he dismissed, and aged friends he cast away. The son of Salvius Julianus, who was in command of armies, he vainly tempted to immodest conduct, and then plotted against Julianus. All the most honourable men he cast aside either by insult or by an unworthy office. He was named by actors as a defiled person and he exiled them so quickly that they did not appear again. The war, also, which his father had almost completed, he abandoned, having accepted the enemy's conditions, and then returned to Rome.

When he came back to Rome he celebrated a triumph, with Saoterus his debaucher placed behind him in the chariot. In the course of the triumphal procession Commodus several times turned his head and kissed him, quite openly. He even did this in the orchestra. He would drink till dawn and squander the resources of the Roman empire. In the evening he even flitted through the taverns to the brothels. He sent to rule the provinces persons who were either his allies in crime or had been recommended by criminals. He became so hated by the Senate that he was filled with a savage passion to destroy that great order; and from having been despised, he became cruel.

Commodus' way of life compelled Quadratus and Lucilla to initiate plans to murder him, with the advice of the prefect of the guard Tarrutienus Paternus ⟨in A.D. 182⟩. But the business of carrying out the murder was given to Claudius Pompeianus, a kinsman. He approached Commodus with drawn sword, when he had the chance of action, bursting out with these words: 'This dagger the Senate sends,' gave away what he was doing, the fool, and did not carry it out; and there were many who had a share in the business with him. After this, Pompeianus first, and Quadratus, then Norbana and Norbanus and Paralius were put to death; and the latter's mother and Lucilla were sent into exile.

Then the prefects of the guard, having seen that Commodus had become so detested on account of Saoterus, whose power the Roman people could not endure, had the man courteously led out of the palace on the pretext of a sacrifice, and murdered him, as he was returning to his own mansion, by means of commissary agents. But that was more offensive to Commodus than the plot against himself. At any rate, at the instigation of Tigidius ⟨Perennis⟩, by the expedient of giving the honour of the ⟨senator's⟩ broad stripe, he removed Paternus from the administration of the prefecture. Paternus not only appeared to be the instigator of this murder but had also, as far as could be seen, been involved in the attempt to kill Commodus himself – and had stood in the way of further punishment of the conspiracy. A few days afterwards he accused him of conspiracy [. . .]. Hence he put to death both Paternus and Julianus and Vitruvius Secundus, a very close intimate of Paternus, who had charge of the imperial correspondence. Besides this, the whole house of the Quintilii was wiped out, [. . .] and savage treatment was meted out in various ways against many others.

After this, Commodus never readily appeared in public, and never permitted anything to be announced to him unless Perennis had previously dealt with it. Perennis in fact, knowing Commodus very well, discovered how to gain power for himself. He persuaded Commodus to free himself for a life of pleasure while he, Perennis, would devote himself to the administration; and this Commodus gladly accepted. Under this agreement, therefore, Commodus began a life of orgiastic abandonment in the palace, amid banquets and baths: he had three hundred concubines, whom he assembled together for the beauty of their person, recruiting both married women and whores, together with youths of ripe age, also three hundred in number, whom he had collected, with beauty as the criterion, equally from the commons and the nobility, by force and by payment.

In the meanwhile, in the dress of a victim-slayer, he slaughtered sacrificial victims, and he fought in the arena with foils and as a gladiator, among the chamberlains, with the swords' points uncovered. By this time, Perennis had arrogated everything to himself: he made away with anyone he wanted, robbed a great many, subverted all the laws, and put all the booty into his own purse. Commodus himself, indeed, killed his sister Lucilla after he had sent her to Capreae [Capri]. Then, having debauched his other sisters, as it is said, and being joined in embraces with a cousin of his father, he even gave one of the concubines the name of his mother. His wife, whom he had caught in adultery, he drove out, then banished her, and subsequently killed her. He used to order the concubines themselves to be debauched before his own eyes, and he was not free from the disgrace of submitting sexually to young men, being defiled in every part of his body, even his mouth, with both sexes.

At this time also Claudius, whose son had once approached Commodus with a dagger, was killed, ostensibly by brigands; and many other senators were made away with, without trial, and rich women as well. In the provinces not a few, having been falsely accused by Perennis on account of their riches, were robbed or even made away with. Those who could not be prosecuted even on a trumped-up charge were accused of being unwilling to name Commodus as their heir.

At that time Perennis gave his own son the credit for successes in Sarmatia won by other generals. Yet in spite of his great power, because he had dismissed senators and put men of equestrian status in command of the troops in the British war, when the matter was made known by the legates of the army this same Perennis was suddenly declared a public enemy and given to the soldiers to be lynched. Commodus appointed

Cleander, one of the chamberlains, to his position of power. Of course, after the execution of Perennis and his son Commodus rescinded many measures, as though they had not been carried out with his authority, on the pretext that he was restoring things back to normal. In fact, he could not keep up this repentance for his crimes for longer than thirty days – what he was to do through the agency of Cleander was more serious than what he had done through the aforementioned Perennis. [. . .] Then, for the first time, there were twenty-five consuls in a single year. All the provinces were sold – Cleander sold everything for cash. He rewarded with office men recalled from exile, and rescinded legal decisions. [. . .]

Eventually, however, Cleander's life too had a fitting end. When Arrius Antoninus was killed on charges that were trumped up as a favour to Attalus, whom Arrius had convicted during his proconsulship of Asia, Commodus was unable to endure the ill-feeling that ensued at that time, for the populace were in a fury. So Cleander was presented to the common people to pay the penalty. At the same time, Apolaustus and other court freedmen were put to death in like manner. Cleander, among other things, had debauched some of Commodus' concubines, on whom he begot sons. They were put to death after his removal, together with their mothers. Julianus and Regillus were appointed to his post. Subsequently Commodus condemned them as well.

When these men had been killed, Commodus put to death [. . .] countless others. He had intended to kill another fourteen also, when the resources of the Roman empire could not sustain his expenditure.

In the meantime, as an act of mockery on the part of the Senate, Commodus was named Pius after he had designated his mother's lover to the consulship, and Felix after he had killed Perennis – amidst a great many murders of many citizens, as if he were some new Sulla. This same Commodus, the 'Dutiful' (*pius*), the 'Fortunate' (*felix*), is said to have invented a plot against his own life as well, to justify the killing of a great many people. Yet there was no other rebellion apart from the one by Alexander, who subsequently took his own life, and those of his family, and by Commodus' sister Lucilla. Commodus was named Britannicus by flatterers, although the Britons even wanted to choose an emperor in opposition to him. He was called 'the Roman Hercules' too, because he had killed wild animals at Lanuvium in the amphitheatre; for it was his practice to kill wild beasts at home. Besides this, he was insane enough to want the city of Rome to be called the 'Commodian Colony': this crazy idea is said to have been instilled into him in the midst of Marcia's blandishments. He also wanted to drive four-horse chariots in the circus. He appeared in public in the Dalmatian tunic and in this garb gave the signal for starting the chariots. Indeed, at that time, when he proposed to the Senate his motion to make Rome *Commodiana*, not only did the senate gladly accept this mockery as far as can be understood, but it even called itself 'Commodian', naming Commodus 'Hercules' and 'god'.

He pretended that he was going to go to Africa too, so that he could exact travelling expenses; and he did exact them and spent them on banquets and gambling instead. He put to death Motilenus, the prefect of the guard, by means of poisoned figs. He accepted statues in the dress of Hercules, and sacrifices were made to him as to a god. He had intended to put many others to death in addition, as was revealed by a little boy who tossed out of his bedroom a tablet on which were written the names of those who were to be killed.

He practised the rites of Isis, even to the extent of shaving his head and carrying the figure of Anubis. He ordered the votaries of Bellona actually to cut off an arm, in his zeal for cruelty. The Isis worshippers, indeed, he forced to beat their breasts with pine-cones, to the point of death. When he was carrying the Anubis figure he used to strike the head of the Isis worshippers hard with the face of the statue. Clad in woman's dress and a lionskin he struck with his club not only lions but many humans as well. Men who were lame in the feet and those who could not walk he dressed up like giants, in such a way that they were covered from their knees downwards with bandages and cloths, to look like serpents, and he dispatched them with arrows. He polluted the Mithraic rites with real murder, although the custom was merely for something to be said, or pretended, to create an impression of fear.

As a boy he was already both gluttonous and lewd. As a youth he disgraced every kind of person that was with him and was disgraced by all of them. Those who mocked him he cast to the wild beasts. One man who had read ⟨Suetonius⟩ Tranquillus' book containing the *Life* of Caligula he even ordered to be cast to the beasts, because his own birthday was the same as Caligula's. [. . .] In his jokes, too, he was destructive. For example, he put a starling on the head of a man who, he had seen, had some hairs that were going white among the black ones, like worms; the bird thought it was chasing worms and made the man's head fester with the striking of its beak. He cut open a fat man in the middle of the stomach so that his innards suddenly poured out. He used to name men 'one-footed' or 'one-eyed' when he had removed one of their eyes or snapped off one of their feet. Besides this, he murdered many others in different places, some because they had met him when they were wearing barbarian dress, others because they were noble and rather handsome. He had among his minions men called after the private parts of either sex, and on them he used to bestow his kisses with particular pleasure. He had, too, a man whose penis projected further than does that of animals; he called him Onos ⟨Donkey⟩ and was very fond of him – he even enriched him, and appointed him to the priesthood of the Rural Hercules. He is said often to have mixed human excrement with the most expensive foods, and did not refrain from tasting it, making a fool of other people, as he thought. He displayed on a silver dish two misshapen hunchbacks covered with mustard; and straight away he gave them advancement and riches. He pushed into a swimming-pool his prefect of the guard Julianus, clad in a toga, in the presence of his staff; and he ordered him to dance – naked, as well – before his concubines, shaking cymbals and with his face contorted. It was seldom that he did not call for every kind of cooked vegetable for a banquet, to provide continuous luxury. He used to bathe seven or eight times a day and eat actually in the baths. He used to enter the temples of the gods polluted with adulteries and with human blood. He even posed as a surgeon, to the extent of letting blood, using scalpels that were deadly in their effect.

The months, too, flatterers renamed in his honour: Commodus instead of August, Hercules instead of September, Invictus instead of October, Exsuperatorius instead of November, and Amazonius, after his own surname, instead of December. He was called Amazonius because of his passion for his concubine Marcia, whom he loved to have depicted as an Amazon, and for whose sake he even wished to enter the Roman arena in Amazon's dress. He also engaged in gladiatorial combat and accepted a gladiator's name, with pleasure, as if he were accepting triumphal honours. He always entered the public shows and as often as he did so, he ordered it to be inscribed in the public records. He is in fact said to have fought seven hundred and thirty-five times.

[. . .] In the meantime, it is recorded, he fought three hundred and sixty-five times under his father and further, he subsequently achieved so many gladiatorial crowns by defeating or killing net-fighters that he reached a thousand. Moreover, he killed with his own hand many thousands of wild animals, even elephants. Frequently it was before the eyes of the Roman people that he did these things.

For such things as these, to be sure, he was strong enough, but otherwise he was weak and feeble, even having something wrong with him in the groin, which stuck out so much that the Roman people could detect the swelling through his silk clothing. Many verses were written on this subject [. . .]. Such was his strength in slaying wild animals that he transfixed an elephant with a pole, pierced a wild goat's horn with a spear, and dispatched many thousands of huge beasts, each with a single blow. Such was his lack of propriety that he very often drank in public, sitting in the amphitheatre or theatre, in women's clothing.

The Moors were conquered during his reign, but, since he himself lived in this way, it was by means of legates; the Dacians were conquered too, and the Pannonian provinces were set in order; while in Britain, Germany and Dacia the provincials rejected his rule. All these troubles were settled by generals. Commodus himself was tardy and careless in signing documents; he used to answer many petitions with a single formula, while in very many letters he used to write merely 'Farewell'. All business was carried out by others, and they are said to have used even condemnations for the benefit of their purses. In fact, through this carelessness, when the men who were administering the republic had been plundering the grain-supply, a tremendous famine arose at Rome, although there was no shortage of crops. As for those who were plundering everything, Commodus subsequently killed and proscribed them. But he himself, pretending that there was a golden age, 'Commodian' by name, declared that prices were to be cheap, as a result of which he caused a greater shortage.

In his reign many persons obtained for cash both punishment for others and acquittal for themselves. He also sold alternative punishments and the right of burial and alleviation of wrongs; and he killed different people in place of others. Provinces and administrative posts he sold also, and in these instances the men through whose agency he made the sale received one share and Commodus the other. To some he even sold the murder of their enemies. In his reign the freedmen sold even the results of lawsuits. He did not long put up with Paternus and Perennis as prefects; even in the case of those prefects whom he had appointed himself, none of them completed three years' tenure, and many of them he put to death either with poison or the sword. Prefects of the city he changed with the same readiness. He took pleasure in killing his chamberlains, even though he had always done everything at their behest. The chamberlain Eclectus, when he saw how readily Commodus put his chamberlains to death, forestalled him and took part in the conspiracy which caused his death.

Commodus would take up the weapons of a gladiator as a 'pursuer', covering his bare shoulders with a purple cloth. Besides this he had the practice of ordering that everything he did that was base, impure, cruel, gladiatorial or pimp-like, should be included in the *Records of the City* [. . .]. He called the people of Rome the 'Commodian people', since he had very often fought as a gladiator in their presence. But although the people had applauded him as if he were a god at his frequent bouts, in the belief that he was being mocked he had instructed the marines who spread the awnings to slaughter the Roman people in the amphitheatre. He had ordered the city to be burned, seeing that it was his own colony; and this would have been done if Laetus the prefect of the guard had not deterred him. At any rate, among his other triumphal titles he was called 'First stake of the Pursuers' six hundred and twenty times.

There were the following prodigies in his reign of both a public and a private kind. A comet appeared. Footprints of gods were seen in the Forum, going out of it. And before the deserters' war the sky blazed. A sudden mist and darkness arose in the circus on the Kalends of January; and before dawn there had been fire-birds too and Furies. He himself moved from the palace to the Vectilian House on the Caelian Hill, saying that he could not sleep in the palace. The twin gates of Janus opened of their own accord, and the marble image of Anubis was seen to move. In the Minucian Portico a bronze statue of Hercules sweated for several days. A horned owl was caught above his bedroom, both at Rome and at Lanuvium. He himself moreover created a not insignificant omen: after thrusting his hand into the wound of a gladiator who had been killed, he wiped it on his head and, contrary to custom, ordered the spectators to come to the show in cloaks, which was usual at funerals, instead of togas, while he presided in dark clothes. Further, his helmet was twice carried out through the Gate of Libitina ⟨through which the corpses of gladiators were removed⟩. He gave largess to the people, seven hundred and twenty-five denarii apiece. Towards everyone else he was very mean, because he had been draining the treasury by his expenditure on luxury. He held many circus races, but for pleasure rather than for religion, and also in order to enrich the faction leaders.

Stirred up by these things, but all too late, Quintus Aemilius Laetus the prefect and Marcia the concubine entered into a conspiracy to kill him. First they gave him poison; and when that was less than effective, they had him strangled by an athlete with whom he used to train.

Physically, at least, he was well proportioned. His expression was vacant as is usual with drunkards, and his speech disordered. His hair was always dyed and made to shine with gold dust. He used to singe his hair and beard from fear of the barber.

Senate and people demanded that his body be dragged with the hook and thrown into the Tiber. But subsequently, by order of Pertinax, it was transferred to Hadrian's tomb. No public works of his still exist except the baths which Cleander had built in his name. Where his name was inscribed on public works of others, the Senate deleted it. Indeed, he did not even complete his father's public works. He did organize the African fleet, which was to be in reserve if the Alexandrian grain-supply happened to fail. He even gave Carthage the name Alexandria Commodiana Togata, after naming the African fleet Commodiana Herculea as well. He made certain embellishments to the Colossus, of course, all of which were subsequently removed. In fact he took off the head of the Colossus, which was that of Nero, and put his own on it, inscribing beneath it an inscription in the usual style, not even omitting those gladiatorial effeminate titles. Yet Severus, a stern emperor and a man like his own name, from hatred of the Senate, as it seems, enrolled this man among the gods, with the grant of a Herculean-Commodian *flamen* ⟨priest⟩ (which Commodus had planned to have for himself while still alive). Three sisters survived him. Severus ordained that his birthday should be celebrated.

There were great acclamations by the Senate after Commodus' death. In fact, so that the Senate's verdict on Commodus may be known, I have included the acclamations verbatim from Marius Maximus, and the content of the decree of the Senate:

> From the enemy of the fatherland let the marks of honour be dragged away! Let the parricide's honours be dragged away! Let the parricide be dragged along! Let the enemy of the fatherland, the parricide, the gladiator, be mangled in the charnel-house! The executioner of the Senate is the enemy of the gods, the murderer of the Senate is the enemy of the gods! The gladiator to the charnel-house, he that killed the Senate, let him be put in the charnel-house! He that killed the Senate, let him be dragged with the hook, he that killed the innocent, let him be dragged with the hook! Enemy! Parricide! Truly! Truly! He that did not spare his own blood, let him be dragged with the hook! He that was about to kill you, let him be dragged with the hook! [. . .] Let the slayer of citizens be dragged along, let the murderer of citizens be dragged along! Let the statues of the gladiator be dragged away! [. . .] Let the remembrance of the parricide, the gladiator, be wiped out, let the statues of the parricide, the gladiator, be dragged down, let the remembrance of the foul gladiator be wiped out! The gladiator to the charnel-house! [. . .] More savage than Domitian, more foul than Nero, as he did to others, let it be done to him! Let the remembrance of the innocent be preserved, restore the honours of the innocent, we ask! [. . .] The innocent have not been buried – let the parricide's corpse be dragged along! The parricide dug up the buried – let the parricide's corpse be dragged along!

When, by Pertinax's order, Livius Larensis, procurator of the patrimony, had given Commodus' corpse to Fabius Cilo, consul designate, it was buried during the night. The Senate cried out: 'On whose authority did you bury him? Let the buried murderer be dug up, let him be dragged along!' Cincius Severus said:

> Wrongly was he buried. I speak as pontifex; the college of pontiffs says this. Since I have recounted glad tidings, now I turn to what is needful: I give it as my opinion that those things which that man who lived only for the destruction of citizens and for his own shame, compelled to be decreed in his own honour, must be wiped out; that his statues, which are everywhere, should be destroyed; that his name be erased from all public and private monuments; and that the months be called by the names by which they were called when that evil first fell upon the republic.

Herodian on the Death
of Commodus

EDITOR'S NOTE: Greek historian Herodian (born ca. A.D. 180) was probably an imperial freedman. His *History of the Empire from the Time of Marcus Aurelius*, not free from factual errors and often highly novelistic but still valuable, covers the period from A.D. 180 to 238 (the accession of Gordian III) in eight books. The following excerpts are from Chapters 16 and 17 of Book 1. Translator's annotations have been omitted. Editor's additions appear in ⟨ ⟩; textual omissions are indicated by [. . .].

Reprinted by permission of the publishers and trustees of the Loeb Classical Library from *Herodian in Two Volumes*, tr. C. R. Whittaker, vol. 1 (LCL 454; Cambridge: Harvard University Press; London: Heinemann, 1969). The Loeb Classical Library is a registered trademark of the President and Fellows of Harvard College.

16. At last it became imperative to check the madness of Commodus and to free the Roman empire from tyranny. [. . .] In the middle of this general festivity ⟨on New Year's Day, A.D. 193⟩ Commodus planned to make his public appearance before the Roman people, not from the palace, as was usual, but from the gladiators' barracks, dressed in armour instead of the purple-bordered toga of the emperors, and escorted in procession by the rest of the gladiators.

Commodus communicated his intentions to Marcia, his favourite mistress. She was treated just like a legal wife with all the honours due to an empress apart from the sacred fire. When she was told of Commodus' extraordinary plan which was so undignified for him, she fell on her knees earnestly begging him with tears in her eyes not to bring disgrace on the Roman empire and not to take the risk of entrusting himself to gladiators and desperadoes. But she achieved nothing by her many entreaties and left in tears. Commodus then summoned Laetus, the praetorian prefect, and Eclectus, the chamberlain, and gave them instructions to make arrangements for him to spend the night in the gladiators' barracks, from where he would start the procession to the festival sacrifices, dressed in armour for all Rome to see. They made every effort to try and dissuade him from any action unworthy of an emperor.

17. Commodus in a fury dismissed the two men and retired to his room as though he were going to take his usual mid-day siesta. But instead he took up a writing tablet (one of the kind made out of lime wood cut into thin sheets with two hinged pieces that close together) and wrote down the names of those who would be executed that night. Heading the list was Marcia; then Laetus and Eclectus, followed by a great many leading senators. Commodus' intention was to be rid of all the remaining, senior advisers of his father, since he felt embarrassed at having respectable witnesses to his degenerate behaviour. He was going to share out the property of the rich by distributing it to the soldiers and the gladiators, so that the soldiers would protect him and the gladiators amuse him. After writing on the tablet he left it on the couch, thinking no one would come into his room. But he forgot about the little boy, who was one of those that fashionable Roman fops are pleased to keep in their households running around without any clothes on, decked out in gold and fine jewels. Commodus had such a favourite, whom he often used to sleep with. He used to call him Philocommodus ⟨"Commodus' Lover"⟩, a name to show his fondness for the boy. This young lad was playing about aimlessly when Commodus left the room for his regular bath and drinking session. He ran into the bed-chamber as he normally did, picked up the tablet, which was lying on the couch – only to play with, of course – and then ran out again. By some extraordinary chance he happened to meet Marcia, who was also very fond of him. She hugged and kissed him and then took away the tablet from him, because she was afraid that he would destroy something vital without realizing it while innocently playing with it. But as she recognized Commodus' writing she became much more curious to have a look at the contents. Finding it was a death warrant, and that she was going to be the first victim followed by Laetus and Eclectus and the others in the same way, she let out a cry. "Ah, Commodus," she said to herself, "so this is all the thanks I get for my loyal

affection and putting up with all your vicious, drunken behaviour for so many years. A fuddled drunkard is not going to get the better of a sober woman." Then she sent for Eclectus, who normally visited her in his capacity as the official chamberlain, quite apart from the gossip which said he was having an affair with her. She handed him the tablet and said, "There you are; that's the festival we are going to celebrate tonight!" Eclectus grew pale when he saw what was written. As an Egyptian he was characteristically given to act upon his impulses and be controlled by his emotions. Sealing up the tablet he sent it by one of his trusted messengers to Laetus to read. He too came to see Marcia in a panic on the pretext of consulting her and Eclectus about Commodus' orders to move to the gladiators' barracks. While they gave the impression they were working in the emperor's interests, they agreed that they must strike first or be struck down, and that there was no time for delay or procrastination. The plan was to give Commodus a lethal dose of poison, which Marcia assured them she could easily administer; she normally mixed and handed the emperor his first drink so that he could have the pleasure of drinking from his lover's hand. Commodus returned from his bath and Marcia put the poison into the mixing bowl, adding some fragrant wine, and gave it to him to drink. Accepting it as a loving-cup which he normally drank after his frequent baths or bouts in the amphitheatre with the animals, the emperor tossed it off without a thought. At once he fell into a coma and went to sleep, thinking that the drowsiness was the result of his exercise. Eclectus and Marcia told everyone to keep away and go home so that they could leave the emperor in peace, they said. This normally happened to Commodus on other occasions after he had been drinking heavily. He would take frequent baths and meals but have no set time for his sleep because he used to get caught up in a non-stop round of various pleasures, to which he was a compulsive slave at any hour. For a while he lay quiet, but, as the poison reached his stomach and bowels, he was attacked by dizziness and began to vomit violently. The reason for this may have been that the food and excessive drink he had taken earlier were reacting to the poison, or it may be that he had taken an antidote to the poison – a practice of the emperors before each meal. At any rate, after a prolonged bout of vomiting, Marcia and the others grew frightened that he would recover by getting rid of all the poison, and destroy them all. So they got hold of a strong, young athlete called Narcissus, and persuaded him to go in and strangle Commodus in return for a large reward. Narcissus rushed into the chamber of the emperor, as he lay there overcome by the effects of the poison and the wine, and strangled him to death.

Such was the end of Commodus after thirteen years' rule since his father's death. More nobly born than any emperor before him; he also had more handsome looks and a better physique than any other man in his day; as for more virile accomplishments, he was a better marksman and had a surer hand than anyone else; but all this talent he debased by corrupt living, as we have seen above.

Aurelius Victor on Commodus

EDITOR'S NOTE: Sextus Aurelius Victor's work *On the Caesars*, written and published around A.D. 360, deals with the Roman emperors from Augustus to Constantius II.

Reprinted from *Aurelius Victor: De Caesaribus*, tr. H. W. Bird (Liverpool: Liverpool University Press, 1994) by permission of Liverpool University Press. Translator's notes have been omitted; his additions appear in ( ). Editor's addition appears in [ ].

17. But his [Marcus Aurelius'] son was considered quite detestable for his despotism, which was savage from its beginning, especially when contrasted with the memory of his predecessors. This is such a burden on successive generations that, apart from our common hatred of the undutiful, they are more loathsome for being, as it were, the corruptors of their kind. Clearly energetic in war, because of his success against the Quadi he had called the month of September Commodus. He constructed a building to serve as a bath that was hardly worthy of Roman might. Indeed he possessed such an utterly harsh and cruel nature that he frequently butchered gladiators in mock battles, since he would use an iron sword, his opponents swords made of lead. When he had finished off very many in that manner, by chance one of them named Scaeva, who was very bold, physically powerful and a skilled fighter, deterred him from this passion. He, spurning his sword, which he saw was useless, said that the one with which Commodus was armed would be sufficient for both of

them. Fearing that in the struggle he might have his weapon torn away from him and be killed, which does happen, he had Scaeva removed and, (now) more fearful of the others, he transferred his ferocity to wild beasts. Since all people were horrified at his insatiable bloodthirstiness through these activities, his closest associates in particular plotted against him. In fact no one was loyal to his regime at all and even his cronies, by whom the power of those men was maintained, while they were wary of a criminal mind that was inclined to cruelty, thought it safer to overthrow him by any means whatever, and actually sought to poison Commodus, albeit very secretly at first, in about the thirteenth year of his reign. The poison's strength was rendered ineffective by the food with which he happened to have stuffed himself; since, however, he was complaining of a stomach ache, on the advice of his doctor, a leader of the group, he went to the wrestling hall. There he died at the hands of the masseur (for, by chance, he too was privy to the plot) by having his throat crushed tightly in an arm-lock as if it were part of the exercise. When this was known the senate, which had gathered in full complement at dawn for the January festival, together with the people, declared him an enemy of the gods and men and (ordered) his name to be erased; and straightway the imperial power was conferred upon the prefect of the city, Aulus Helvius Pertinax.

Chronology: The Roman Empire at the Time of Commodus

All dates are A.D.

161

August 31: Lucius Aurelius Commodus born to Emperor Marcus Aurelius and his wife, Annia Galeria Faustina (II).

166

October 12: Commodus becomes Caesar.

175

January 20: Admission to all priestly colleges. May 19: Departure for Germany. July 7: Commodus assumes the *toga virilis* and enters adulthood; becomes *princeps iuventutis* (Leader of the Youth).

175–6

Journey to the east with his father. Fall 176: Initiation into the Elysinian Mysteries.

176

October 28 or November 27: First acclamation as *imperator*. December 23: Triumph over Germans and Sarmatians, possibly together with his father.

177

Before June 17: Elevation to rank of Augustus; honorary title of *Pater Patriae* ("Father of the Country"). Official name: Imperator Caesar Lucius Aurelius Commodus Augustus.

178

Before August 3: Marriage to Bruttia Crispina. August 3: Departure for second expedition to Germany.

180

March 17: Death of Marcus Aurelius. Commodus becomes sole

ruler. October 22 (?): Triumph over the Germans. Official name: Imperator Caesar Lucius (since October: Marcus) Aurelius Commodus Augustus. Office of Pontifex Maximus (since 177, according to inscriptions; since 183 on coins).

181
Second half of the year (?): Conspiracy of Lucilla, his sister (born March 7, 149). She is banished to Capri, then executed.

185
April or May (?): Fall and death of Perennis.

185–6
Further border campaigns.

187
Before March 25: Conspiracy of Maternus.

188
Third German expedition.

189
Fall and death of Cleander, probably late in the year.

191
Name change: Imperator Caesar Lucius Aelius Aurelius Commodus Augustus.

192
October (?): Rome refounded as Colonia Commodiana. Months renamed after Commodus. Fall: Bruttia exiled to Capri, then executed. Her memory is condemned (*damnatio memoriae*). December 31: Assassination of Commodus.

193
Early January: Pertinax, Commodus' successor, reburies Commodus' body in Hadrian's tomb. Commodus suffers *damnatio memoriae*.

195
Spring: Emperor Septimius Severus deifies Commodus (Divus Commodus) and declares himself brother of the Deified.

217
April: Commodus suffers a second *damnatio memoriae* under Emperor Macrinus (until June, 218).

Commodus held the consulship seven times and was proclaimed *imperator* eight times. His official surnames (*cognomina*) were *Germanicus*, *Sarmaticus*, *Germanicus Maximus*, and *Britannicus*. He was *Pius* ("Dutiful"), *Felix* ("Fortunate"), *Pater senatus* ("Father of the senate"), *Invictus Romanus* ("Invincible Roman"), and *Hercules*. Other honorary names and titles were unofficial. Commodus had no children.

Source: Dietmar Kienast, *Römische Kaisertabelle: Grundzüge einer römischen Kaiserchronologie*, 2nd edn (Darmstadt: Wissenschaftliche Buchgesellschaft, 1996), 147–51.

Further Reading

EDITOR'S NOTE: The following lists are intended to provide readers interested in specific topics with first suggestions; they are therefore not comprehensive. All items listed contain additional references. Works already mentioned in the essays above are not included here.

1. On Roman Culture and History

Beacham, Richard C. *Spectacle Entertainments of Early Imperial Rome*. New Haven and London: Yale University Press, 1999.

Birley, Anthony R. "Marius Maximus: The Consular Biographer." *Aufstieg und Niedergang der römischen Welt*, 2.34.3 (1997), 2679–757.

Campbell, J. B. *The Emperor and the Roman Army, 31 BC–AD 235*. Oxford: Clarendon Press; New York: Oxford University Press, 1984.

——. *The Roman Army, 31 BC–AD 337: A Sourcebook*. London and New York: Routledge, 1994.

The Colosseum. Ed. Ada Gabucci; tr. Mary Becker. Los Angeles: Getty Museum, 2001.

Friell, Gerard, and Stephen Williams. *The Rome That Did Not Fall: The Survival of the East in the Fifth Century*. London and New York: Routledge, 1998.

Gabucci, Ada. *Ancient Rome: Art, Architecture and History*. Ed. Stefano Peccatori and Stefano Zuffi; tr. T. M. Hartmann. London: British Museum; Los Angeles: Getty Museum, 2002.

Gibbon, Edward. *The History of the Decline and Fall of the Roman Empire*. Abridged edn. Ed. David Womersley. London: Penguin, 2000.

Gilliver, Catherine. *The Roman Art of War*. Stroud: Tempus, 1999; rpt. 2001.

Goldsworthy, Adrian Keith. *The Roman Army at War: 100 BC–AD 200.* Oxford: Clarendon Press; New York: Oxford University Press, 1996; rpt. 1998.

——. *Roman Warfare.* London: Cassell, 2000; rpt. 2002.

Grant, Michael. *The Antonines: The Roman Empire in Transition.* London and New York: Routledge, 1994.

Hadot, Pierre. *The Inner Citadel: The* Meditations *of Marcus Aurelius.* Tr. Michael Chase. Cambridge and London: Harvard University Press, 1998.

Kyle, Donald G. *Spectacles of Death in Ancient Rome.* London: Routledge, 1998.

Le Bohec, Yann. *The Imperial Roman Army.* 1994. Rpt. London and New York: Routledge, 2000.

Liberati, Anna Maria, and Fabio Bourbon. *Ancient Rome: History of a Civilization That Ruled the World.* New York: Stewart, Tabori and Chang, 1996.

Lintott, Andrew. *Imperium Romanum: Politics and Administration.* London and New York: Routledge, 1993.

Rutherford, R. B. *The* Meditations *of Marcus Aurelius: A Study.* Oxford: Clarendon Press, 1989.

Sumner, Graham. *Roman Army: Wars of the Empire.* London and Herndon: Brassey's, 1997.

Syme, Ronald. *Emperors and Biography: Studies in the Historia Augusta.* Oxford: Clarendon Press, 1971.

——. *Historia Augusta Papers.* Oxford: Clarendon Press, 1983.

Veyne, Paul. *Bread and Circuses: Historical Sociology and Political Pluralism.* Tr. Brian Peirce. 1990. Rpt. London: Penguin, 1992.

Warry, John. *Warfare in the Classical World: An Illustrated Encyclopedia of Weapons, Warriors and Warfare in the Ancient Civilisations of Greece and Rome.* Ed. Philip de Ste. Croix. London: Salamander Books; Norman: University of Oklahoma Press, 1995.

Welch, Katherine E. *The Roman Amphitheatre: From Its Origins to the Colosseum.* Cambridge: Cambridge University Press, 2003.

Wells, Colin. *The Roman Empire.* 2nd, corrected edn. Cambridge: Harvard University Press, 1997.

2. On the Germanic Tribes

Thompson, E. A. *Romans and Barbarians: The Decline of the Western Empire.* Madison: Unversity of Wisconsin Press, 1982; rpt. 2002.

3. On History and Historiography

Bann, Stephen. *The Inventions of History: Essays on the Representation of the Past.* Manchester: Manchester University Press, 1990.

Fulbrook, Mary. *Historical Theory.* London and New York: Routledge, 2002.

Southgate, Beverley. *History: What and Why? Ancient, Modern, and Postmodern Perspectives*. 2nd edn. London and New York: Routledge, 2001.

4. On Film and History

Barta, Tony. "Screening the Past: History Since the Cinema." In *Screening the Past: Film and the Representation of History*. Ed. Tony Barta. Westport and London: Praeger, 1998. 1–17.

Ferro, Marc. *Cinema and History*. Tr. Naomi Greene. Detroit: Wayne State University Press, 1988.

May, Lary. *Screening Out the Past: The Birth of Mass Culture and the Motion Picture Industry*. New York: Oxford University Press, 1980.

Saab, Joan. "History Goes Hollywood and Vice Versa: Historical Representation and Distortion in American Film." *American Quarterly*, 53 (2001), 710–19.

5. On Film

Bordwell, David, Janet Staiger, and Kristin Thompson. *The Classical Hollywood Cinema*. New York: Columbia University Press, 1985.

Maltby, Richard. *Hollywood Cinema*. 2nd edn. Oxford: Blackwell, 2003.

Monaco, James. *How To Read a Film: Movies, Media, Multimedia: Language, History, Theory*. New York and Oxford: Oxford University Press, 2000.

Thompson, Kristin. *Storytelling in the New Hollywood: Understanding Classical Narrative Technique*. Cambridge: Harvard University Press, 1999.

Index to Chapters 1–10